STAYING TUNED

DANIEL SCHORR

STAYING TUNED

A LIFE IN JOURNALISM

POCKET BOOKS

New York   London   Toronto   Sydney   Singapore

POCKET BOOKS, a division of Simon & Schuster, Inc.
1230 Avenue of the Americas, New York, NY 10020

Library of Congress Cataloging-in-Publication Data

Schorr, Daniel, 1916–
    Staying tuned : a life in journalism / Daniel Schorr.
        p. cm.
    Includes index.
    ISBN 0-671-02087-0
        1. Schorr, Daniel, 1916– 2. Journalists—United States—Biography. I. Title.
    PN4874.S335 A3 2001
    070'.92—dc21
    [B]   2001021014

First Pocket Books hardcover printing May 2001

10 9 8 7 6 5 4 3 2 1

POCKET BOOKS and colophon are registered trademarks of
Simon & Schuster, Inc.

Designed by Lindgren/Fuller Design, Inc.

Printed in the U.S.A.

For my wife, Lisbeth, my son, Jonathan, and my daughter,
Lisa, who give meaning to the second half-century of my life.
And for my mother, Tillie, and my father, Louis,
who did not live to see how far
the son of Jewish immigrants could go.

CONTENTS

ACKNOWLEDGMENTS

My gratitude goes first to my own family, who not only inspired this book, but made constructive suggestions along the way. To my brother, Alvin, my only sibling, and sister-in-law, Ann, who helped me clarify my family history, joining me in a nostalgic visit to the Bronx as he worked on his own memoirs, *Passion and Policy.*

To good friends, starting with William Safire and Judith and Milton Viorst, who helped to revive impetus when writing flagged.

To those who compensated for my computer illiteracy by being my word processors. Ed McNulty, my assistant at National Public Radio, did the lion's share of the manuscript and revisions. Then, other assistants at home and at the office: Sarah Beyer Kelly, Alicia Montgomery, Ruth-Ann Keister, Amy Holmen, and Meg Saunders.

To Tim Seldes, my agent, and Nancy Miller, my editor, whose unflagging enthusiasm for this book helped carry me over several rough sports of discouragement.

To my colleagues at NPR, who displayed support and understanding when these labors interfered with my broadcasting duties.

Finally, to the Rockefeller Foundation, at whose wonderful Bellagio study center on Italy's Lake Como I started this work in 1995.

INTRODUCTION

I am pretty good at turning out copy speedily under deadline pressure. But this book took me six years to write.

The reason became clear as I worked on it. I am a news junkie, fascinated by what is happening today, less excited about raking up the past. Almost any event, at home or abroad, could lure me away from the typewriter. (Yes, I still use a typewriter, but an electric one.)

I would sometimes wince as I returned to the huge stack of radio and television scripts and newspaper clippings, dating back to the 1930s, that cluttered my study. (I needed them to jog my memory since I had kept no diary.)

But, all along, I knew the memoir had to be written. For one thing, to help people remember an era fast disappearing from view in the miasma of ever new sensations. I am actually aware of having outlived many—perhaps most—of the principal actors of my epoch. Gone are Eisenhower, Kennedy, Johnson, and Nixon; Paley, Murrow, and Sulzberger; Khrushchev, Adenauer, and de Gaulle. I feel a little like the recording secretary for my generation.

For another thing, to fulfill a family responsibility. Having married at the age of fifty, I felt an obligation to fill in my wife, son, and daughter about all the global gallivanting I did while still single. At an elegant party, my wife, Li, threw in a Washington hotel for my eightieth birthday in 1996, my son brought home what it was like to become a senior-citizen father. He toasted me for having had my midlife crisis before he was born.

So, Jonathan and Lisa, let me tell you about when I met Greta Garbo...

That's a good opening line, but, alas, the story goes downhill from there. In 1957, author John Gunther invited me to lunch in the courtyard of his home in the East Fifties in Manhattan. He promised me a surprise in thanks for my help with his book when he'd visited Moscow.

Soon there materialized a tall woman with a floppy hat, dark glasses, and a nervous manner. John introduced her as his neighbor Greta Garbo. I had not recognized her. Her handshake was limp. She resisted all efforts at conversation. I told her I had recently arrived from Moscow, where her movie spoof of life in the Soviet Union, *Ninotchka*, had just been released.

"Oh, really?" she said.

Not staying for lunch, she glided away, without even any "I want to be alone."

Hang on, Jonathan and Lisa, the book gets better. But I must warn you that this memoir is a lot more professional than personal. You won't find much about bachelor romances. I marvel at the way some of my colleagues can write discursively about their affairs with women. Something makes me resist that—perhaps the journalist in me, perhaps a respect for privacy, perhaps something else.

What you will find, I hope, is the story of a multimedia journalist who has spent some sixty years observing a multifaceted world. What you will discover, I hope, is a dedication to defending reality against the ever more clever tools of media manipulation and the ever sharper competition for ratings and circulation that have consigned news-gathering into an ever smaller corner of a vast entertainment stage.

My own inability to take the principal actors on this stage at face value seemed inevitably to land me on somebody's enemies list. It must mean something that I was targeted, at various times, by both the KGB and the FBI. It must mean something that, unable to accept the dictates of my bosses, I ended up in confrontations with Bill Paley after a quarter century at CBS and with Ted Turner after six years with CNN.

It may be that I am just hard to get along with, but to me it always seemed that some principle was involved. Now I look back from the relative tranquillity of life as a news analyst for National Public Radio, trying to help people make sense of the torrent of information that deluges them, unleashed by a communications revolution.

I try to imagine whether America would have stood by passively if satellite television had been available to show the brutal crackdown on the anticommunist revolution in Hungary in 1956 or in Czechoslovakia in 1968. Today the "CNN effect" describes the way reluctant officials are prodded into action by the knowledge that the public is seeing, live, the anguish in Somalia, Sierra Leone, or Kosovo.

I try to imagine the Cuban missile crisis of 1962 and whether Kennedy and Khrushchev would have been able, by secret diplomacy, to step back from the brink of nuclear war or whether they would have been exchanging bellicose statements on television every hour on the hour.

On the other hand, I wonder whether the Berlin Wall would have come down with such a crash in 1989 if East Germans had not been watching West Berlin television with glimpses of what life could be in a free country.

But I end up worrying about the downside of advancing media technology and economics, the pressures from media conglomerates to transform journalism into a quest for the vivid, the violent, the scandalous, and the sensational.

If, in writing this book, I have formed some conclusions about the evolution of journalism, I have also gained some insights into myself. I came to realize how, being poor, fat, Jewish, fatherless, I came to feel like the quintessential outsider, fighting my way into journalism, which I have always thought of as an outsider's profession.

Conrad Black, proprietor of a large chain of Canadian newspapers, has called journalists "the rogue elephants of Western society," whose "overarching journalistic objective is to attract public attention by almost any means."

I respond to that description. I achieved identity through my stories. My superiors may not have liked me—too pushy—but they had to like my scoops. In 1991, CBS News chief Richard Salant, five years after firing me and then trying to rehire me, wrote me on my seventy-fifth birthday that he considered me "the greatest reporter CBS ever had." Not TV personality, mind you, but reporter.

Looking back, I perceive that my identity also came from generating controversy about myself. How else to account for so many confrontations—with Presidents Nixon and Ford, with Senator Goldwater, with the CIA and the House of Representatives? (I could go on.) All of these conflicts underlined my position of quintessential outsider.

I was always aware that I was not invited to many of the intimate breakfasts and soirees where powerful people ladled out "deep background" to social equals. I guess I could not be relied upon not to bite the hand that fed me.

I have, over the years, received a great many journalistic awards. They are emblazoned with words like *courageous* and *uncompromising*. Yet, I know myself to be not courageous, and perhaps even to be a coward. So what propelled me into the controversial situations I describe in the chapters that follow?

Stormy as it was, I wouldn't trade my career for anyone else's. And, in my wonderful family, I am the quintessential insider.

CHAPTER 1

IN THE BEGINNING

"Write the easy part first," said my perceptive friend William Safire. "Then you can go back and do the hard part."

This is the hard part—a jumble of long-submerged memories of childhood poverty, a polio-stricken young brother and a struggling widowed mother, memories of how I felt fat, unattractive, Jewish, an outsider struggling for a way in. I had a strong temptation to skip the early years and cut to the career chase. But then you would not understand why I became a journalist and the kind of journalist (combative? abrasive?) that I became. It was, in the end, the journalist in me that demanded that I fill in the early background.

Part of that background is the immigrant experience. While writing this chapter, I went for a visit to Ellis Island, trying to imagine the bewilderment my parents must have felt when they came to this country. They came from Telechan, a *shtetl* (village) in the Pinsk area of what is now Belarus. I would have gone back to the shtetl, too, but it no longer exists. It was wiped out, and all my remaining relatives were murdered in the Holocaust.

In September 1912, my parents married in Telechan, my father then twenty and, I think, a year younger than my mother. From relatives I learned how he had courted her, once taking her for a ride in a horse-drawn wagon, usually, but not always, chaperoned by her

1

brother, Naftali. They had waited, according to tradition, for my mother's older sister, Chaya, to marry. But then, with her encouragement, they decided to wait no longer.

With what prescience I do not know, my parents came to America in May 1914, three months before the outbreak of World War I. They had been staked to steamship tickets, as a loan, by a relative already in the United States, about whose identity I am very vague.

My mother's maiden name was Tillie Godiner (from the Yiddish *Gott-Diener*, meaning "servant of God"). My father's name was Gedaliah Tchornemoretz ("Black Sea" in Russian). An immigration officer arbitrarily conferred on my father the more manageable name of Louis Schorr. (Little did he know that a half century later I would be in his debt for not having to sign off my broadcasts with "This is Daniel Tchornemoretz, CBS News, Washington.")

Relatives have told me that when I was born on August 31, 1916, my parents were having a hard time. Like many immigrants they were learning that America was not the advertised *goldeneh medina* (golden domain). My father, artistic, poetic, apparently had no trade. He worked as a waiter. He opened a dry-goods store in Hackensack, New Jersey, that failed. He later joined with a partner in a Delancey Street real estate brokerage that also was not successful. During some of that time my mother ran a bakery on St. Nicholas Avenue in Washington Heights and, later, worked in a factory as a dress finisher.

My father must have been ill quite early because, in 1917, he was rejected for military service on medical grounds. By 1922 he was in the hospital, suffering from a kidney infection that would today be treated with antibiotics. He died two days after my sixth birthday. My brother, Alvin, was sixteen months old.

I have dim memories of my father, whose brown eyes and love of music I share. I remember—or think I do—lying on the living room floor, chin cupped in hand, looking up while my father played the violin. I even recall—or think I do—that he played the Dvořák "Humoresque." (Inheriting his violin, I would take violin lessons for fifty cents a session in a class in elementary school, but would give it up after showing no great promise.)

My father's last wish, my mother said, was to make sure that the boys would go to college, to which end she saved most of the $2,000 in insurance that he left.

My father's death undoubtedly had a shattering effect on me. I have no memory of the funeral other than the rainy day and my first ride in an automobile and the ferry ride (to Staten Island). Of the rest—who was there, what was said, how the casket was laid in the ground—I have no recollection whatsoever. I have come to believe that, unable to cope with such a loss, I banished it from my mind. (Denial, I think they call it.) In later years, I wondered about my sense of detachment from tragedy and customary lack of emotional response.

My first reimbursement as a journalist came at the age of twelve when a woman fell or jumped from the roof of our apartment house, landing outside our ground-floor window. I called the police, waited for them to arrive, interviewed them about what they had found out about the victim, and coolly telephoned the *Bronx Home News*, which paid $5 for news tips. I felt no particular sense of awe or emotion about the first dead body I had ever seen.

This sense of detachment from the woes and trials of strangers would serve me when I came to report from the death camp in Auschwitz or the urban slums of America.

Early on I made a financial contribution to the household by selling magazines on the street, by tending to an after-school newspaper delivery route, by canvassing neighborhood stores selling printing for a mail-order house.

Most of my ventures were law-abiding. One got me arrested. On sunny Sunday mornings I offered sunglasses to motorists stopped for a red light in the Botanical Gardens and facing into the sun. For many weeks I managed to elude Detective Corby, trying to arrest me for peddling on park property without a permit. I could spot his police car, stuck in the long line of traffic, and flee. One morning, however, he was in an unmarked car, and I walked right up to him, offering him a pair of sunglasses. He grabbed my wrist, and next thing I knew I was in a police wagon with other transgressors against the peddling ordinance, on our way to be locked up, waiting to be arraigned in Manhattan night court. My only sustenance was from the ice cream peddler, who saw his stock melting anyway.

At 10 P.M. a dozen of us malefactors came before the judge. He asked the police officer how long we had been locked up.

"They've been punished enough," he said. "Let 'em go."

I had been permitted one telephone call—to my mother. She was waiting in the courtroom in tears to receive the first member of our family with a police record—all in the cause of helping to support my family.

Money was the easiest thing to give. Giving of myself was harder.

In the 1920s we were joined by three uncles and an aunt, who came from Europe, one by one, and boarded with us until they found jobs and married. In the traditional manner of children of immigrants striving for assimilation, I bristled at their ignorance of my American language and my culture. To meet the changing needs of our family for space, we moved from one apartment to another in the East Bronx. The last of the family to arrive was my maternal grandmother in 1925, who was needed to help care for my brother. She never did learn to speak English, and she irritated me by leaving her dentures in the bathroom.

Alvin needed special help because his early years were marked by a succession of misfortunes—scarlet fever, diphtheria, and finally, polio, which, after a series of operations, left him with one leg attenuated. I can remember the quarantine notices posted on our door, which kept me out of school, but not out of the movies.

I must have visited my brother in Fordham Hospital with my mother but, typically, have no memory of having done so. One Sunday my mother, needing some free time with other family members, asked me to take Alvin to the movies, and an uncle offered to pay for the tickets. I refused, saying, "I am an American and I have the right to do what I want."

At that point, Uncle Srolik, a law student, the youngest and mildest mannered of my mother's siblings, banged the table and said, "That's the trouble with you Americans. You know all about your rights and you don't know anything about your responsibilities!" That I remember the incident to this day indicates how surprised, if not chastened, I felt.

The family spoke mainly Yiddish, to which I vociferously objected as a ghetto jargon. I mounted frequent campaigns to speak English or Hebrew, the language of a future Jewish state in Palestine. I, attending *heder* (Hebrew school) five days a week after school, was quite fluent in Hebrew. As a prize student in the Bronx Jewish Center I was awarded a gold watch with Hebrew numerals and a railroad trip (my first time outside New York) to the 1926 Philadelphia Sesquicentennial Exposition.

At my bar mitzvah in 1929 I read from the Torah and got to deliver a speech. I was praised extravagantly by Rabbi Charlap. (Alvin would later refuse to undergo the bar mitzvah ritual.)

In the interest of full disclosure, let me also report that I sang soprano in the synagogue choir on the high holy days and, occasionally, at weddings for fifty cents.

Hebrew school, where I was the rabbi's pet, served my need to be noticed, but in P.S. 6, on Tremont Avenue, the teachers seemed less enamored of my wit and wisdom. Years later my mother recalled (though I did not) that I talked out of turn so often that she would be called to school and asked to discipline me. My mother said this happened several times, costing her a half day's work each time. Finally, more peremptory than was her wont, she ordered me to desist from talking in class.

Looking back, I wonder how I could have been so oblivious to her desperate efforts to keep the family afloat. I did not realize how important was the check she received from Governor Franklin D. Roosevelt's New York State relief program, the precursor to the federal welfare system.

In 1929 I entered DeWitt Clinton High School as a sophomore, having saved a year in junior high school. DeWitt Clinton was housed in a brand-new building on Moshulu Parkway in the northern reaches of the West Bronx. For me, living in the East Bronx, this meant a subway ride down to 149th Street and up again on the Jerome Avenue line. The forty-five minutes allowed me time for last-minute homework. My extracurricular interests were the Hebrew Society, of which I was president, the History Honor Society, and of course, the school paper, the *Clinton News*. I was also managing editor of the senior yearbook, the *Clintonian*.

In high school, mentored by faculty adviser Ray Philipson, a retired newspaperman, I settled on journalism as my vocation in life. My mother had qualms about a profession requiring no advanced degree, such as law or medicine. "Isn't it a little like being an actor?" she asked hesitantly. But, in the end, she withdrew her objections. (And, forty years later, basking in her son's fame, she would recall with pleasure how wrong she had been.)

Love of journalism meant long evenings in the commercial printing plant, listening to the soft tick-tick of the letters dropping into place on the Linotype machine, laying out the pages and seeing them cast in hot metal. For the *Clintonian*, I reviewed the little blurbs that went under the seniors' pictures. My own blurb was written by others on the staff and I was not allowed to see it until the yearbook appeared. It read:

> I love me, I love me,
> I'm wild about myself.
> I love me, I love me,
> I've got my picture on my shelf.

I also learned an early lesson in journalistic ethics. Because of the long lead time for the yearbook, I undertook to write a vivid story about the senior prom before it was held. When the event was cancelled because of the deepening depression, all I could think to do was to include, next to that page in the yearbook, a slip of paper with the Whittier lines:

> For all sad words of tongue or pen,
> The saddest are these: "It might have been!"

One other memory remains with me of my 1933 graduation amid the Great Depression. The nearby delicatessen put out a sign, "Eat here or we'll both starve."

To make some money, my best high school friend, Bernard Zamichow, and I decided to start a news syndicate. We would dig up stories and try to sell them to the big newspapers. One of the first scoops of the Collegiate Press Service was about the impending resignation of a famous football coach. It was published by the *New York Daily News*. Unfortunately, it was not true, and our enterprise quietly folded, leaving us with a lot of unused stationery. Our confidential source had been a member of the team, whether fantasizing or playing a practical joke I shall never know.

Pudgy as I was, I nevertheless did some youthful dating. With press tickets for a lavish Zionist pageant called "The Romance of a People," I invited a particularly attractive girl whom I had recently met. The show was in the Kingsbridge Armory, not far from my home in the Bronx. She lived in the outer reaches of Bensonhurst in Brooklyn. When I called to make arrangements to meet, she cut me off with peremptory word that she expected to be picked up. That meant two round-trips of more than an hour each by subway, to Brooklyn and back, to pick her up and afterward to take her home. I got home at 2 A.M., with school the next day.

My uncle Naftali said, "This should teach you not to date a girl who lives further than Freeman Street." That was one subway stop away from ours. (Some thirty years later I met the woman I would marry, who lived a few blocks from me in Georgetown. Li teased me that I was still heeding my uncle's advice.)

I was graduated from Clinton with an average good enough for tuition-free admission to the College of the City of New York. CCNY in those days was a hotbed of radicalism. In the basement area, called the Alcoves, arguments about Stalin and Trotsky vied for attention with lunchtime Ping-Pong. On the campus there were frequent demonstrations for "Books, Not Battleships." I, with my customary detachment from struggle, covered the demonstrations for the college newspaper, *The Campus*. Short of money, I also sorted library slips for fifty cents an hour from the National Youth Administration, one of the New Deal agencies. And I constantly looked for paying opportunities in journalism.

The *New York Times* allowed me to do occasional music reviews and articles for the Sunday music page. Once, I was invited to meet with Olin Downes, the most famous critic of his time. In the subway on the way to Times Square, I read a Downes review of a Carnegie Hall performance by the violinist Josef Szigeti. Downes had written that Szigeti's tone was fine, but that the "profile of his tone" left something to be desired. Awed by the dimension of musical understanding that this indicated, I asked Downes what the line meant.

Cheerfully he said, "Don't give it a second thought. That's just the kind of bullshit you put down when you're up against a deadline."

I decided that being a music critic was not an honorable profession.

Another opportunity presented itself in the form of a newly launched venture called the *Jewish Daily Bulletin*. It was the first (and last) English-language Jewish daily, founded by the Vienna-born Jacob Landau, head of the Jewish Telegraphic Agency. His hope was that the daily would appeal to people feeling increasingly Jewish with the rise of Hitler, but no longer reading Yiddish.

My mother expressed the fear that I would quit college, and she reminded me of her promise to my father on his deathbed that his boys would get a college education. I reassured her that I would graduate, but I switched to night school, which meant that I was graduated in 1939 instead of 1937.

I started at the *Bulletin* as a "stringer"—that is, a freelancer paid by the number of inches my article occupied. (I believe the word *stringer* derived from the early practice of measuring column inches with a piece of string.) I was the most productive stringer the *Bulletin* had. I covered Sunday sermons of Reform rabbis, Zionist conferences, and did shipboard interviews with celebrities arriving on ocean liners. (I had a ship news reporter's pass authorizing me to go out to the ships with the Coast Guard cutter carrying the customs and immigration officers.)

Among my other contributions was a six-part exposé of rackets in Jewish charities. But my most remunerative assignment, although risky, was covering demonstrations of the local Nazis, the German-American Bund, who rallied in Yorkville and Queens, heiling Hitler and threatening the extermination of the American Jews.

Like many of the media before and since, the *Bulletin* regarded fear as a circulation builder. The *Bulletin* thrived on Nazi threats, and the Bund thrived on clippings it could send to Propaganda Minister Joseph Goebbels to show what impact it was having.

I piled up so many column inches that I was earning more than a staff reporter. Whereupon I was appointed to the staff. But the *Bulletin* was a money-loser that not even the Nazis could save. After some two years the paper folded. The last weeks were grim as the paper ran out of money to pay wages. As a charter member of the American Newspaper Guild, I picketed the *Bulletin*'s office—the Guild's first strike. Our demand was modest indeed—our back pay. We got a small part of it.

With the death of the *Bulletin*, I transferred to its parent organization, the Jewish Telegraphic Agency. My principal work was cable rewrite—expanding brief messages from Europe and Palestine into stories that could be served to the American news agencies. (The adjoining desk served the Yiddish press.)

I received an intensive education in the arcane language "cablese." Since cablegrams had to be paid for by the word—and even press rates were expensive—the practice was to affix Latin prefixes and suffixes to make one word do the work of several. Thus, an imaginary cable might read, DUBNOW ARRIVED LONDON BAGGAGELESS EXPOLAND NEWYORKWARDING TOMORROW HOPING PROENTRY ALTHOUGH VISALESS. Translation:

Rabbi Jacob Dubnow, a leader of the Jewish community in Lodz, has escaped from Nazi-occupied Poland and arrived safely in London. He was obliged to leave his baggage behind. He is planning to sail for New York tomorrow, hoping that he will be admitted by the immigration authorities as an asylum seeker although he lacks an American visa.

I have a vivid memory of editor Victor Bienstock's reprimand to a correspondent who overfiled: PROCRISSAKE OFFLAY. Cablese is long since gone, a victim of the Teletype and, eventually, the fax machine. DOWNPLAY, for "play down," was a cablese word that survived in the American language.

At JTA we received chilling cable reports of anti-Semitic depredations in Europe from refugees, Jewish organizations, and neutral travelers. These reports occasioned screaming headlines in the Yiddish press, but were largely ignored by the general newspapers. Editors were being counseled by the State Department to be wary of Jewish propaganda. Years later, declassified records would show how far the American and British governments went to keep Americans in ignorance of the extermination of the Jews in Europe. For fear of distracting the Allies from pursuit of the war, it was said.

My job also included providing a weekly packet of mimeographed news and editorial material for several dozen Anglo-Jewish weekly newspapers around the country. Their demand was as great as their financial resources were small. So, I churned out copy using several pseudonyms, as well as my own name. The rule was to emphasize the "Jewish" angle. In my music column I favored conductor Bruno Walter over Leopold Stokowski, pianist Arthur Rubinstein over Claudio Arrau. (For free concert tickets and phonograph records I had relented on my contempt for music criticism.) Each week I summarized "The War and the Jews." Each year I did an article asking, "Was Columbus a Jew?" (No, but his navigator may have been Jewish.)

After seven years of this I began to bridle about this contorted view of a world in crisis. I made my discomfort evident enough so that Landau finally suggested it might be time for me to move on. Fired, you might call it. For the first time, but not the last. Anyway, I would rather be sending cables than receiving and rewriting them. With my language aptitude and my fascination with a Europe in torment, I wanted to be a foreign correspondent, like Vincent Sheean, H. R. Knickerbocker, and Walter Duranty.

The time was the summer of 1941. Expecting soon to be drafted (I had a deferment as the sole support of my widowed mother), I did not try hard to find a permanent job. For a few weeks I worked on the copy desk of Hearst's *New York Journal-American*, where I first learned about efficiency experts. One of those employed by Hearst had the doors taken off the stalls in the men's room on the theory that people would spend less time there. That's all I remember of my experience with the "Lord of the Press."

A mutual friend introduced me to Arnold Vas Diaz, a bouncy, bearded Hollander who was establishing, in the Associated Press building on Rockefeller Plaza, a bureau of ANETA, the news agency of the Netherlands East Indies (today, Indonesia). He explained that, with Holland occupied and its national news agency spewing out Nazi propaganda, ANETA had set up headquarters in London, where Queen Wilhelmina and her family were living in exile. ANETA wanted now to have an outlet in America, and I was offered the job of news editor, rewriting cables for American consumption.

I volunteered that I knew little about Holland and less about its colonial possessions. Vas Diaz said he considered that a qualification for a job that required an American perspective.

This was weeks before the December 7 Japanese attack on Pearl Harbor. As the Japanese moved southward toward the Philippines and the Indies, my work took on an unpremeditated form. At 7 A.M. daily, the ANETA bureau in Batavia (now, Jakarta) would call on the telephone and dictate news stories, which we would record, transcribe, and rewrite. With the outbreak of war, the Dutch government in the Indies exercised strict military censorship, and I could sense when my Batavia colleague slowed down or paused for a second that there was something he could not say.

One morning (there, night) our man in Batavia went through his news budget and then, as though adding a feature story, said, "The American airmen, with their crushed caps, are becoming a familiar sight on the streets of Batavia." What American airmen? We knew that several squadrons of the U.S. air force were operating from Australia. I realized that my colleague had slipped something through censorship.

I put out a bulletin on our wire, "Elements of the American air force have arrived in Java to aid in the defense against the oncoming

Japanese." Seeing little ANETA credited on the front pages of American newspapers was the most thrilling moment of my year and a half with the little Dutch news agency.

The AP building was also a place for journalistic camaraderie. Around the corner from us on the fifth floor was the Canadian Press bureau, where I met Sydney Gruson, a reporter from Toronto, who would later become, as a *New York Times* correspondent, my most enduring friend in journalism. I was on hand when he met and married a brilliant young AP diplomatic correspondent, Flora Lewis.

We crossed paths and worked together many times in many places—Holland, where, as a stringer, I would succeed Sydney; in Poland; in Geneva and in Germany, where Sydney sold me his Mercedes when he left. I went to Mexico on vacation when Sydney was stationed there, leading the high life and making a big splash at the racetrack with his ownership of two horses. Urbane and smooth, son of a rabbi who had migrated to Ireland and later Canada, Sydney had one particular talent as a journalist. In Geneva, while the rest of us scrounged around for word of the American position at the four-power conference on Berlin, he went out to play golf with a member of the American delegation and returned casually flaunting the secret document detailing the American position.

Together, in 1955, we covered a Nicaraguan invasion of Costa Rica that ended abruptly when the United States provided Costa Rican president José "Pepe" Figueres with two outdated P-51 fighters. Together we did stories from Panama and reported on a meeting of the Organization of American States in Caracas at which Secretary of State John Foster Dulles rammed through a resolution condemning the left-wing regime in Guatemala, a preliminary to a CIA-organized coup that ousted the regime and set the stage for thirty years of repressive military rule.

But Sydney's real ambition was to be a *Times* executive, and he eventually became one—a loss to journalism. A personal loss to all of us was his divorce from Flora, breaking up one of the great reporting teams of our time.

At ANETA, I developed a warm feeling for my Dutch bosses and colleagues. When, finally, in January 1943 my draft number came up, I was sent off with sentimental farewells and my promise to return after I had helped to liberate the Netherlands and the Netherlands Indies.

To say that I disliked life in the army would be a considerable understatement, but I found ways of coping with it. Undergoing basic training at the replacement center at Fort Riley, Kansas, I contrived to make the experience a little easier on myself. For example, when my platoon was called out of barracks to march to the dispensary at the other end of the post for inoculations, I stayed behind and took the camp bus, falling into place when the others arrived. A sergeant who saw me get off the bus shook his head unbelievingly.

The climax of our training cycle was a weeklong bivouac on ground sodden with Kansas's winter rains. I managed to persuade the top sergeant that he needed someone back in barracks to bring out the mail and other messages, so I was designated "company clerk" and slept no night in the mud.

I was—let's face it—not a very good soldier. Named "acting corporal," I was soon dismissed when I displayed absolutely no leadership ability. It took me longer than most soldiers to clean and assemble a rifle. I came close to being killed when I ventured across a shooting range while returning from the latrine.

I disliked guard duty and stable police (Fort Riley was a cavalry post, in transition between horses and jeeps). I disliked that bane of the GI called kitchen police, the mess-hall cleanup detail on which, it sometimes seemed, I spent half my waking and some of my semiwaking hours. A Polish-American man from Chicago, a rough and ready sort, became my undying friend. Paired with me in the kitchen, he helped me with the soapy water as well as doing the clean-water rinse. He would refer to me, affectionately, as "you fuckin' intellectual."

Fuckin', I learned, was a word with no specific meaning, simply a form of emphasis. I remember the comrade-in-arms who returned from his first trip to town on a weekend pass. He talked of "going into this fuckin' bar," ordering a "fuckin' beer," meeting "this fuckin' dame," taking her to "this fuckin' hotel," and "up the fuckin' elevator to a fuckin' room." There, he said, "we had intercourse."

One thing basic training did for me was to cure me forever of being a light sleeper. After a day of guard duty (two hours on, four hours off) followed by KP or stable police, followed by a night march with full gear, I could instantly fall asleep when the sergeant said, "Fall out by the side of the road. Take ten. Smoke if you got 'em."

It was also in basic training that I learned to drive. After one lesson in "double clutching" to shift gears, I was put into a three-quarter-ton armored personnel carrier and told to follow the vehicles ahead of me in a column. Preoccupied with trying to drive the behemoth, I did not watch the vehicles ahead. Suddenly I found myself nearing what looked like a deep pool of water. I hastily tried to jam on the brake, but hit the accelerator instead. My vehicle zoomed into and out of the water. A lieutenant came up in a jeep to compliment me on doing "exactly the right thing" when faced with water on the road.

Having completed basic training (and lean at last), I was assigned to the Eighth Armored Division, training at Camp Polk, Louisiana, for movement overseas at some indeterminate time. Arriving at Camp Polk after a furlough, I found myself waiting outside headquarters with a couple hundred other replacements. Deciding to see if I could influence my fate, I walked into headquarters and looked for the public relations office. There I told a young lieutenant that he might be able to use an experienced journalist who could write press releases and such. He requested my assignment to his office, which saved me from some uncomfortable infantry platoon.

One weekend I went to Houston to meet a friend from New York, Jacques Abram, a talented pianist. He was stationed in a special services (entertainment) unit at Randolph Air Force Base, in San Antonio. Jacques said he thought he could get me transferred to San Antonio because he knew the commanding general of the Fourth Army, who had authority over my division. To my surprise, a few weeks later I was transferred to Headquarters, Fourth Army, Fort Sam Houston, because of "special skills."

The Eighth Armored soon shipped off to Europe and ended up in Czechoslovakia. I, with my "special skills," was promoted to sergeant and placed in the Fourth Army's G-2 (intelligence) section. If I could not be a correspondent for *Yank* or *Stars and Stripes,* San Antonio was not a bad place to be. The headquarters occupied a quadrangle around a lawn graced with peacocks and deer (an enthusiasm of the commanding general's).

A headquarters detachment, while waiting for an army to be shipped overseas, had little function other than to observe the training of subordinate units. We were receiving large quantities of briefing materials in the expectation of going to the Pacific. I volunteered to condense some of this material into a treatise on the psychology and traits of the Japanese.

I was sent for a five-week course at the intelligence training center at Fort Ritchie, Maryland. Several of us were sent out on a field exercise that required us to find our way back to camp, using only map and compass. When I realized that none of us had the foggiest idea how to do that, I did the forbidden thing—asked a gas station attendant where we were and which way to Ritchie.

Being stationed in Maryland also enabled me to make visits to Washington. One evening I stood in the back of the Stage Door Canteen in Lafayette Square near the White House watching Lana Turner perform. A young sailor asked if I knew Washington and whether it was true that there were four women for every man in the nation's capital. I said I had heard some statistic like that.

"Well," the sailor said, "then some son of a bitch must have eight."

I returned to San Antonio to find my headquarters detachment gone—alerted and one day later on its way to the Pacific. I became part of the new Fourth Army headquarters detachment. As luck would have it, I was in the hospital when this group packed up and started off to the Pacific.

When the war was over and I was asked where I had served, I would say, "In the army of occupation in Texas." And when someone pointed to my one decoration, the Good Conduct Medal, and asked what I got it for, I would say, "I think for not getting syphilis for a whole year."

What, more than anything else, made San Antonio bearable was the presence of a couple, Frank and Florence Rosengren, who ran the best bookshop in town and made their rambling house a salon away from home for those who liked books and music. I spent many a Sunday evening there, and sometimes a whole weekend. Frank, in a wheelchair, suffering from rheumatoid arthritis, and Florence became my dear friends. We corresponded after the war, but I did not get to see them again before they died. Young Frank ("Figgi") and his wife still live in that wonderful house on Anastacia Street, and I was able to visit with them a few years ago.

It may not be customary for a nonviolent civilian who prizes comfort and privacy to be sentimental about any part of his enforced military service. But I associate San Antonio not only with the relative comfort of a permanent garrison, but the friends with whom I shared the climactic closing days of the war.

It was there, on April 12, 1945, that our detachment was called to attention while an officer told of the death of President Roosevelt in Warm Springs, Georgia. Our mourning was mixed with apprehension. We had lost not only our commander in chief, but also our father.

It was there, on August 5, that we learned that a new weapon, the atomic bomb, had been dropped on Japan. And, whatever considerations of morality would trouble me in later life, our predominant feeling as soldiers was joy at the prospect that Japan would surrender without our being involved in an invasion.

In candor I must say that, passionate as I was about the war against Hitler, destroyer of Europe and a generation of Jews, and his allies, that passion did not extend to relishing the idea of combat. Call me a coward, but every time a contingent of troops went overseas without me, I felt only a sense of relief. I felt detached from the maelstrom of war as I felt detached from so many human activities. I guess my mother didn't raise her son to be a hero.

Had the opportunity presented itself to be a war correspondent for *Yank* or *Stars and Stripes*, I would have overcome my antipathy to trenches and foxholes. But the army ignored my offer to volunteer for duty overseas as a journalist.

Once the war had ended, the army offered us courses to fill the time before our discharge. (I chose Spanish.)

I used some of my free time to write an article for *The New Republic* on the rampant discrimination against Mexican-Americans in south Texas. That drew a reprimand from an officer, who said soldiers were not supposed to write for civilian publications—especially left-wing ones.

One curious thing I must report: As the date for my separation approached, I began to feel more apprehensive than exhilarated. For two years I had been fed, clothed, and directed by the army, with few decisions to make for myself. Now, nearing thirty, I had to reorient myself to the idea of autonomy. No more barracks, no more mess halls, no more PX, no more free dispensary. And I would have to decide what I would wear every day.

I would return to living with my mother in the Bronx. Yes, but for how long? I would return to ANETA, but for how long, now that Holland and Indonesia had been liberated?

Unsure of many things, I was sure of one thing—I wanted to be a foreign correspondent. I had grown up nourished by the boldface bylines in the *New York Times*—Frederick Birchall, Arnaldo Cortesi, Herbert Matthews, Otto Tolischus. I dreamt of seeing my name among them on that front page. That was my clear goal as I reentered civilian life.

CHAPTER 2

GOING DUTCH

The Netherlands, that neat and orderly country wrested in large part from the North Sea, was where I first experienced the outside world. The ANETA news agency, to which I returned after being mustered out of the army, asked me in 1946 to spend a year in Holland reorganizing its service to America. Arriving in Rotterdam on the Holland-America liner *Westerdam* in October, I found a country still reeling from war and occupation. Textiles, meat, butter, and even cheese were still rationed. So was newsprint, doled out at a quarter of the prewar level, starving the many lively underground newspapers that had sprung up during the occupation.

Decent, God-fearing, and law-abiding, the Dutch could deal with material privation. There was relatively little black-marketing. They found it harder to deal with the disloyal among them—the "collaborators" who had worked, passively or actively, for the Nazis. The musical world was torn apart when the famous conductor Willem Mengelberg sought his pension and rehabilitation. Under occupation aegis, he had conducted the Amsterdam Concertgebouw, boycotted by the resistance. The three-judge Central Court of Honor found him guilty of collaboration and denied him rehabilitation.

My assignment in Holland brought me up against some of the ambiguities of the postoccupation period. ANETA had been the

Dutch news agency in exile while the Algemeen Nederlands Persbureau, A.N.P., the general news agency of the Netherlands, had operated under Nazi license during the occupation. Headquartered in the A.N.P. building on the Parkstraat in the center of The Hague, I had the job of restoring a working relationship with A.N.P. for purposes of filing news reports for America.

It wasn't easy. My best journalistic friends were from resistance newspapers—underground heroes such as Dries Ekker of *Het Parool* and Jaap Hoek of *Trouw*. I distrusted the daily file of the A.N.P., which, from long habit, specialized in official handouts. In turn, the managers of A.N.P. resented me, especially for spreading subversive ideas of independent journalism among the younger staff. At the end of a year we felt well rid of each other, and I returned to New York.

But, if I did not like the residue of occupation journalism, I did like the Netherlands. I liked the way, in the most crowded country in Europe, the Dutch maintained respect for each other and avoided intruding on each other. I liked the directness with which they spoke—and, after a while, even the literalness. It took me some time to learn not to say "Let's have lunch sometime" to someone I didn't really want to see, because the invariable answer would be "Fine! When?"

(A tourist guide whom I knew catalogued the addresses of all the Americans who had, at the end of their tours, told her heartily, "You be sure to come see us if you are ever in the States!" She flew to New York for a cross-country trip, showing up at their homes without advance notice. On her return to the Netherlands, she said she had had a wonderful time, but was puzzled by the double takes she got from some who had told her they would never forget her.)

I liked the industriousness of the Dutch. In 1947 the fast-growing nation of almost 10 million had expanded its industry to 90 percent of prewar. Neatly dressed burghers, smoking just-derationed cigars, pedaled their freshly-tired bicycles that a year before had been clanking down the streets on their rims. A congressional committee headed by Rep. Chris Herter came to Holland on a European tour of Marshall Plan progress. A staff member marveled at how the Dutch were willing to keep a lid on consumption in order to boost exports. After Italy, France, and Belgium, a committee staffer told me, "It's like a refreshing breeze to come to Holland."

Most of all I liked the tolerance of the Dutch. Later, with an influx of dark-skinned people from the lost colonies in the East and West Indies, would come some ethnic tensions. But, the Holland I first came to know was a country proud of its centuries-old hospitality to exiles. It was the only country I have ever known where the words *Jew* and *Jewish* were used admiringly, most often to denote cultured people. It was a country whose Jewish families went back to fugitives from the Spanish Inquisition, a country that grieved for families lost in the Holocaust.

When *The Diary of Anne Frank* was published in its original Dutch, I was one of the first to visit the *achterhuis*—the garret concealed behind a bookcase where her family, refugees from Germany, had lived for two years. Isaac Stern, the violinist, arriving in Amsterdam from Israel, where he had just married a German refugee, asked whether I could arrange for him to visit the Anne Frank house. We went there together, escorted by Miep Gies, the onetime employee of Otto Frank who had sustained the family until the Nazi police found them. Not yet turned into a museum, the bare attic rooms left both Isaac and me hardly able to speak. Isaac observed that the smells of six-year-old cooking spices and condiments were still faintly in the air. Looking out the window to the nearby Westerkerk (Western Church), whose bells Anne had listened to, we recalled the line from the diary, "I see the eight of us in the Annex as if we were a patch of blue sky surrounded by menacing black clouds."

That night, soloist with the Amsterdam Concertgebouw Orchestra in the Beethoven Concerto, Isaac walked back and forth in the dressing room, practicing some phrases. At one point he stopped at the piano, where, in his open violin case, I could see a picture of Anne Frank. Softly he said, "This one tonight is for you."

I would return thirteen years later to No. 263 Prinsengracht (Princes' Canal) as a CBS News correspondent working on a documentary on Nazi war criminals titled *Who Killed Anne Frank?* In the garret, whose wall still displayed the photos of Anne's favorite movie stars and a map showing the D-Day landings, I interviewed her seventy-five-year-old father, Otto Frank, the only survivor among the eight Jews who had lived there in terror for twenty-five months. In Vienna, with the help of Nazi hunter Simon Wiesenthal, I had found the Austrian policeman, Karl Silberbauer, who had been Anne Frank's captor. His only visible reaction was surprise at the fuss the world was making over a few more Jews rounded up. He professed not to have known where they would end up. "I was just doing my job," he said.

Otto Frank, who had returned from his home in Switzerland for the interview, told me how Silberbauer (a name new to him) had broken into the attic with drawn revolver, had looked for money and jewelry, dumping the contents of a briefcase on the floor. Included was Anne's diary—found still lying there after the war.

Frank talked bitterly of Germans today, who seemed so "ordinary," but may have been murderers and sadists during the war. I reminded him that his daughter had written in her diary that she believed in the good in all men. "Well, my daughter was of an age of great optimism," he replied, "but I think she didn't mean that. We know that bad people exist."

The date of the interview was November 22, 1963. I left the house on the Princes' Canal and, on the radio in my car, heard that President Kennedy had been shot in Dallas. Every American remembers where he or she was that day. I was in Amsterdam, documenting bygone murders.

I would return to the Anne Frank House once again in 1985, no longer a bachelor, but with my wife, son, and daughter. Now 263 Prinsengracht was an official museum, and a long line of visitors stretched around the corner. Much had been changed on the lower floors, but the garret remained untouched. This was a way of sharing with my family one of the moving experiences of my bachelor professional days.

But I have gotten far ahead of my story. In the fall of 1947, I completed my year for ANETA, returned to New York, and took an amicable leave of the Dutch news agency that had tided me over during my postwar readjustment. I resumed my quest to become what I wanted most in the world to be—a foreign correspondent for the *New York Times*.

Theodore Bernstein, assisting managing editor, told me I could not have picked a worse time. Swollen wartime bureaus were being reduced or dismantled and foreign correspondents were in great surplus. Bernstein suggested that if I had my heart set on being a *Times* foreign correspondent, the best thing I could do was to find other remunerative work in some not overcovered part of Europe and wait for the breaks.

That decided me—I would return to the Netherlands, expanding my domain to include Belgium and Luxembourg, working at whatever freelance assignments I could muster. These turned out to be for the *Christian Science Monitor*, the American Broadcasting Company, and *Time* magazine, to which I later added the *London Daily Mail* and the *New York Times*. Still later *Newsweek* replaced *Time* and CBS replaced ABC.

Also in my bailiwick was the International Court of Justice, the judicial arm of the United Nations, housed in the Carnegie-endowed Peace Palace. It betokened the postwar dream of a rule of law in the world. But soon it fell under the shadow of the Cold War. For a year its fifteen black-robed judges waited for someone to submit its first case. Finally, in 1947, Britain lodged a complaint against Albania for the mining of the Corfu Straits, which had damaged two British destroyers at a cost of forty-four lives. Month after month the hearings droned on. Eventually a majority found in Britain's favor, awarding reparations that the pugnacious little Soviet satellite refused to pay.

Later I would sit through cases involving the right of asylum in Latin America, American commercial rights in French Morocco, and a British-Norwegian fishing dispute. I found the *Christian Science Monitor* receptive to detailed coverage of tedious argumentation about peripheral issues. The gathering clouds of the Cold War hardly reached the serene corridors of the Peace Palace because most countries (including the United States) did not accept automatic jurisdiction of the court. An exciting moment occurred in 1951. The Iranian government of Mohammed Mossadegh, which had unseated the Shah, sent delegates to counter a British complaint over the nationalization of the Anglo-Iranian Oil Company. But, before the rule of law could be applied, Britain and the United States applied the rule of cloak-and-dagger and had Mossadegh toppled and the Shah restored.

The fifteen old men, ranging in age from fifty-five to seventy-eight, sighed over the case that had got away. They did not enjoy the enforced idleness that was their usual lot. They were forbidden to engage in any other professional activity. They could leave The Hague, subject to recall if and when a case cropped up, but mostly they spent their time in academic work, reading or just sitting around the lounge of the Hôtel des Indes.

I settled down in a rented top-floor room in a house owned by a Dutch widow on the quiet blind alley Surinamestraat in The Hague. (Because of the housing shortage, house owners were obliged by law to rent out rooms.) I shared office space on the nearby Javastraat with Nel Slis, correspondent of the Associated Press, with whom I developed a close personal as well as working relationship. I was concerned whether I could subsist on freelance earnings in a region that had been a quiet European backwater between the world wars.

I need not have worried; the next five years would produce the drama of the American-financed recovery program called the Marshall Plan, the stirrings of European unity, the birth of the North Atlantic alliance, the traumatic Dutch separation from Indonesia, royal crises in Belgium and the Netherlands, and finally, a flood of historic proportions in Holland.

My first week back in Holland, in May 1948, I covered a Congress of Europe, keynoted by former prime minister Winston Churchill with a ringing call for European unity in the face of the Soviet shadow falling over Eastern Europe. This conference of non-governmental organizations would be remembered as the first step toward bringing defeated Germany and Italy back into the family of nations, and as the precursor to the European Union.

The Congress of Europe was the occasion for my first network-radio broadcast—live from a tiny studio in The Hague for the ABC

World News Roundup. The shortwave connection crackled and faded in and out. The editor in New York told me I would hear the program in my headphones, that I should start when I heard myself introduced and not, on any account, go over two minutes. I heard my name and rattled through my script with an eye on a stopwatch, ending on the nose of two minutes with "Now back to ABC News in New York." I waited for the editor's comment and heard only silence and crackle. "Hello, New York; hello, New York," I called. Finally the editor, by now busy working other circuits, came on the line. "How did I do?" I asked. "Great!" he said. "You got off in time." That was my first lesson in the priorities of electronic journalism.

My next story broke unexpectedly—the announcement of sixty-seven-year old Queen Wilhelmina that she would abdicate in September because of "fatigue" and "the complex problems facing the kingdom." She spoke on the radio from Soestdijk Palace in a voice tremulous with emotion. Two cabinet ministers sat together to hear her. One covered his face with his hands. The other left the room to avoid showing his emotion. My stolid charwoman said, "She's done it long enough, and it couldn't have been easy."

How to explain, in this day of royal scandal, how reverently the Dutch felt about their widowed queen? From wartime exile in London, she had maintained the House of Orange as a symbol of unity and anti-Nazi resistance. Her broadcasts over Radio Orange had helped the Dutch keep faith in liberation when the prospects seemed dim. She had made a historic broadcast from London to prepare her people for a different relationship with the colonies when the war was over. Restored to her throne after the war, she had conducted herself with a simplicity that had endeared her to her nation.

Like most Americans, I stood in awe of royalty, never having met any. My first encounter with Dutch royalty had come the year before when I'd joined a journalistic vigil at a country inn near Soestdijk Palace, where Crown Princess Juliana was expecting a fourth child. This was a source of enormous tension. Princess Juliana, herself an only child, had three daughters. A fourth would mean three queens in a row—Wilhelmina, who had reigned for almost half a century, to be followed by Juliana, and then by her oldest daughter, Beatrix. The Dutch wanted, at long last, a future king.

The prayers of the Dutch did not prevail. It was a fourth girl. I interviewed the father, Prince Bernhard, who said the predictable things about how nice it would have been to have had a boy, but how happy they were with their girl. The media-savvy prince and I also laid the basis for future informal meetings.

Not immediately known was that Princess Maria Christina, familiarly called Marijke, had been born partially blind. Princess Juliana, while pregnant, had contracted rubella while performing one of her royal chores—greeting in Rotterdam a shipload of troops returned from revolution-torn Indonesia. The conflict between royal duties and mother's duties would, in time, precipitate a crisis in one of the most stable monarchies in Europe—a crisis in which I would become deeply involved. But that is getting ahead of the story.

The first time I found myself playing a role in a story I was covering was when I was blamed for the scuttling of the Dutch-Indonesian peace talks. I had flown to Indonesia, in May 1948, to report on the deadlocked negotiations and the threatened breakdown of a five-month-old truce.

On the way I found myself skirting another war. When the KLM Constellation from Amsterdam landed at Cairo's Farouk Airport, we were told by excited officials that the Arab states were at war with the newly proclaimed state of Israel, and we had violated a newly announced ban on night flying. Thinking to report on the atmosphere in darkened Cairo, I wrote a dispatch to ABC and the *Christian Science Monitor*, but was told that all cables now had to be submitted to censorship—and the censor had not yet been appointed. At the airport hotel where we spent the night I got a pilot headed for Amsterdam to take my dispatch with him—my first evasion of censorship.

Indonesia, my introduction to Asia, provided an experience in culture shock. It took me some time to understand that many Indonesians have only one name. The president of the unrecognized republic, Sukarno, a Balinese, had no other name. *Time* magazine cabled, insisting that I provide a first name. I cabled back "Achmed." In subsequent years, I was awed at how "Achmed" stuck to him in the American press for years thereafter, even showing up in his Associated Press obituary.

One of my first Indonesian Republican friends was (no first name) Dr. Leimena, a Dutch-educated physician who spoke excellent English. From him I learned my second never-the-twain lesson. In a long teatime talk I tried to grasp the strategy of the nationalists by surmising how they would respond to various contingencies. At each suggestion, Dr. Leimena nodded his head, as though in affirmation. When my scenario turned out to be totally wrong, I felt betrayed. An old Indonesian hand among the resident correspondents explained that my mistake had been to make positive assertions that would require my host to tell me I was wrong. To a cultured Indonesian that would be impolite. So he had nodded politely rather than be rude. And I had totally misunderstood.

In May 1948, after a five-month truce, the United Nations had failed to find a basis for negotiation between the Indonesian Republicans, seeking sovereignty over the far-flung archipelago, and the Dutch rulers, demanding a federal structure that preserved the rights of the non-Javanese (and more pro-Dutch) islands. The United Nations was represented by the Good Offices Committee, including a pro-Dutch Belgian, a pro-Indonesian Australian, and an ostensibly neutral American, a retired consul named Coert DuBois. The talks shuttled every three weeks, by wood-burning train, between the capital, Batavia (Jakarta), and the cool mountain resort of Kaliurang in Republican-held central Java. In the old colonial dining room of Batavia's Hôtel des Indes, one still called the waiter *djongos* (boy). In Kaliurang, one was well advised to call him *bung* (comrade). Along the way on the fourteen-hour train ride, young Indonesians were turned out to shout *"Merdeka!"* (freedom).

Although the United Nations had set the end of 1948 as the target for independence, freedom was nowhere in sight. The Dutch, who had ruled the Netherlands East Indies for more than three centuries and exploited its oil, rubber, tobacco, and tin resources, talked of a gradual transition toward a federal state, but they seemed in no hurry. They also sought to organize the outlying islands such as Celebes, Borneo, and Bali into a separate federation as a buffer against the dominant Javanese.

Despairing of early agreement, fearing a renewal of fighting, the American and Australian mediators decided on an initiative of their own, violating the committee's unanimity rule. Over the objections of the Belgian, they offered a confidential "compromise proposal" for elections throughout the archipelago, leading to the formation of a constituent assembly. Premier Mohammed (a real first name) Hatta accepted for the Indonesians. Dutch governor-general Hubertus J. van Mook rejected it out of hand and demanded that it be withdrawn and suppressed.

At that point, someone slipped a copy of the plan to me. I summarized it in a cable to *Time* magazine. Soon I found myself vaulted to center stage. In the U.N. Security Council, Dutch ambassador Eelco N. van Kleffens denounced the leak and asserted that the Netherlands was suspending negotiations. This was before *Time* had even appeared. When the magazine did come out, it said that the Dutch, by jumping the gun, had admitted that "somebody was snooping into correspondents' outgoing cables." Years later, Dutch officials admitted to me that this was true. They also said they had been looking for the first available pretext to call off the sterile talks and resume the war, or "police action," as they called it.

I still remember the heady feeling of being catapulted from freelance reporter to the center of the story, discussed by name in a U.N. debate. I am aware that, half a century later, historians are still interested in finding out who leaked the document—the Dutch, to justify breaking off negotiations, or the Indonesians, to force the issue into public debate. I still find it almost viscerally impossible to expose a source. But, for the benefit of the historians, let me say that the leak did not come from either of the contending parties.

A melancholy footnote to my six-week tour of Indonesia: A year later, in 1949, Charles E. Gratke, foreign editor of the *Christian Sci-*

ence Monitor, wrote me in The Hague that he had been invited by the Netherlands government to join a group of journalists for a trip to Indonesia. He offered to defer to me as the paper's expert on Indonesia, but, sensing that he really wanted to take the trip, I urged him to go. And thus he was one of the fourteen who toured Indonesia and were all killed when their chartered KLM plane crashed near Bombay on the way back to Amsterdam. In their memory, the Dutch government established an annual journalism award called the William the Silent Prize ($2,500 and a large gold medallion). *William the Silent* may sound like a strange name for a journalistic prize, but that was how the taciturn William of Orange, founder of the Netherlands, was known. As irony would have it, I was the first winner of that prize in 1950 for an article in Gratke's paper. I sometimes think about Chuck Gratke, my first foreign editor, and a splendid one, and I wonder about there, for but the grace of...

I returned from Indonesia to Holland in June 1948, in time to cover the first Dutch postwar election. There was some interest back home in what advances the Communists were making, whether the Marshall Plan was effectively immunizing the liberated countries against subversion. (A query from *Time* magazine asked whether any great upset was to be expected; I replied, "Holland is too flat a country for a landslide.") The election confirmed the basic moderation of the Dutch, bringing to power a centrist Labor-Catholic coalition, led by the mild-mannered, droopy-mustached Laborite Willem Drees. His first task was to try to find a way out of the deadlock with the Indonesian nationalists.

Indonesia was to dominate my reporting for the next year and a half. The Drees government, in vain, tried out various formulas for a federation that would leave the outlying islands of the archipelago with considerable autonomy. Complicating the situation was an abortive uprising of the Indonesian Communists. In June 1948, I had interviewed Alimin, the Moscow-trained leader of the PKI (Indonesian Communist Party) in Solo, central Java. Clad in a sarong, sitting on a straw mat, he said that "our present policy is to support the nationialist revolution" and that "the time will come for socialism in

Indonesia, but no one can tell when." Months later he led an unsuccessful revolt—against the Indonesian nationalists. The display of Communist muscle in Indonesia helped harden the Dutch position.

Finally, in December 1948, the Dutch launched a renewed military action, occupying the Republican capital of Jogjakarta in central Java and arresting its leaders. This dismayed the friends of the Netherlands and angered the United States. The U.N. Security Council demanded a cease-fire, and as I was able to report, the Truman administration threatened a suspension of Marshall Plan aid for Holland.

The Dutch authorities, as many times before, accused me of being antagonistic to them and serving Indonesian interests. I responded that, as an American, I was aware of the sweep of history dismantling colonial empires, but sympathized with the Dutch desire for an orderly transition. More persuasive, it turned out, was what the Dutch found when they pored through the Indonesian files they had captured. Memorandums of nationalist officials expressed suspicion that I was working for the Dutch. Finally a Dutch official told me, "We thought you were working for the Indonesians. But they seemed to think you were working for us. We were reluctantly forced to conclude that you were evenhandedly a pain in the neck to both sides."

The Dutch justified their "police action" as aimed at eliminating "terrorists" and setting the stage for negotiation. But, in the end, the international pressures on them proved irresistible, and they had to pull back. Their attempt to impose their will by force represented the death throes of colonial rule. In 1949, under incessant American pressure, a six-week U.N.-mediated Round Table Conference in The Hague painfully wrote the charter for a "sovereign Indonesia."

I found myself reunited with friends I had made in Indonesia— Indonesian premier Mohammed Hatta, Health Minister Leimena, and members of the U.N. Good Offices Committee, on which the ineffective American member, Coert DuBois, had been replaced by Ambassador H. Merle Cochran, who became the powerhouse of the strenuous negotiations.

The last hitch, which almost stalled the conference, was typically Dutch. On grounds of conscience they resisted surrendering Dutch New Guinea, saying that would only abandon a primitive people to a new colonialism. In the end, an arrangement was worked out for New Guinea to remain under Dutch control for a transitional period. (During that period, Secretary of State John Foster Dulles, seated next to Dutch foreign minister Joseph Luns at a NATO dinner in Copenhagen, asked Luns, a member of the Catholic People's Party, how missionary work was progressing in New Guinea. Luns replied, "Fine, Mr. Secretary. On Friday the natives now eat only fishermen.")

It was with a sense of being a witness to history that I watched from the balcony of the medieval Hall of Knights on November 9, 1949, as the leaders of the Indonesian Republicans, the Indonesian Federalists, and the Dutch signed documents creating "the Republic of the United States of Indonesia," a name chosen by the Indonesians as a gesture of recognition of the role played by the United States. Thus ended three and a half centuries of Dutch rule and four years of revolution against it.

I congratulated Indonesian Premier Mohammed Hatta. "So, your battle is over," I said. "The battle only begins," he replied.

Perhaps Dr. Hatta foresaw that the Sukarno government, originally installed by the Japanese as a kind of time bomb for the West as they withdrew in 1945, would be rent by civil war once independent. In 1965 the chief of the armed forces, General Suharto, conducted a massacre of ethnic Chinese, ostensibly to thwart a Communist coup against Sukarno. Suharto then unseated Sukarno and established a military dictatorship, declaring himself president for life. And that he might well have been if his greed and corruption had not caused him to be overthrown in 1998.

Do I betray the pro-Dutch side of my ambivalence about Indonesia when I say that the warnings of the Dutch, pooh-poohed in anticolonial America, came true in many respects? The nationalists, so fond of quoting Washington and Jefferson, turned out to be authoritarian once they had power. The Javanese established their own colonial rule over peoples of many ethnic strains in an archipelago of 13,500 islands. They gobbled up everything around them—Dutch New Guinea and Portuguese East Timor. In East Timor, the independence aspirations of a mainly Christian people were suppressed by the Indonesian military with greater brutality than the Dutch masters had ever shown.

The Netherlands, forced to give up its overseas empire, turned toward integration in Europe. Economic integration came relatively easily. I covered dozens of conferences in which Holland, step by step, blended its economy with those of Belgium and Luxembourg, first in a customs union, finally, in 1950, in a complete economic union. Benelux was the trailblazer for what ultimately became the European Community.

Participation in a military alliance came harder. The Netherlands had been neutral in World War I and would have remained neutral in World War II had it not been invaded by the Germans. Now, the Dutch, along with other so recently occupied territories, were asked by the United States, in the person of Secretary of State Dean Acheson, not only to raise standing forces for a military partnership, but to accept Germany into that partnership.

Along with Acheson, I was present at the creation of NATO in Brussels in December 1950. A heavy snowstorm delayed Acheson's arrival for a day as foreign and defense ministers of twelve NATO countries gathered to sign the one-for-all-all-for-one defense pact, which, in effect, put them under the American nuclear umbrella and authorized German rearmament. The Christmas lights and the falling snow turned Brussels more into a fairyland than the scene of fateful decisions. The ebb and flow of crowds in the Place Brouckère mocked the Belgian army motorcycles revving their motors and trying to shepherd limousines to the dowdy Hôtel Métropole.

Eventually Acheson and various other missing ministers arrived from the Paris and other airports to which they had been diverted. They gathered in a huge mirrored room in the provincial legislature, around an oval table so large that one could not see through the cigar and cigarette smoke from one end to the other. But, two days later, the die was cast. The decisive element was the promise that

Gen. Dwight D. Eisenhower would be called out of retirement by President Truman to become the supreme commander of the NATO force. Less than a month later, the charismatic hero of World War II was there, setting up headquarters in Paris.

I accompanied him on parts of his European tours, the first one in January 1951. Wearing the famous short "Eisenhower jacket" with only one row of his many ribbons, he talked only perfunctorily to the press, but more vigorously in private sessions with government ministers and defense chiefs. A bevy of colonels had been sent to West European capitals in advance with word that the supreme commander wanted a minimum of publicity—a brief arrival statement at the airport without opportunity for questions.

Only once during that tour did I get to talk to General Eisenhower—while he was waiting in the Luxembourg hotel lobby to be picked up for a dinner at the residence of American envoy Perle Mesta. He asked me if Luxembourg had a golf course. I said I didn't know. And his car drove up. I guess he didn't have important business with Luxembourg's two-battalion army. When I asked Mrs. Mesta for a briefing about the dinner, she said she had addressed the supreme commander as "Ike" and he had greeted her as "Perlie." Anything else? Well, she had hired a five-piece musical ensemble and wanted them to play selections from *Call Me Madam!*, the musical comedy based on her. Not necessarily "The Hostess with the Mostest," but, at least, "I Like Ike." But the music had not arrived in time, and Mrs. Mesta had apologized to the general, who had said it was another lesson in readiness.

(At that, the supreme commander fared better with the unpredictable minister than some. Once she gave a reception for a delegation of young farm people representing the American 4-H clubs, who had spent the summer working on Luxembourg farms. Vain about wearing glasses in public, Mrs. Mesta read from her prepared text, "There are no people more representative of the best in American life than these young people of the 4-F Clubs of America.")

My favorite memory of Eisenhower as supreme commander was on a visit to a Belgian army supply depot. He asked about two piles of blankets of different quality. "These are for the officers," a Belgian

general said, pointing to the higher-quality blankets. General Eisenhower asked, in even tones, "Do the officers get colder?"

By the time Eisenhower left Europe in May 1952, a NATO military structure was in place. For Queen Juliana's birthday on April
30, Dutch Sherman tanks paraded and jet fighters screamed over-
head. A Hollander in the crowd said, "It took five days to occupy
Holland last time. Next time it will take ten."

CHAPTER 3

THE QUEEN,
THE FAITH HEALER,
AND I

Queen Juliana's investiture (the democratic Dutch don't call it a coronation) on September 6, 1948, had one downbeat note—the new sovereign herself. The event followed a weeklong celebration of the fifty-eight-year reign of the abdicating Queen Wilhelmina. Crowded into Amsterdam's medieval New Church were the crowned heads of Europe and a lot of top hats (including the one I had to rent in order to report the ceremony). Princess Juliana, in sapphire blue, entered on the arm of the resplendently uniformed Prince Bernhard, looking as though she were being led to the gallows.

It was widely known that the diffident Juliana, an only child, hated the idea of being monarch. As a child she was said to have expressed the hope that when she grew up, queens would no longer be needed. Unlike her mother, who had received a hothouse palace education, Juliana had been permitted to go to Leiden University, with commoners as friends, and had loved it. She had spent the war years in Canada and gotten accustomed to its easy going ways.

Queen Wilhelmina, in her farewell speech offered her thirty-nine-year-old daughter the consolation that she would reign as "a child of her time." But the new sovereign, addressing the assemblage in muted, tremulous tones, spoke of her "inner struggle" about ascending to the throne and announced that she considered her motherly duties as important as her royal duties. Just before taking the oath, she reflected her turmoil by asking, "Who am I that I may do this?"

Soon the new queen established an unpompous royal style. The curtsy was banned from her court. When she moved around her crowded country, no motorcycle escort roared ahead, and her car halted for stoplights with those of her subjects. When she went to the theater, no announcement to the audience of her presence was permitted. When I visited her with other foreign correspondents at Soestdijk Palace, we were told that the protocol of not leaving until dismissed by the queen no longer applied because she would often neglect to end the audience.

Outwardly, though, the succession in Holland stood in vivid contrast to the troubles of other European monarchies. In England, Edward VIII, appeasement-minded before the war, had been obliged to surrender the throne for love of an American divorcée. Belgium, part of my beat, was tormented by the effort of King Leopold to recover the throne. Unlike Queen Wilhelmina, who had joined her government in exile in London, Leopold had spent the war in Belgium under German occupation. After liberation, he went into exile in Switzerland with his unpopular Flemish wife, the Princess de Rethy. (His beloved first wife, Queen Astrid, had died in an automobile accident.) Leopold's restoration effort, backed by the Catholic party, tore the country apart. Finally, under the threat of a general strike from Paul-Henri Spaak's Socialist party, Leopold abdicated in 1951 in favor of his son, Prince Baudouin. Covering the *crise royale* in Belgium brought home to me the stability of the Dutch monarchy.

But beneath the placid surface a royal crisis of another sort was simmering, kept from the public by a benevolent conspiracy of official and press silence. The queen had taken up with a weird faith-healer and was hearing voices, believing she was in direct contact with God. And what the voices were telling her threatened to put her in conflict with her government. This began to evidence itself early in 1952 during planning for her first official visit to the United States. The itinerary called for speeches to a joint session of Congress, to the United Nations, and in several cities across the country and in Canada. For the government, led by Laborite Premier Willem Drees, this was an occasion to stress that the Netherlands, neutral until World War II, was now a sturdy member of the North Atlantic alliance. Queen Juliana had other ideas.

In March I learned and reported for the *New York Times* that the queen, departing from the constitutional rule that the monarch speak in public only for the government, was drafting her own speeches for America. I said that she wished to express "her personal credo, her spiritual and humanitarian outlook on life."

What I did not know was that a real battle royal was in progress. The government was strenuously opposed to much of what she wanted to say. Foreign Minister Dirk U. Stikker refused to accept responsibility, threatening to stay home from the trip and possibly resign. After long bickering, compromises were reached and the speeches were watered down. Knowing nothing of the battle, I was aware only that the speeches had an otherworldly, pacifist, and even neutralist tone. Before Congress, Juliana spoke of "the nightmare of our time." Before the United Nations, she talked of an overly technological society, a world run by "brains on wheels." She talked of Soviet-bloc countries not in NATO terms as potential aggressors, but as "concentrating on their own defense." Soviet delegate Jakob Malik congratulated her. A State Department official told me, "Her sentiments sent shivers down our spines."

When the queen came home in April, the constitutional conflict began to bubble to the surface. The widely circulated Laborite newspaper *Het Parool* sent me an advance copy of a front-page editorial containing an unprecedented attack on royal conduct. The queen being constitutionally inviolable, it took the form of criticism of the government for having permitted her speeches. Captioned "A Queer Country" in English, the editorial said, "Attentive reading leads one to ask what the government means by these speeches...."

One seeks in vain for any resolute expression of the stand that the Netherlands takes in these times as a member of the NATO alliance. . . . Views hailed by pacifists . . . and some mystics . . . Do they hear voices in The Hague and are they haunted by visions?"

I had lived in Holland long enough to respect the privacy of the royal family. But after this bombshell, clearly the time had come for some investigative reporting. Why was the queen bucking her government and where was she getting her subversive ideas? That investigation, over three months, led me down some uncharted paths of probing palace secrets. Eventually, as four years before in Indonesia, I again became the center of my own story and found myself facing dire warnings that I might single-handedly bring down the monarchy.

My first lead came from Mrs. Eleanor Roosevelt, a friend of Juliana's from wartime. She had been invited the previous fall to join a circle of the queen's friends for a weekend retreat at her mother's palace, known as Het Oude Loo, in central Holland, to discuss a religious outlook on current world problems. Among those present was Margareta Hofmans, described as a close friend of the queen's, and a schoolteacher named Johan Kaiser, who led the discussions. The group called itself Religion without Name, or the Oude Loo Movement. Its stated purpose was "the establishment of peace based on the sole acceptance that God is invincible."

Queen Juliana, after giving a short introduction, sat unobtrusively in the corner of the chapel-like eleventh-century room. The talk was about submission to God's will, personal connection with God, with some discussion of the dangers of rearmament. When one participant asked whether an unarmed Western Europe could be overrun by the Russians, Kaiser replied that the human spirit would survive occupation.

Mrs. Roosevelt was appalled by what the queen was involved in. She wrote in her newspaper column, "I felt that it was almost arrogant to expect to establish with the Almighty a direct and conscious connection." She was also concerned that Juliana would attribute to God ideas that might come from other sources. The former first lady told me she had written the queen expressing her concerns. When Juliana came to America in the spring of 1952, Mrs. Roosevelt invited her to Hyde Park for a weekend, took her for a long walk, and warned her forcefully about her dangerous ideas and associations. Mrs. Roosevelt told me that she did not succeed in swaying the queen from her conviction that "the answers to life's problems can only be found in one way"—by submission to the will of God, with whom she had direct contact.

I learned that there had been earlier confrontations with the government. Opposed to capital punishment, the queen had refused to ratify the warrant of execution for Willy Lages, the wartime chief of German security in Amsterdam, who had ordered the shooting of Dutch captives without trial and the shipment of seventy thousand Jews (probably including the family of Anne Frank) to extermination camps. To avoid a public showdown, the minister of justice had commuted Lages's sentence to life imprisonment.

Government liaison officers with the palace spoke to me guardedly of their worries about the willful queen. Members of her personal staff at Soestdijk spoke with the conviction of true believers about Miss Hofmans as a miracle worker. The queen's secretary, Baron van Heeckeren van Molecaten, on whose estate the faith healer lived, said, "To us she is everything." Others said she had healed thousands of people by helping to establish their contact with God. One said Miss Hofmans had looked at a photo of her cousin's three healthy children and correctly predicted that one would come down with a lung infection.

As word got around about my inquiries, I received a telephone call from an intermediary for Prince Bernhard, inviting me to meet with the prince privately. In a parlor in The Hague's dowdy Hôtel Vieux Doelen, he put a bottle of Scotch on the table and, without prompting, started to tell of his troubled wife. He said the near blindness of Princess Maria Christina (Marijke), whose birth I had covered five years before, had thrown the queen into a deep depression. Hoping to ease her depression, Bernhard said, he had introduced the faith healer to the queen and could now kick himself for having done so.

Juliana found herself immediately attracted to the serene, soft-spoken woman, who offered not only a cure for blindness, but a spiritual answer to the great riddles of life. With Miss Hofmans came her friend, Johan Kaiser, a student of religion and Hindu mysticism, who added a mélange of "third way" neutralism and antimilitarism to Miss Hofmans's doctrine of submission to God's will.

In 1949, Queen Juliana invited Miss Hofmans to live in the palace. The court soon split into adherents and detractors of the faith healer. Crown Princess Beatrix lined up with her father against "the mystics." Miss Hofmans told the queen that healing Marijke's eyes required the unreserved faith of both parents, intimating that Bernhard's skepticism was hindering the cure. Thus a wedge was driven between husband and wife. They quarreled constantly.

Prince Bernhard said he had recently succeeded in getting Greet Hofmans thrown out of the palace, but she had taken up residence near Soestdijk and was still seeing the queen.

I wondered why Prince Bernhard was telling me all this, with no suggestion that it was off-the-record. I surmised that he might welcome some disclosure that might help bring his wife to her senses.

Pursuing my investigation further, I went to see Miss Hofmans in Baarn, where she lived on a quiet lane in the home of a friend of the queen's. Johan Kaiser was on hand ostensibly to serve as English interpreter. He also prompted her, polishing and extending her remarks. Miss Hofmans, sitting in a straight-backed chair, her hands clasped in her lap, looked at me with a serene, fixed expression, but her eyes burned with an inner fire.

She told me she was 58 years old, never married, had worked for many years in an Amsterdam textile factory until 1946, when "it happened." She said, "Suddenly I felt a veil lift in my mind and I was in contact with God. It was not like hearing voices or seeing visions, but something of both, and more—something of another dimension."

As to how she conducted her faith healing, she said, "A sick person comes to me. As soon as he enters the room, I know what his illness is and I tell him. Then I say, 'I commit you to Christ.'" And that, she said, was all. Kaiser volunteered that she would see as many as six hundred persons a day, and that she had helped many thousands.

She explained the connection between faith healing and ideology. "A disease is not a thing in itself. It is a manifestation of a spiritual disorder. Thus, cancer in a person is connected with the spiritual disorder called war. Therefore I cannot cure cancer until war is eliminated. But I can definitely remove the pain." And how was the war to be eliminated? "By submission to God's will." There was a lot more about "psychic fluids" and "spiritual regeneration," but I frequently lost the thread of the Hofmans-Kaiser discourse.

She would not discuss specifically her relations with the queen and her efforts to cure Princess Marijke's near blindness, but she said, "In the case of young children, it is the parents who must have faith. You see, the parents are linked with the child by psychic fluids. This is a well-known fact. For example, it is not unusual for a child to feel ill when a parent is sick."

She added that the healing of a sick child required complete faith of both parents. When I asked whether that was why she had not been able to heal Princess Marijke, she stared at me without replying. But I could see how she had turned the queen against Prince Bernhard.

I came away convinced that this Rasputin-like story, with overtones of East-West conflict and constitutional conflict and marital conflict, had to be written. *Life* magazine had already expressed interest in it, and in May, I flew to New York and delivered it to Emmet J. Hughes, an editor of the magazine. I had tried to write the article with the sympathy I felt for the tormented queen, "haunted by personal unhappiness and an inability to grasp the wanton fate heredity had thrust upon her." "At a moment of susceptibility," I wrote, "she had reached out to a religious fanatic who seemed to have all the answers. This might have remained a private aberration had the relationship not spilled over into affairs of government, presenting Miss Hofmans and her mystical friend in the role of unlikely Rasputins."

The Netherlands government was apparently not part of Prince Bernhard's plan to administer shock treatment to his wife by public disclosure. Before my departure for New York, my friend Han N. Boon, secretary-general of the Foreign Ministry, told me at lunch that if such an article was published, it would shake the foundations of the monarchy. I would be cut off from all government contacts and—if a suitable law could be found—might be expelled from the Netherlands.

The government was aware I was working on the article, but not for whom, and apparently assumed it was the *New York Times*, my primary customer. Arriving in New York, I was told at the *Times* that the publisher, Orvil Dryfoos, had been contacted by Netherlands ambassador J. H. van Royen with a plea to kill the article. Dryfoos replied—truthfully—that he knew nothing about it.

The embassy's number two, Minister Jacob G. de Beus, came to New York from Washington with his press aide, Han Friedericy, a friend of mine, for a weird lunch at the elegant Brussels Restaurant. De Beus gravely read me a formal diplomatic note, in Dutch, representing Prince Bernhard as wishing me to know that his conversation with me (subject not mentioned) had been off-the-record and His Highness hoped I would not use it to engage in "irresponsible reporting." When I asked for a copy of the note, the minister said it was an "oral note," not to be handed over. I asked whether protocol permitted him to read it again, slowly, while I took notes, which he did while Friedericy tried to stifle his amusement.

Returning to The Hague in June, I was called in for several more meetings to receive stern warnings that I was abusing the hospitality the Netherlands had shown me and endangering the monarchy. To all of these I replied that the story of the queen and the faith healer was bound to come out, and better in the sympathetic form in which I had written it. There were more government pleas, warnings, and now also the suggestion that I would not lose financially if I killed the article.

Life had collected photos of the faith healer, and the article was scheduled for publication at the end of September. In early September, covering a Benelux conference in Luxembourg, I was taken aside by Foreign Minister J. W. Beyen for a long conversation, this time without threats, but with a plea not to do something that would shock the Dutch people. I gave him no reason to hope that I would change course.

Then an extraordinary thing happened—or rather two extraordinary things. In Amsterdam, I had dinner with my dear friend Lou de Jong, director of the Netherlands Institute for War Documentation—the one who had introduced Isaac Stern and me to the Anne Frank House. The gentle, soft-spoken scholar said the pressure tactics of the government had been stupid, and that I was probably right in believing the faith-healer story could not be contained. Still, he said, I could not be the one to explode a bomb that might shake the foundations of the monarchy.

Why not I? Because the Dutch considered me a friend, almost a member of their family. Because I had won the William the Silent Prize, named for the founder of the kingdom. Because the Dutch— not only the government, but the people—would see the article as a hostile act. Because... because... because. And late that night, and for the first time in my life, I agreed to try to kill a legitimate story, already in type and fully paid for.

My son, Jonathan, a newspaper reporter, has said that I have never adequately explained a decision that violated my principles and my image of myself as the uncompromising purveyor of truth. And, almost a half century later, I still wonder. Did I yield to soft soap and flattery? Was it a sense of debt to the second homeland where my career had started? Sympathy for the tragic queen and antipathy for her jet-set husband? I still don't have the answer.

Next morning I cabled *Life*, asking, with abject apologies, to withdraw my article, and offering to return the fee. Then the second extraordinary thing happened. *Life* replied that the magazine was happy to kill the article and wanted me to keep the fee, it being understood that it would not be published anywhere else.

Only twenty years later did I learn why *Life* had been so accommodating. In early September my friend Han Boon had become Dutch ambassador in Rome. The American ambassador was Claire Luce, and her husband, Henry Luce, publisher of *Time* and *Life*, spent much of his time in Rome. At a diplomatic dinner, Boon arranged for his wife to sit next to Luce and appeal to him to kill my article in the interest of the stability of the North Atlantic alliance. He readily agreed to do so. Thus, when I cabled asking that my article be killed, it was already dead.

Four months later, on February 1, 1953, catastrophe struck Holland in a way that seemed to validate the queen's doomsday mysticism. A ferocious North Sea storm, coinciding with the high tide and the monthly spring tide, broke the dikes and flooded large parts of the country. Holland, a third of which lies below sea level and a half below flood level, had been no stranger to floods, but this was the worst in centuries. Some eighteen hundred persons drowned, and hundreds of thousands were evacuated to high ground.

The queen seemed to be everywhere in the stricken area, flying in by helicopter, touring in hip boots. To a woman in Zeeland who addressed her as "Your Majesty," she snapped, "This is no time for Majesty!" An echo of Oude Loo dogma could be heard in her radio broadcast to the nation: "Our highly developed technology could not avert this disaster." The Foreign Ministry, in distributing translations of the speech to the foreign press, omitted some of the odder sentences about the flood's having created a foundation for a brotherhood of man that would end East-West hostility.

In 1955, now a CBS correspondent in Washington, I was advised that the queen had conferred on me a decoration, Officer of the Order of Orange-Nassau. In the same honors list Henry Luce received the higher degree of Commander. Well, there are nonjournalism prizes, too.

Prince Bernhard had apparently not given up on trying to get a story out that would blast the Juliana-Hofmans relationship. In 1956, he met in Stockholm with Sefton Delmer, a longtime friend on the *London Daily Express*. Once again an article was written— this time with the added feature of an allegation that Miss Hofmans and her mentor, Johan Kaiser, were under Communist influence, peddling subversion to the queen.

Once again an appeal from government to a publisher, this time Lord Beaverbrook. Delmer agreed to withhold his article only if it did not appear elsewhere. Two weeks later the story turned up in the German weekly *Der Spiegel*. Delmer denied that he had been the German magazine's source.

I was, by this time, CBS correspondent in Moscow, far from palace turmoils. But Dutch colleagues told me that this time the controversy had assumed new dimensions. Earlier in the year Prince Bernhard had visited his friend CIA director Allen Dulles, in Washington, and there was some suspicion of a CIA role in trying to root out the neutralist nest.

Premier Willem Drees and Foreign Minister Beyen called in editors in chief of Dutch newspapers for a confidential briefing, asking them to ignore the coming *Spiegel* revelations—which they agreed to do. The queen was reported to believe there was a government conspiracy to drive her from the throne, naming, as ringleader, Minister Beyen. He was forced to resign from the cabinet. The government named a confidential investigating commission, and the queen named her own.

In the end the controversy simmered down, and Juliana remained on the throne until 1980, when, like her mother, she abdicated in favor of her daughter. And Beatrix became the third successive queen of the Netherlands.

In 1982, the Dutch magazine *Vrij Nederland* asked whether my thirty-year-old article could now be published. After consulting editors of *Life* magazine, none of whom seemed to remember my article, I gave permission.

Among those who read it was Han Boon, now in retirement from the foreign service. The one who had worked so hard to get my article killed now said that I had written "about the troubles and worries of our sovereign with such delicacy that one is almost moved."

Still, he said, "It remains my conviction that publication would have had disastrous consequences for the dynasty. If the article had been written in a vulgar or obscene way, it might not have done a great deal of damage. But the understanding way in which you write about the problem makes it all the more devastating."

To this day I wonder whether I was right to let the big one get away. The more I think about it, the less I am convinced that the stability of the Dutch monarchy rested on my decision. To my writer son, Jonathan, who pressed me to justify my decision, all I could say was that there are other values that have to be weighed against journalistic values—sometimes.

And all I have to show for one of the toughest decisions of my professional life is that tiny orange-blue rosette in my buttonhole.

CHAPTER 4

THE LAST OF
THE MURROW BOYS

After some five years in Holland I felt quite at home. I had mastered the Dutch language well enough so that a professor of linguistics, at a party in Amsterdam, trying to identify which part of the country I came from by my accent, concluded, "You can't fool me—you're not Dutch at all. You're Flemish!" But the flap over my suppressed article about the queen and the faith healer had left many of my relationships awkward and constrained. As the year 1953 dawned, I looked forward to a change that I had been awaiting for six months.

During my trip to New York the previous June, I had bearded Turner Catledge, managing editor of the *New York Times*, in his office, pointed to my two-year record of scoops and bylines as a stringer, and made the case that it was time I was hired as a staff correspondent. He said that might be possible, but that he wanted to end the tradition of an elite corps of foreign correspondents. What he wanted, he said, was an all-purpose type of reporter who could cover any kind of situation.

Catledge made me this offer: Spend three days of my vacation working for the city desk, and if City Editor Robert Garst found me

competent, I would be named to the staff. As happens on the *Times*,
the first two days I sat around without an assignment. For the third
day I was asked to cover a ceremony in the morning at City Hall in
which the first contracts would be signed under Title I of the Federal
Housing Act, providing an infusion of federal money to help in privately executed slum clearance.

After the signing ceremony I accepted the invitation of Robert
Moses, construction coordinator, to tour some of the Manhattan sites
marked for projects that might ultimately reach $200 million. One of
those sites was at Columbus Circle, where the plan called not only for
new housing but for an auditorium complex that would eventually be
called Lincoln Center. After lunch with Moses I returned to the office
to be asked, at the city desk, where I had been all day. I outlined my
story. The editor suggested I sit down and start writing. Next day I saw
my story with a two-column headline on the front page.

Catledge said I had passed his test, and that I should return to
Holland as a stringer while he completed plans for hiring me as part
of a reorganization that might take several weeks.

Since then, six months had passed, and Catledge had responded
to my monthly inquiries by saying he needed a little more time.

Then, on Sunday, February 1, 1953, came the flood.

The previous evening I had attended a concert at the Kurhaus in
The Hague's seaside suburb of Scheveningen. I found my little Cit-
röen car, parked on the seaside boulevard, being drenched by waves
that swept over the beach. At four in the morning I was awakened
by a Dutch reporter colleague, who said the storm had gotten worse
and the dikes were in danger.

I drove to South Holland. Standing atop the great Wierdrecht
dike below Rotterdam, I could see the water lapping up on one side.
On the other side, fifteen feet below, lay fertile farmland and a
group of farmers showing no sign of leaving. I called to them to alert
them to the danger of the rising tide. One of them yelled back,
"Where should I go? This is my home. I would rather drown here."

In the ensuing week hundreds of thousands from South Holland
and the Zeeland islands were evacuated with the aid of the Allied

forces in Germany. I flew on one of the American army helicopters, picking desperate, but somehow never hysterical, people from rooftops and trees. Eight years earlier they had been liberated from the Nazis. Now they had been invaded by their most ancient enemy, the sea. Once again they would fight back.

Within a month the hydraulic engineers were planning the counteroffensive. They would repair the dikes and dry out the land. Then they would build a huge sea wall connecting the Zeeland islands, thus shutting out the North Sea forever. When the floods returned in February 1995, it was by a flanking attack—through the rain-swollen Rhine and Maas Rivers. Once again, forty-two years later, the Dutch were up against the fury of the elements that would not forgive their insolent conquest of the sea.

Covering the flood left me physically and emotionally exhausted. It was now truly time for a change, and I was still waiting to hear from the *Times*. I had also covered the flood as a stringer for CBS, and some of my more vivid reports had been carried on Edward R. Murrow's evening newscast. Now, in March, out of the blue, came a cable from Murrow that I can still remember: "Would you at all consider joining the staff of CBS News with an initial assignment in Washington?" I was flattered, but thought of broadcasting as no more than a sideline, and I was not to be diverted from my primary goal of joining the *Times*. However, using the CBS offer as leverage, I cabled Catledge saying I needed a firm date for my *Times* appointment because I had another offer that I would otherwise have to consider.

To my astonishment, Catledge cabled back that I would be well advised to accept the other offer. Shaken and uncomprehending, I agreed to join CBS. Only three years later would I receive an explanation of the mysterious *Times* reversal. On a visit to New York, now a CBS Washington correspondent, I was invited to dinner by *Times* foreign editor Emanuel Freedman, who had handled my dispatches, and Assistant Managing Editor Ted Bernstein—the one who had advised me to go to Europe and await my opportunity.

Bernstein said they had an embarrassing confession that they felt was owed me. I had not been named to the *Times* staff because, at the time when my appointment was to be made, Catledge had ordered a freeze on the hiring of Jews as correspondents. Catledge was concerned that the disproportionate representation of Jews on the staff might hamper *Times* coverage of some future Middle East war. The ban was soon canceled, Bernstein said. And I was the only person directly affected by it. The two Jewish editors said they had acquiesced in the short-lived quota and deeply regretted it.

I thanked Ted Bernstein and Manny Freedman for their candor. Until then, I had not thought to count Jewish noses among *Times* correspondents. But, yes, there were some prominent ones—Meyer Handler, Sydney Gruson, A. M. Rosenthal (who had been asked not to use *Abraham* in his byline from the United Nations), and later, Max Frankel, who would become my colleague and friend in Moscow.

In 1975, Frankel, then Washington bureau chief, and on his way to becoming executive editor, sought to turn the clock back and rectify the twenty-two-year-old injustice. At CBS I had covered Watergate and was now deep in the official investigations of CIA misdeeds. Max asked me if I would be interested in joining the *Times* as diplomatic correspondent. That was a title that only two had held—himself and James N. Reston. Reston was the one who had in 1953, kidded me about my defection to broadcasting by asking periodically, "Had enough?" And I had periodically joked in response, "Not yet, Scotty, but soon."

Now the *Times* post-Catledge generation, Executive Editor Reston and Bureau Chief Frankel, were bidding me to come home, and so great was the tug of old dreams that I spent several days thinking about the offer and discussing it with my wife. I went to New York to talk to *Times* executives, half-minded, but only half-minded, to accept. During a long dinner with Scotty alone, I brought up various mundane problems such as retirement benefits and health insurance. Finally Reston said, "I don't think you really want this." And I agreed that he might be reading me better than I had read myself. Perhaps I was too old to start, or to resume, a print career. Perhaps television exposure, and remuneration, had become too seductive. But there was no returning from 1975 to 1953 and the road not taken because it had been blocked by an anti-Semitic aberration.

Instead, the 1953 road led from Holland and the uncertain life of a stringer to CBS in Washington. First to Paris, where longtime correspondent David Schoenbrun welcomed me at a lavish lunch in the Bois de Boulogne on behalf of the fabled Murrow team, to which I would be a belated addition. Wineglass hoisted, David wanted me to know what a signal honor it was to be joining the cream of broadcast journalism—Eric Sevareid, Howard K. Smith, Winston Burdett, Alexander Kendrick, Richard C. Hottelet—and David Schoenbrun.

From Paris to Le Havre for a voyage on the SS *America*, docking in New York late on a Friday afternoon. Reporting to CBS News headquarters on Madison Avenue, I found executives gone for the weekend, but a message from News Director Wells "Ted" Church. It said that before proceeding to Washington I should anchor the Saturday 7:45 P.M. network news, a "sustaining" (noncommercial) version of the weekday Murrow program.

Just off the boat from Europe, I had not the foggiest idea of what anchoring a newscast entailed and took this to be some sardonic initiation rite. On Saturday I sought the help of the desk editor, Ed Bliss, who also wrote scripts for Murrow. He said the routine was reasonably simple—I would read the news agency wires and write a newscast of exactly 14:30 minutes, rehearsed with a stopwatch. An associate producer would be in the studio with me and would hand me a two-minute watch counting down to my close to make sure I got off in time.

One complication—this was the day of the Kentucky Derby, so about halfway through the newscast, Bliss told me, I would have to "switch to Louisville" for a report on the results. "How do I switch?" I asked. Patiently, Bliss explained that I needed only to introduce the reporter in Louisville and a technician would see to the switching. I asked the associate producer for a two-minute watch to the midway point, which I mistakenly supposed I had to hit precisely.

Nervously I wrote my newscast, finishing too late for a rehearsal before airtime. On the air I found, to my horror, that I had written too much copy for the first half, up to the midway point, and started frantically discarding pages when I was given the two-minute watch. But, after Louisville I was short of material and found myself on my last page, waiting desperately for the two-minute watch. I broke into a sweat, slowed down my reading, and wondered whether several minutes of dead air would abruptly end my broadcasting career.

As I reached the last line, the door opened and there entered into the studio an angel in the form of Ed Bliss, who placed some neatly stapled wire-service copy before me. He had been watching through a glass partition and was fully aware of my predicament. Not to worry, he said—he had performed similar services for Ed Murrow.

I would later learn that while I had gone through a bad bout of beginner's fright, no one was immune to studio tension—not even the fabled Murrow. I often watched Murrow from the control room. He would stride into the studio in shirtsleeves, open collar, and red suspenders and sit calmly down at the microphone. Then, even as he was being introduced by the announcer, he would break into a sweat. As he read his script in authoritative cadences, his feet would shuffle back and forth in a steady rhythm under the table. I would never again worry about stage fright.

Following my Saturday baptism of fire, I proceeded to Washington and reported on Monday morning to the CBS bureau, located then in the office building of the Warner Theatre, near the National Press Club. I was coolly received by Bureau Chief Ted Koop, later learning that the turf-proud bureaucrat did not appreciate an utter stranger from Europe being imposed on him because of some whim of Ed Murrow's. He suggested that I spend some time getting re-Americanized and Washingtonized.

No re-Americanization could prepare me for the experience, on my first day, of witnessing Sen. Joseph McCarthy's hearings on Communist influence in government. As luck would have it, I arrived in the hearing room just in time to see him destroy a United States Information Agency officer whom I had known in Europe. Soon I found myself assigned, with my colleague George Herman, to covering the McCarthy hearings and assembling taped excerpts for an evening recap on radio.

It was a chilling experience to sit at the press table of the Senate Caucus Room day after day while McCarthy brutalized people who may have had left-wing leanings at some time in their lives. Lawyer Joseph Welch became our hero when he challenged McCarthy's persecution of a young lawyer, Fred Fisher, saying, "Have you no sense of decency, sir? At long last, have you left no sense of decency?"

And it made me proud of CBS when Ed Murrow and Fred Friendly, his producer, devoted an hour-long *See It Now* production to exposing McCarthy in all his recklessness.

Because of my European experience, I was soon assigned to cover the State Department and the diplomatic beat. Thus I came to know Secretary John Foster Dulles, who remained an unreconstructed anticommunist moralizer despite the death of Stalin in the second month of the Eisenhower administration. In fact, at a private breakfast with me in 1955, Dulles indicated some nostalgia for Stalin. I asked whether Dulles would help Nikita Khrushchev stay in power by helping him gain some success for his policy of "peaceful coexistence." The secretary instantly responded that he would not lift a finger to save Khrushchev and that he really preferred Stalin. His reasoning was that Stalin, however tough, was cautious, controlled, and predictable. Dulles cited the Berlin blockade of 1948 as an example of measured pressure that had stopped short of provocation to war. Khrushchev, said Dulles, was emotional, impulsive, and dangerous, and the United States had no stake in his political survival. (Khrushchev, who could recognize an adversary when he saw one, once called Dulles a "rascal" in my presence.)

Dulles spent his years trying to contain international Communism, but mainly through slogans such as "rolling back the Iron Curtain" (which spurred the Hungarians into their suicidal uprising in 1956) and "massive retaliation" against conventional attack (which spurred the Soviets in their nuclear buildup). Dulles's willingness to take risks, at least verbally, attached the word *brinkmanship* to him. He talked of using tactical nuclear weapons like conventional weapons, which led the Soviets to warn that any use of nuclear arms would lead to all-out nuclear war. His phrase "getting a bigger bang for a buck," led Eric Sevareid to note that, meanwhile, the Russians might be getting "a bigger rumble for a ruble."

Dulles had little patience with India and other nonaligned countries, regarding neutrality as simply immoral. He devoted himself to trying to patch together NATO-like alliances in the Pacific, Latin America, and other regions. Aware of Dulles's anticommunist zealotry, President Eisenhower withheld from him until the last moment the arms control proposals he was preparing to make at the Geneva summit with Khrushchev and Bulganin in 1955. The Eisenhower plan, called "open skies," would have permitted Soviet and American planes to fly over each other's country to monitor any military buildup. The Soviets rejected the proposal.

In 1959, it would fall to my lot to report on CBS that Secretary Dulles, terminally ill with cancer, was planning to resign. It was true, but several of Dulles's friends expressed anger that I had anticipated the official announcement. Reporting that Dulles was dying did not enhance my popularity in the administration, but I don't think I had any alternative.

During my time on the State Department beat, I had some other foreign assignments.

I was sent to cover what was billed as a civil war in democratic Costa Rica, which turned out to be a small-scale invasion instigated by President Luis Somoza of Nicaragua. The war ended abruptly when the United States furnished to Costa Rica two antiquated P-51 fighter planes—the only airpower in the area. Flown by hastily instructed Costa Rican civil pilots, the planes dipped low in a salute over the presidential palace. I was standing in the courtyard with the popular President José "Pepe" Figueres. Without missing a beat, he looked up and said casually, "Two of ours." That day the government issued "Communique No. 1 of the Costa Rican Air Forces."

How I wished I had a camera crew so that television could show this cozy, little, almost bloodless war south of our border! But we were still in that era when radio news controlled most of the correspondents, often refusing even to share information with television.

Radio news director Ted Church treated TV news director Sig Mick-elson like a pariah. Meanwhile, TV news, leaned toward press con-ferences and other low-cost staged events—what historian Daniel Boorstin would call "pseudo-events."

But then television discovered the "live event." In 1953, the American Broadcasting Company, lagging behind the other networks in daytime soap opera ratings, decided to fill the unprofitable time with the hearings on Senator McCarthy's stormy controversy with the army. The Army-McCarthy hearings attracted an unusually large daytime audience, some of whom became addicted to this new kind of soap opera.

The networks made efforts to get President Eisenhower's press conferences opened up to television. The White House news confer-ence, starting with a handful of reporters gathered at President Franklin D. Roosevelt's desk, had remained, until Eisenhower, under a rule of "background only." That meant no direct quotations and, obviously, no use of the president's voice.

News Secretary James Hagerty decided to experiment with hav-ing the president seen and heard. Broadcasters were told they could film and record the morning news conference, but the film and tape could not be broadcast until after a Hagerty briefing in the after-noon aimed at clarifying Eisenhower's sometimes tangled language and obscure utterances.

At one new press conference I tried to draw the president into discussing French president Charles de Gaulle's crisis in revolution-ary Algeria. Eisenhower said he would have absolutely no comment. I asked him if he would simply share his memories of de Gaulle, his wartime comrade in arms. Eisenhower laughed and proceeded to speak of de Gaulle warmly, concluding with the words "I always liked him." This implied endorsement of de Gaulle in his conflict with the Algerian nationalists was headline news.

Leaving the high-ceilinged Indian Treaty Room of the Executive Office Building, scene of the press conferences, I asked Scotty Reston how he imagined Hagerty might deal with the presidential indiscretion. Lighting his pipe contemplatively, Reston said, "On this one I think Jim will probably have to say that President Eisenhower does not necessarily speak for this administration."

In two years in Washington, I had bought a car, rented an apartment, and come to like the life of a diplomatic correspondent. But, once again my life took an unpremeditated turn. On August 6, 1955, returning to the office from an assignment, I passed a woman in the hall who said, "I see you're going to Moscow."

"How's that again?" I asked.

"There's a news release on it."

Indeed there was. It said News Director John F. Day had cabled Nikita Khrushchev requesting my accreditation as Moscow correspondent. "We beseech you," it said, "in the name of peace, goodwill, and understanding," to permit the reopening of the bureau that Stalin had closed in 1947. CBS was hurting competitively because NBC's Irving R. Levine had traveled to the Soviet Union with an American agricultural delegation in July and had been permitted to stay, broadcasting from the studios of Moscow radio. CBS had only the services of freelance journalist William Worthy, who had entered with the farm delegation. In the afterglow of the East-West summit, CBS invoked the "spirit of Geneva" in its efforts to catch up with NBC. But it had all happened without a word to me.

Stunned, I walked into Ted Koop's office and asked what was going on and why I hadn't been consulted. He said, "We assumed you would not want to miss this opportunity." In any event, he said, the cable was only exploratory and other names might be submitted. What Koop did not then tell me was that a staff reduction in the Washington bureau was planned, that I was on a list of those to be dismissed, and that CBS executives in New York had thought to solve two problems by sending me to Moscow and getting me out of Koop's nonexistent hair.

So, once again subject to random forces, my fate now rested with Nikita Khrushchev, new-style Soviet leader, garrulous and gregarious salesman of "peaceful coexistence." But, the personal plea to the top man, this business of "we beseech you," struck me as naive. I made a formal application for a visa and two weeks later got a call from the Soviet consulate to come and get it. Translated (which I was unable to do) it provided for a stay of two weeks in September. When I asked about permanent accreditation, a Soviet attaché said he knew nothing about that and that I could discuss that in Moscow.

It gradually became clear that the Soviet government, encouraging East-West contacts, had a policy of freely issuing short-term visas to cover important official visits. A visit by West German chancellor Konrad Adenauer was coming up in early September, and Richard C. Hottelet, CBS correspondent in Bonn, also received a visa to cover the trip. Thus, my visa told me nothing of my prospects for establishing a permanent bureau. News Director John Day agreed with me that, under the circumstances, I could not dispose of my Washington apartment and car, but, if I received accreditation, would have to return to Washington to settle my affairs.

My thirty-ninth birthday on August 31 was a turbulent time for me as I prepared to fly to Moscow via Helsinki, Finland, for what might be a two-week trip and a dubious CBS future or a new career. Ordinarily a reporter being assigned to Moscow would be given many months to learn the language and history. Several old Moscow hands, such as Harrison Salisbury of the *New York Times*, told me how severely handicapped I would be, unable to read the press or to talk to ordinary Russians, having to rely on a government-furnished translator who would regularly report to the KGB, the Soviet secret police.

At this point, I was introduced to television news, which had now been officially merged with radio news. Because I could not count on being permitted a cameraman in Moscow, I was given a crash course in the operation of the Bell & Howell 16mm handheld camera. I was also given a heavy, hand-operated, windup Magnemite tape recorder. The tape recorder could be used to record radio features, and also to provide narration for the film that TV news executives confidently expected me to shoot. I also bought a Leica still camera to record my coming adventure for posterity.

Few journalists have crossed the Iron Curtain so freighted with equipment and doubts. I had not asked for this assignment and I was far from ready for it. Yet, I knew that if I somehow succeeded in becoming Moscow bureau chief and making a success of it, I would be confirmed on the Murrow roster. More than that, I might join that elite group—Eric Sevareid, Howard K. Smith, David Schoenbrun, Richard C. Hottelet, Alexander Kendrick, Winston Burdett—who sat around a table with Murrow at year's end for a global review on television called "Years of Crisis."

The day before I left, Murrow called to wish me good luck, and that helped my spirits.

CHAPTER 5

MOSCOW CORRESPONDENT IN WAITING

My first and most enduring impression of Moscow, where I arrived on September 5, 1955, was the smell—a pall generated by the burning of soft coal. My first meal in Moscow was a caviar-laden lunch at the pretentiously sumptuous Praga Restaurant as the guest of E. Clifton Daniel, the *New York Times* correspondent. He was about to leave in ill health, would meet and marry Margaret Truman, the former president's daughter, and would not return to Moscow.

In the first-class Hotel National, I had a room overlooking the Kremlin walls.

My first visitor was Boris, who came knocking at my door without notice, carrying a bottle of vodka and saying he was there to greet me on behalf of the Soviet Journalists' Union. "How is Mr. Paley?" he boomed to show he had boned up on CBS. He had also studied the American idiom. Raising a glass of vodka, he toasted, "Well, Mr. Schorr, here's mud down your hatch!" Boris came often during those first weeks, quizzing me about the American media and telling me how life was improving in the Soviet Union. I suspected that he was not representing the journalists so much as the KGB.

NBC's Levine had permission to broadcast from Radio Moscow. I did not. My first cabled dispatch on September 6 reflected the ambiguities of the early coexistence days. The Soviet press was criticizing American politicians (mentioning Vice President Nixon by name, but not President Eisenhower) as going back on "the spirit of Geneva," generated by the groundbreaking East-West summit three months earlier. But, at the same time, a visiting group of senators— John Sparkman, William A. Purtell, and George W. Malone—and Supreme Court Justice William O. Douglas were taken for a tour of the Stalin (still) Auto Works, and I was allowed to accompany and film them with my handheld camera. The manager denied that the *Zis* limousine on display had been copied from the prewar American Packard, calling it a "parallel development." He also explained that the Soviets had not developed an automatic transmission because it was not suited to cold weather.

I became keenly aware of the pervasive use of euphemism, reflecting the defensiveness of a people anxious for contact with the outside world but sensitive about invidious comparison. When I tried to film run-down housing in the shadow of Stalinesque wedding-cake skyscrapers, I was stopped by "indignant citizens," presumably KGB agents who had been trailing me. Universities and other institutions that I asked to visit were often said to be *in remont* ("in renovation"), a standard phrase that became a standing joke. Outside the National Hotel, police, protecting Soviet dignity, shooed away youngsters begging for ballpoint pens and other Western products. On each floor of the hotel there sat a stern *dezhurnaya* (literally, "woman of the day"), guarding against visits to guests by unauthorized Russians. (That was how I knew that Boris was authorized.)

Nevertheless, I managed a few unauthorized contacts. CBS stringer Bill Worthy, who is black, arranged for me to meet Robert Robinson, who had lived in the Soviet Union since 1930, when he was recruited from his job as a toolmaker at the Ford Motor Company in Detroit to go and teach his skills in Russia. As a token black, he was elected to the Moscow Soviet (city council) and found himself in groups that met with Stalin, Molotov, and Bulganin. But having seen the Stalin purges and endured the war in Russia, having also seen racism more virulent than that he had left behind in America, he was totally disaffected after a quarter century as a Soviet citizen. Robinson gave me forbidden information about current strikes in Soviet factories. He told me of the skepticism of Russian workers that the post-Stalin era would bring them better conditions.

(Having repeatedly been refused permission to return to the United States, Robinson finally managed, in 1974, to go to Uganda on vacation. He spent fourteen years there under the patronage of President Idi Amin before finally making it back to the United States and recovering his American citizenship. At a news conference in 1987 marking the publication of his book, *Black on Red*, he said he was wearing the shoes I had given him when I left the Soviet Union thirty years earlier.)

Another contact, Slava Repnikov, had never been outside his country, but worshiped all things American—a form of anti-Soviet protest. He carried Russian cigarettes in empty Marlboro packages. He called Gorki Street "Broadway" and said "good-bye" and "okay" to Russians. He wore pegged pants, platform shoes, and a rainbow tie—the American zoot-suit fashion of the times. He wore his hair long, as he had seen in a Tarzan picture. And he cultivated a look of utter boredom with his surroundings. He was one of a group called *stilyagi*—literally "stylish people," but generally a term of contempt. This was the group that Soviet leaders had in mind when they called for elimination of "alien influences." And many of the leaders had firsthand knowledge of the *stilyagi* because, as often as not, they were the spoiled children of "new class" luxury. The newspaper *Soviet Culture* called them "parasites" and "moral monsters."

My *stilyag* friend asked me to take back and mail in New York a fan letter to a stridently anti-Soviet commentator for *Newsweek* magazine named Leon Volkov, and I stupidly agreed to do so. *Newsweek* published the letter in his original handwriting, and Slava was arrested and sent to jail. This I learned twenty years later when he turned up in New Jersey and called me to say he had finally made it to America—which was not as wonderful as he had thought when we used to meet outside the Hotel National.

The Hotel National, for me as for NBC's Irv Levine, was the center of operations. We kept lists of tourists and their scheduled departure dates so that we could ask them to carry out the film and audiotape that we could not legally ship from Moscow. (The procedure was to cable our New York offices asking to have a "friend met and extended courtesies" on arrival in a Paris, London, or Stockholm airport. These messages went through censorship. I believe that the Soviet authorities divined the meaning of the many "friends" of television correspondents, but preferred not to make an issue of our smuggling operations for lack of any approved procedure for shipping film and tape.

The National was also important because there we would find VIP guests—the physician, Paul Dudley White, impresario Sol Hurok, and members of Congress whose exchange missions made up much of the news of these early post-Stalin days. (Tenor Jan Peerce, invited to sing with the Bolshoi opera, occupied a suite at the National reputedly once the residence of Lenin, with a grand piano in a huge living room.)

In my first week in Moscow, Sen. Estes Kefauver led a delegation of five senators to meet with Premier Nikolay Bulganin and Party chief Khrushchev. Khrushchev complained about the "reactionary circles" in America undermining the "spirit of Geneva." Senator Kefauver, at my request, raised with the Soviet leaders the question of my accreditation and later reported that Khrushchev had promised to do something about it. I also persuaded Kefauver's aide Bill Haddad to take my handheld camera with him on a visit to Moscow University, with drastic consequences that I learned about forty years later. Vladimir Nadein, a student in training to join the KGB and studying English, acted as Haddad's volunteer guide. Because of Haddad's filming, Nadein was denounced by someone as an accomplice to American spying and exiled to Siberia for ten years. So Nadein told Haddad when they met in 1995 in Washington. Nadein, having been rehabilitated during the Gorbachev era, was now chief Washington correspondent for *Izvestia*. Even forty years later I felt a pang of remorse for my unwitting contribution to his exile.

My first week in Moscow was dominated by Chancellor Adenauer's visit. A member of the West German delegation carried with him a hard-to-get map of Moscow. He said, without embarrassment, that he had used it as a Wehrmacht officer when his unit had come within thirty miles of the capital. But the Germans found the Russians as tough in peace as in war. Adenauer had come hoping to trade diplomatic and trade relations with the Soviet Union for the release of almost 150,000 German war prisoners and civilian internees and to get agreement on some step toward German reunification. The chancellor had to satisfy himself with the prisoners alone. Not only did the Soviet government remain dead set against reunification, but then proceeded to sign an agreement with East Germany extending full recognition to the Communist regime.

My most vivid memory of that hectic week was a ballet performance in Adenauer's honor in the Bolshoi Theatre. The program featured Tchaikovsky's *Romeo and Juliet*. During the curtain call a spotlight lit up the box where the notables were sitting. Khrushchev raised Adenauer's hand clasped in his to the cheers of the Soviet audience. A Soviet spokesman was on hand to explain the significance of the gesture in case we had missed it. Germans and Russians, like the feuding Montagues and Capulets, reconciled over the bodies of their slain children. Get it?

I later learned that, in conversation with Adenauer, Khrushchev had made another point about reconciliation. He talked of ideological difficulties with China's Mao Tse-tung and predicted that, at some not distant time, the Western alliance and the Soviets would find themselves joining hands to meet the menace from the East. This was two years before Soviet-Chinese friction surfaced. Adenauer had Khrushchev's message passed on to Secretary Dulles, who didn't believe a word of it.

Because of the Adenauer visit we were permitted to have the CBS German camera crew in Moscow, and we used it to cover not only the Adenauer story, but everything in sight. There was an evident hunger in the United States just to see Russian faces, Russian stores, schools, subways. With the menacing Stalin gone, it was as though a curtain were parting on a hidden country. Americans found it exciting just to see and hear the sights and sounds of this forbidden land. Dick Hottelet and I worked hard on assembling all the film we could and produced a half-hour television special that provided a window on Russia, exciting in its novelty. Our camera crew took the film and on-camera narrations with them when they departed. We neglected to submit them for censorship. In fact, in those early days, there was no procedure for reviewing unprocessed film.

The camera crew gone, with no sign of my accreditation and no permission to broadcast, I returned in frustration to sending cable dispatches to be read on radio. I soon learned that the relaxed censorship rules for a state visit no longer applied. During the Adenauer visit, the censors excised nothing from my cables—not even personal references to their leaders. I reported that Bulganin, his offer of a cigarette declined by Adenauer, had made a heavy-handed joke: "Too bad you don't smoke because then you could hide behind a cloud of smoke." And I reported that when Bulganin had started a statement to Adenauer by saying, "As prime minister of the USSR," Khrushchev had interjected, "He's only saying that because he wants to keep the job."

These curious gibes suggested that the heavy-drinking Bulganin was in some trouble and might not last long. Two years later he would be ousted in an internal leadership struggle.

But soon the hand of the censor began to fall more heavily. All dispatches of Western correspondents had to be brought to the Central Telegraph office, there presented at a counter to a clerk who turned around and slipped them through a slot to an unseen censor. The pages would come back sooner, later, or not at all, untouched or with words, lines, or paragraphs crossed out in heavy black pencil.

My first bout with the censor was on the subject of censorship. I reported in a cable that Senator Kefauver had raised the subject of censorship with Khrushchev as an obstacle to improved relations with the West, and that the Soviet leader had promised progressive elimination of censorship, saying, "Everything cannot be done over-night." The censor held my cable for a full day, then released it untouched, presumably having checked with the Kremlin.

Censorship was exercised by a KGB department known as Glavlit, the literary bureau. Glavlit darkened my two and three-quarter years in the Soviet Union. It was a unique institution. Oddly, no other Communist-ruled country—not even China—maintained official censorship of foreign correspondents. Today, it seems hard to imagine, visiting the Central Telegraph on a recent Moscow trip, that through one door funneled everything that some thirty corre-spondents wanted to tell the noncommunist world about this vast empire, and that here we would sometimes spend half our waking hours waiting to see what would be permitted.

The maintenance of censorship seemed to reflect an obsessive sense of secrecy and lack of self-confidence. What Soviet leaders wanted most to suppress provided clues to the thinking of the men in the Kremlin: any indication of internal unrest or discontent. Any suggestion of disharmony between the Soviet Union and other members of the Soviet bloc. Any personal reflection on Soviet lead-ers—a rule so inflexible that it was impossible even to say that Khrushchev was *not* a habitual drunkard. And any suggestion of pol-icy conflict among members of a collective leadership supposed to function in smooth tandem.

Thus, early in my Moscow stay, I was hindered in reporting on an ideological conflict of major importance.

In 1946, soon after the first atomic bombs were dropped on Hiroshima and Nagasaki, Premier Stalin had laid down the line that Russia would not be intimidated by the new American weapon. He said, "Atomic bombs are intended to frighten the weak-nerved, but they cannot decide the outcome of war." In March 1954, a year after Stalin's death, his handpicked successor, Premier Georgy Malenkov, acknowledged that the Soviet Union might not survive a nuclear war, thus laying the groundwork for a policy of coexistence and arms control. He said that a conflict, under modern conditions of war, "would mean destruction of world civilization." But Malenkov was ousted as premier by the fast-rising Khrushchev and was replaced by Nikolay Bulganin. In September 1955, Foreign Minister Vyacheslav Molotov, the principal Stalin heir surviving in the cabinet, suddenly took the position, in a party theoretical organ, that the Soviet Union could survive a nuclear war. That appeared to challenge the premise for Khrushchev's coexistence policy. Molotov was soon obliged to make a public recantation.

Such disputes are frequently a surface reflection of struggles for personal power. Molotov was scheduled to go to Geneva for the four-power foreign ministers' follow-up to the East-West summit. I wrote in a cable that despite his rebuke on a serious ideological question, Molotov was nevertheless still slated to go to Geneva. The censor cut the reference to the rebuke, but sent the rest, prompting an editor in New York to query why the reconfirmation that Molotov was going to Geneva. My reply that something in my message had been killed by the censor was itself killed. I then cabled that we correspondents were suffering from "tightening censorship." The censor deleted the word "tightening," probably enjoying a chuckle at my frustration.

Other frustrations stemmed from the difficulty American editors and producers had in grasping that the kind of interviews and man-in-the-street reactions normal in our country were almost unobtainable in a country emerging from Stalin's regimentation. A Russian confronted with a camera and microphone was likely to freeze. An urgent cable from New York on September 26 asked for Soviet reaction to President Eisenhower's heart attack. The request was natural enough, Eisenhower was warmly remembered as having stood with Stalin reviewing the victory parade in Red Square in 1945, and he had recently opened a new era in Soviet relations with the Geneva summit. But, from Red Square, I had to report that Russians were learning about the heart attack from me—it had not yet been reported in the Soviet press—and Russians, fearing some provocation, were disinclined to react to unofficial information. One Russian responded to my mention of President Eisenhower by showing me a copy of *Pravda* with Eisenhower's name—but the paper only referred to his having received a letter on disarmament from Premier Bulganin. The Foreign Ministry press department said the government had no comment—Khrushchev and Bulganin were away on vacation.

"In fact," said my frustrated report, "in Russia there is no one you can call for comment, and reaction will come when the government decides to give it."

Some of my frustrations stemmed from my own organization. The Sunday CBS radio program *Church of the Air* asked whether I could record the liturgy in a Russian Orthodox church now that repression of religion was being eased. With the help of an American embassy friend, Nathaniel Davis, who was a student of Russian religion, I took my wind-up Magnemite tape recorder into a church for a service conducted by the Metropolitan Nikolai. I managed to get an acceptable recording. Weeks later I got a message from the producer of it saying that it had been killed because the president of CBS Radio thought it might give too favorable an impression of religion in the Soviet Union.

My two-week visa had, meanwhile, expired and I could not get an appointment at the Foreign Ministry to discuss my accreditation—nor even an extension of my temporary visa. Senator Kefauver's intervention with Khrushchev had had no effect. At a diplomatic reception, I appealed to Bulganin, telling him I was uncomfortable with my illegal position. He patted my cheek and said, "Illegal? A real criminal face!" At another reception the hard-bitten head of the Foreign Ministry Press Department, Leonid P. Ilyichev, told me not to worry about not having a visa. "When we want you to go, we will tell you," he said brusquely.

Unaccredited, I was not entitled to employ a government-furnished translator. Marguerite Higgins of the *New York Herald Tribune*, on temporary assignment, turned over her translator when she left, and he agreed to work for me unofficially. The smooth-talking Victor Louis, as I would learn years later, was at the beginning of a remarkable career of press liaison for the KGB that would make him rich and famous. In those days he presented himself as a dissident just released from a labor camp, ready to feed me tidbits of clandestine information about rumored high-level disputes that usually ended up on the censor's cutting-room floor. In 1964 he would sell a big scoop to a London newspaper—the ouster of Nikita Khrushchev.

On October 10 I wrote Ilyichev a long letter asking him to expedite action on my accreditation, explaining to him that my apartment was standing empty in Washington and pointing out that I was handicapped in my work by not being invited to events open only to regular correspondents. I asked him also to allow regular broadcasting from a studio and a permanent camera crew for television coverage. I explained to him, also, that CBS had an audience of many millions. I had come to suspect that NBC was faring better than we because to Soviet officials, unfamiliar with America, *National* sounded more official than *Columbia*.

There followed a long silence, but then my expired visa was extended, indicating that some attention was being paid. Finally, on December 14, three days before the expiration of my latest visa, I was invited to the Press Department, where a subordinate official told me, "I am glad to be able to inform you that, as of today, you are accredited as a permanent correspondent for the Columbia Broadcasting System." I said I planned to fly to New York at the end of December to settle my affairs in Washington and to appear on the CBS year-end roundup. The official assured me I would have no trouble getting a return visa.

That increased the American press contingent in Moscow to nine, including two Associated Press, two United Press, one NBC, one International News Service, two *New York Times* (but with the ailing Cliff Daniel absent and due to be replaced). B. J. Cutler of the *New York Herald Tribune* would soon join us to make it ten.

We were more than a contingent—we were a closely knit community on an island in a sea of Russian humanity around us. We spent endless hours together at the Tzentralni Telegraf, writing our stories, waiting for the censor's verdict, and comparing what phrasing he had killed and what he had passed.

I say "he" from long habit, having always assumed that the wielder of that thick black pencil had to be a man. Actually, Masha Geffen, chief correspondent of the Moscow magazine *Itogi*, told me a few years ago that my censor had been her grandmother, who sometimes talked at the dinner table of what she had felt obliged to cut from my copy.

Much of our professional and social life centered around the U.S. embassy. We went to the Friday-afternoon briefings of the breezy Ambassador Charles E. "Chip" Bohlen, who was constantly in trouble with Secretary Dulles because he believed in the post-Stalin détente. (He also prophesied, incorrectly, the durability of the post-Stalin collective leadership.) Friday evening we went to the Spaso House residence for poker with Chip. In dollars only, so that no one would benefit from black-market ruble rates.

Thrown constantly together in a pressure-cooker atmosphere, we formed strong friendships and strong enmities—which sometimes shifted. Factions formed, usually around the American news agencies, whose access to the Tass agency wire made us dependent on them. Thus, Irv Levine of NBC was friends with Richard O'Malley and Stanley Johnson of AP; I was friends with Henry Shapiro and Whitman Bassow of United Press. A few of us reached out, adventurously, to Reuters of Britain and Agence France Presse. Alexis Schiray of AFP, a Russian émigré, became a close friend of mine. (The nasty press officer, Ilyichev, once asked me, "Why is it, do you think, that French correspondents in Moscow tend to be White Russian émigrés and American correspondents tend to be Jews?")

On Christmas Eve, as planned, I left for New York, stopping for two days in Leningrad to cover the Russian opening of the touring Gershwin opera *Porgy and Bess*, the climactic event of the year in the burgeoning cultural exchanges. As a former music critic, I had also been asked to review it for the *New York Times*.

Truman Capote was covering the *Porgy* tour for *The New Yorker* and a book. He came into my room while I was dictating to Moscow a story to be cleared by the censor and filed to New York. So, I had the unusual experience of becoming a character in a piece of novelistic nonfiction:

"Now in Room 111," Capote wrote, "Schorr, a heavy-set man in his late thirties, was trying simultaneously to correct a typescript, keep a pipe lighted and dictate over the telephone to a stenographer in Moscow. 'O.K. here's the story, you put in the slugs. Let's go.' " (I don't know what slugs are, and I doubt I used the word.)

He then quoted, more or less accurately, what I was dictating, including every side remark. For example, "Long lines of Leningraders have waited many hours in the snow to buy tickets. The top price was sixty rubles ($15), a figure that doubled and tripled on the black market. Hey, what's the synonym for 'black market' that we can get past the censors? O.K., make it 'curb price.' "

The elfin little man who, uninvited, sat quietly taking notes, quoted me further as describing how members of the *Porgy* cast had gathered around a Christmas tree singing carols. He had me adding, "Yeah, I know I'm overfiling this story. But I got excited. Real excited. You can see it. The impact of one culture on another culture. And, by the way, listen, I'm having a hell of a time. They're a great bunch, these *Porgy and Bess* people. Like living with a circus."

I have no doubt that Capote got it basically right. I can also endorse his description of me during the hour-long ceremony before the curtain went up. He had me on the stage, alternating between camera and tape recorder as I tried to capture the event.

He quoted "a baffled Daniel Schorr" as complaining to someone during the performance, "It's not going over!" I remember the fervent performance and the strange silence of the audience, even for showstopping songs such as "Summertime" and "I Got Plenty o' Nuttin'." I could guess the reason. Thrilled as they were at this opening of the Iron Curtain, the Russians, brought up on Stalinist puritanism in the theater, were simply thrown by the open sensuality of the opera.

Next morning I was off for New York and Washington—knowing my future, for once. After three months in limbo that had revived the insecurities of my stringer days, I could now close my apartment in Washington and appear with the Murrow boys on "Years of Crisis." On New Year's Day, 1956, wearing professionally applied makeup for the first time ever, and with a sense of having reached some Olympic peak, I joined the roundtable along with Howard K. Smith

(London), Richard C. Hottelet (West Germany), David Schoenbrun (France), Alexander Kendrick (Africa), Robert Pierpoint (Asia), Bill Downs (Rome), and Eric Sevareid (Washington).

Let me not pretend that the program was any model of spontaneity. The individual and collective reputations at stake dictated a careful run-through of questions and answers the day before that an unkind critic might call a rehearsal. Murrow introduced me with a sense that, after three months in the Soviet Union, I could unfold the riddle wrapped in a mystery.

I said that Russians were not as secure as they looked to Americans across the ocean. To Murrow's question of what change I had observed in Russia, I said that the most significant change was "the opening of windows to the West and the way Russians flock to those windows for a breath of fresh air."

"The Russians," I said, were "groping for new freedoms," and I added, "All this may go further and faster than the rulers intended. The thaw has reached a point where it would take some grave international crisis to turn it off."

Asked what the Russians were laughing at these days, I told of a joke circulating at Moscow University. A student says that Adam and Eve were Russian. Asked for proof, he says, "Well, they had no clothes, they had to share an apple, and they were supposed to believe they lived in paradise."

At the end of an hour, with no commercials, we were off the air, and we sat back to unwind. Murrow strode around the inside of the circular table, exchanging a few words of praise with each in turn. He came to me, paused a moment for effect, and said, "Schorr... you'll do!"

Then we adjourned to the Murrow apartment off Central Park West for the traditional poker game and a buffet supper arranged by Janet Murrow, who greeted us and then discreetly withdrew from the "boys" game. Murrow lost consistently because he refused to "fold" any hand. I suspect that losing to his "boys" was part of noblesse oblige.

We waited up for the reviews. In the *New York Times*, Jack Gould called us "the ablest news staff in broadcasting" and said that we had "an absorbingly mature and articulate analysis of the world scene." In the *New York Herald Tribune*, John Cosby spoke of "tremendous depth and range" and "a truly surprising literacy of expression."

Nice to hear. But we knew that. After all, this was Murrow's team that I had so proudly joined.

I was a latecomer to the Murrow team, whose greatest days of glory had been during World War II and its prelude. I am the last of that team still active in daily journalism. Murrow, struck down by his cigarette habit, remains an icon to broadcast journalists too young to have ever heard him. He was Mr. Authenticity, which is why he never really liked television and its theatrics. He was more at home in radio, and I like to think that if he were alive today, he would be working for National Public Radio.

As a broadcaster without previous journalistic experience, he displayed deference to reporters, many of whom had come from news agencies and newspapers. A typical invitation to one who happened to be around 485 Madison Avenue after his evening broadcast was "Brother Schorr, would you have time for several drinks?"

For many years I have approached ethical and professional problems by asking myself, "What would Murrow have done in this situation?" Not that I always knew the answer.

CHAPTER 6

RUSSIA'S YEAR
OF TURMOIL

I returned to Moscow on February 11, 1956, permanent press card No. 138 firmly in hand, to cover a Communist Party congress that was expected to usher the Soviet Union into the post-Stalin era. "Cover" was only in a manner of speaking because press cards, even permanent ones, did not get "bourgeois" reporters inside the Kremlin walls. Although Moscow television started a second channel that week, there was no live broadcasting of the congress. We had to depend on delayed broadcasts and running transcripts distributed by the Tass news agency. It was hard even to track down delegates, who ate in restricted dining rooms.

My own living arrangements took a turn for the worse from my comfortable Hotel National room. I had made the mistake of giving up the room while home on leave to save CBS money. NBC's Irv Levine, more farsighted, if less economy-minded, had held on to his. With Moscow jampacked for the congress, I was shunted off to a room without bath in the second-class Savoy Hotel.

My professional arrangements, however, took a turn for the better. In response to my importuning for broadcast facilities like those Levine enjoyed at Moscow Radio, the government equalized our situation downward by announcing that no one could use Moscow Radio anymore, and a studio would be provided instead in the Central Telegraph office. That turned out to be a telephone booth with a primitive microphone and earphones.

The first time I tried to use the glass-enclosed cell, the CBS technician in New York advised that the plate glass was producing so much resonance that I couldn't be made out. He suggested that I wrap my fur-lined coat around my head and the microphone to muffle the echo. By the time I achieved a marginally acceptable signal, my head was completely encased in the coat, and in the dark, I could not read my censor-approved script. For the censor's benefit, in case he was listening, I announced in loud tones what my predicament was and said I planned to ad-lib but as close to my script as possible. If he was listening, he took pity. Some weeks later blue velour curtains were draped around the booth, which alleviated the problem.

A greater problem was getting a script past the censor intact. What Khrushchev and his little band of modernizers were trying to achieve at the Twentieth Party Congress was controlled decontrol, a peaceful revolution against the dead Stalin that would not lead to insurrection and chaos. Under the circumstances the censor himself seemed at times confused about what he was supposed to allow under the new rules.

One could quote speeches calling Stalin "arbitrary," but not "tyrannical." One could quote a Russian worker who said, "I still think Stalin was a great man," but not a taxi driver who said, "They talk about him that way because he is dead, but if he were alive..." When I referred to the people under Stalin as "the long-suffering Russians," *long-suffering* was deleted. When I wrote of Stalin victims being "posthumously rehabilitated," the word *posthumously* was excised.

I could imagine the censor scratching his head and wondering how much revisionism he was supposed to permit. What he clearly knew he was supposed to allow was Khrushchev's buildup for himself. I had no trouble reporting an episode such as Khrushchev telling the congress not to applaud every time he entered, saying,

"Behave like Communists! You are the masters of this congress!" or, at another point, criticizing bureaucrats for wasteful use of automobiles, then looking up and noting sarcastically, "I don't hear any applause." Whereupon the delegates broke into loud applause.

I managed to get through censorship a report that the latest volume of the *New Soviet Encyclopedia* had been delayed in publication—the volume for the letter *S*, which, of course, included "Stalin."

Out of frustration I played games with English idiom just for the fun of beating the censor. I got away with saying that the delegates, hearing a report that life expectancy had increased to age sixty-four, seemed "cheered to learn from the new leadership that they could expect to live longer." To express skepticism about the size of an announced cutback in troops, I said, "Tell that to the soldiers, tell it to the sailors, and above all, tell it to the marines."

A blanket censorship ban was occasioned by Khrushchev's unscheduled secret speech denouncing Stalin. I reported, without hindrance, on the CBS "World News Roundup" on Saturday, February 25, that the congress had met in all-night session, with all foreign delegations and observers barred. I said that, because of delegate fatigue, a Saturday closing session and rally had been canceled. That was all I knew, and the last report before the censorship boom fell.

From foreign Communist delegations and from diplomats, word began to spread that what had occupied the delegates that night and shocked them into canceling further proceedings was an extraordinary unscheduled speech by Khrushchev. He depicted Stalin as a monster who had created a "cult of personality" that had derailed the Soviet Union from its Marxist-Leninist course. Khrushchev's effort, clearly, was to paint the Stalin epoch as a massive aberration from a still valid Communist ideal. He said that Stalin had murdered not just citizens, but thousands of "good Communists." And far from having been the architect of victory in World War II, he had left the country almost defenseless and had ignored warnings of the impending German invasion.

It was said that at one point a delegate shouted, "And, Nikita Sergeyevich, where were you while all this was happening?"

Khrushchev had looked up and snapped, "Who said that? Stand up!" When no one rose, Khrushchev said, "That's where I was, comrade."

An electrifying story—the most momentous we Moscow correspondents might ever have—and not a whisper of it could we get through the censor. Not the slightest reference to "secret speech" or even "supplemental speech on Stalin." And when I told an editor in New York on the telephone there was a big story we couldn't transmit, the censor cut me off.

Word of the speech began to spread across the country in briefings for local party cadres and in factory rallies. Still, the censor kept us mute. There was widespread public agitation. We couldn't report that, either. I could say that the public was "taking time adjusting to the new climate." But, two weeks after the speech, in a feature about the celebrated pianist Emil Gilels, I noted that he no longer wore his Stalin Prize medal and added, "The expunging of Stalin's name apparently dates back to the recent Party congress at which Khrushchev reportedly delivered a three-hour speech denouncing Stalin." No luck. The censor was awake.

Tension reached a peak with the third anniversary of Stalin's death on March 5. No longer was the date noted in the press. A policeman stationed outside the Lenin-Stalin mausoleum in Red Square told visitors, some of whom had come hundreds of miles, "Sorry, no visitors today." The censor let me report that, but not to add, "Stalin has been forgotten, but not by those who stood before the tomb in reverence."

In Georgia, there were riots on the anniversary in homage to the native son and as an expression of nationalism. Our first indication came when trains from Tbilisi arrived in Moscow with bullet-riddled windows. A reliable clue to trouble was the closing of that region in the Caucasus to foreign visitors. A month later, when correspondents were allowed to visit a cleaned-up Tbilisi, we learned firsthand what had happened: Students staged a banned rally in front of a Stalin statue. Police fired with machine guns, killing more than a hundred persons. Our belated reports from the scene did not get through the censor unmangled, even though we quoted from official sources such as the university rector. We also went to see Stalin's birthplace in Gori, a humble cottage now enshrined in marble. Stalin may have been a tyrant, but he was their tyrant, and they did not like his image being spat on by Russians and Ukrainians. But it was hard to report that.

Georgians knew of the Khrushchev speech. By now the speech, with various expurgations, was being read to Communist cadres and factory groups everywhere. We heard that, in a second or maybe third stage, it was being communicated to Communist parties in Eastern Europe, and even in the West. And yet we correspondents in Moscow were still gagged by the censor. The only way for one of us to report on it was to leave the country—and undoubtedly be expelled on returning. We wondered which of us might try that, and we didn't discuss it among ourselves. Finally, a young Reuters correspondent, John Rettie, went to Finland on vacation. A few days later Reuters carried an unbylined story under a Frankfurt dateline, summing up what was known of the Khrushchev speech. And John Rettie did not return to Moscow.

More than three months after the speech, in June, the CIA put us out of our misery. Messages from our home office advised that a text had been published in the *New York Times*. Later we would learn of the propaganda coup of CIA director Allen Dulles, who had made obtaining the speech a high-priority project and had succeeded with the aid of Israeli intelligence and a Polish Communist source. The text was then offered to the *Times*. There was still no open Soviet acknowledgment. When I asked press spokesman Ilyichev ironically if he was pleased by the publication of the speech, he responded, "I don't know who should be more pleased— the Soviet government or the American government."

It now became possible to report steps in an orchestrated campaign to tear down the image of Stalin. The party theoretical magazine, *Kommunist*, published a long-suppressed Lenin testament calling Stalin "rude" and saying he should be replaced as Party secretary. A professional military magazine detailed how Stalin had almost lost World War II. On July 1, a month after the speech had become known throughout the world, I was finally permitted by the censor to refer to "the publication abroad of the Khrushchev secret speech."

Meanwhile, cultural and professional exchanges continued to expand. Isaac Stern, born in Russia, came back to the Soviet Union and took the country by storm. Not only with his musical prowess, but with his warm talks in Russian to his audiences. Movie producers came to Moscow with projects for joint productions. Mike Todd, who had recently made *Around the World in Eighty Days*, arrived with a proposal to produce Tolstoy's *War and Peace* in Russia with American stars and the Red Army as extras. The idea was a nonstarter. I was, however, impressed to see Todd talk his way through three lines of police into Red Square for the May Day parade by flashing his private cigar label as his credential. He also brought from Paris his new wife, Elizabeth Taylor, recently converted to Judaism. I sat between them at a lavish dinner in the Georgian Aragvi restaurant as he motioned toward her décolleté and said, "Those Jewish gals have big tits, don't they?"

As part of the general thaw in Soviet-American relations, a cautious effort was made to start a military exchange. Gen. Nathan Twining, air force chief of staff, accepted an invitation to the annual Tushino air show, a much-trumpeted event where the latest Soviet aircraft were exhibited. General Twining observed to American correspondents that there were new fighters, but no new bombers. He thought the Russians were trying to create the impression of downgrading bombers in favor of missiles.

The air show was important to Irving Levine and me as one of the infrequent occasions we could bring in camera crews for a couple of weeks. Aside from covering the air show, we tried to shoot as many unrelated stories as possible. My crew was out doing scenic shots on the Moskva River when I heard that Levine had arranged a pre-departure interview with General Twining in his hotel.

I demanded equal treatment, and the general readily agreed to an interview with me as well. But my camera crew was out of contact. In the end Levine found himself obliged to let me use his crew. He was not happy about it. American network coexistence was no easier than East-West coexistence.

The Twining visit did not advance Soviet-American relations. At a lavish reception given by Defense Minister Zhukov, Twining found himself almost joining in a toast to Red China before Ambassador Bohlen signaled him to put his glass down. Amid the free-flowing brandy and champagne, I heard Khrushchev say to General Twining, "We want to cooperate with you even though you send spy planes over our country." Twining did not respond. Later he told me he didn't know what Khrushchev was talking about.

It was one of the times I should probably have taken Khrushchev more seriously, even with a glass in his hand. Three weeks later the Soviet government officially charged intrusion by Germany-based American reconnaissance planes. The Eisenhower administration, while not acknowledging it, asked for the return of downed pilots. Not until January 1961, was the two-man crew of a downed RB-47 reconnaissance plane released by Khrushchev as a gesture to the incoming President Kennedy.

Meanwhile, I was importuning my CBS News bosses to approve the budget for my bureau, submitted shortly after my return to Moscow. The standard budget for an American news operation in Moscow called for a combined office-apartment in one of the militia-guarded diplomatic buildings, a car purchased abroad, a Russian chauffeur (the government discouraged us from driving) provided by the government bureau that served diplomatic missions, and a translator-secretary selected by the same bureau.

CBS continued, unaccountably, to drag its feet on approving my budget. Finally, CBS News president Sig Mickelson came to Moscow and, with deep embarrassment, told me that corporate executives had decided against having an official bureau in Moscow.

"The thinking is," Sig stammered, "that CBS is still too close to the troubles it suffered from the McCarthy Red scare to risk having 'Moscow' listed in the corporate directory."

CBS had been a particular target of the anticommunist campaign, many of its personnel included in the blacklist called Red Channels. But most people thought the era of the Red scare was over.

When I had recovered from the shock of that bizarre statement, I asked whether CBS was, in that case, willing for me to remain head-quartered in a hotel, charging all my living expenses to the company, and riding in Intourist cars. Mickelson, almost blushing, said that was the way things would have to be.

And so, for more than two years, I lived with a windfall from a shell-shocked network. I banked virtually my entire salary since, as a foreign resident, I paid no American income tax, and only a nominal Soviet tax.

Only nine months earlier, the snarling Foreign Ministry press chief, Leonid Ilyichev, had summoned us to his first-ever press con-ference, limited to the one-line announcement that we were hence-forth subject to the Soviet income tax. We quickly ascertained that this was in reprisal for a U.S. Treasury ruling that Soviet correspon-dents, not enjoying diplomatic status, had to pay American tax. The Soviets, having made their point, had no mechanism to assess the tax and told us simply to pay 10 percent of our declared income. It may be safe now to reveal that we considerably understated our incomes, with many deadpan references to capitalist exploitation.

To make sure the Soviets couldn't check on us, we sent no accounts—or any other personal correspondence, for that matter—through the Soviet mail. The American embassy permitted us to use its diplomatic pouch. That protected our correspondence from Russian snooping, but not from American snooping. Congressional investigations two decades later would reveal CIA scanning of our mail in the embassy pouch. Photocopies of some of my envelopes were returned to me on a Freedom of Information application.

I moved into Rooms 390 and 392 of the venerable Hotel Metropol, at the end of a long corridor with a window looking out on the ruins of an old Chinese wall. My translator, Paul Shikman, Cleveland-born, became companion and friend, not only translating, but performing a variety of chores such as carrying my camera case and unloading film. Because room service was slow to nonexistent, I cooked simple meals from provisions that foreign correspondents were permitted to import from diplomatic supply houses in Helsinki and Stockholm.

One lack I felt was a refrigerator. That need was filled when *New York Times* correspondent Welles Hangen, ordered expelled on forty-eight-hour notice, offered to sell for $50 a General Motors original bell-top Frigidaire that correspondent Brooks Atkinson had brought in during Word War II. I routinely charged the purchase on my monthly expense account. When CBS News auditors disallowed the item as household rather than office equipment, I listed it in my next expense account as a water-cooler. Meeting the accounting executive in New York at the end of the year, I asked him if he had found the refrigerator in my account. "It will cool water, won't it?" he replied.

Installed in the Metropol, I led a professional life that started daily with Paul Shikman translating at sight from *Pravda*, the party organ, *Izvestia*, the government organ, and three other newspapers. (On weekends, my translator was Marvin Kalb, moonlighting from his job in the American-British Joint Press Reading Service.) I had started taking Russian lessons after my return to Moscow, but was so often obliged to cancel because of news events that I finally gave up.

Out on the street one day, Paul warned me to be cautious about what I said to him in the office because he was obliged to report weekly to the government bureau—which could check on him from eavesdropping tapes. He also cautioned me about Russian visitors. So, when three Russians, evidently cleared through the third-floor monitor, appealed to me to help them leave the country, I looked up at the chandelier and announced, "I am here as a guest of your government and would not dream of violating its laws." Paul nodded approval of my performance.

I also made minimal use of the telephone, in part because of assumed wiretapping, in part because it was simply so hard to hear—probably causally related.

Everyone has a favorite eavesdropping story, many of them involving talking to lamps and chandeliers as the most direct way to deliver a message. Mine is about becoming frustrated at all the static on the line one day while I was trying to talk to someone at the American embassy, finally shouting, "If some of you clowns would get off the line, I might be able to say something that the rest of you could hear." If memory serves, the line cleared up magically.

My day usually ended at the Central Telegraph office, working on my portable typewriter or waiting for the censor to do his thing. These sessions could last until the early-morning hours, thanks to the eight-hour time difference with New York. And then back on foot to the Metropol by dawn's early light, along streets shared with the women plying their twig brooms.

Tourists often asked me if I was afraid. The answer was, not of private crime. The KGB agents who occasionally followed me, rather conspicuously, seemed to afford more protection than menace. Street crime was rampant in those days (and is more rampant in these), but the Soviet authorities went to some length to make foreigners feel safe. An American tourist told me her camera had been stolen from her Intourist hotel room in Kiev, and I suggested she report it to the Intourist agency in Moscow. When it was restored to her the next day, she expressed gratification and surprise. Her Intourist guide said, "One thing about a police state—it's well policed." That joke from a Soviet employee in 1956 would have been inconceivable even a year earlier. The thaw was having some effect.

If Russians were slow to believe in a new era when repression would be ended, it was because they had seen such new eras before, turned on and abruptly turned off. What Khrushchev needed to demonstrate was some dramatic evidence of the irreversible end of Stalinism. Nothing would serve that purpose better than to bring to the Soviet Union the one East European leader who had stood up to Stalin, preached a more liberal form of socialism, and lived to tell the tale. That was Josip Broz Tito of Yugoslavia.

On June 2, 1956, as President Tito's train crossed the border into the Soviet Union, the Kremlin announced the resignation of Foreign Minister Vyacheslav Molotov. In 1948, Molotov had signed, with Stalin, the letter that read Yugoslavia out of the Communist camp.

(Unruffled and still vice premier, Molotov told me at a reception that maybe he would now have time to write his memoirs. But, in fact, he would have other ideological battles still to fight.) The Tito tour was a smashing success—almost too smashing for a Soviet bureaucracy unprepared for the surge of popular acclaim that would greet him.

In powder-blue marshal's uniform, he radiated a sense of authority. He strode through the Lenin-Stalin tomb with hardly a glance at Stalin's waxen figure. At a rally of workers in the Moscow (formerly Stalin) auto plant, he said pointedly, "We note that today there is a smile and a bold look on the faces of citizens of the Soviet Union. They walk straight, they look better." In the evening, he and Khrushchev stopped in at a Gorki Street ice-cream parlor while crowds gaped at the unheard-of scene.

Arriving by train in Stalingrad, Tito was almost swamped by the crowd that broke through police lines, shouting, "Ti-to, Ti-to!" Clearly concerned at invidious comparisons with Khrushchev being made abroad, the Soviet authorities now tried to discourage us Western correspondents from continuing on the trip. When Khrushchev and Tito boarded a boat to go down the Volga to a dam site, passing the huge copper statue of Stalin that Khrushchev had denounced at the Party congress, we were escorted to a press boat that stayed tied up at the dock.

A colleague and I, seeing the official boat disappearing in the distance, jumped off our launch, raced along the Volga in our rented car, barely caught a ferry, then ran a mile to the dam, where Khrushchev was standing on the rim, flailing the air in a speech denouncing capitalism. He flickered a smile in our direction and, without missing a beat, said, "And I am glad that the bourgeois press has come here to hear what I have to say about capitalism." The crowd howled with laughter. Tito knew nothing of how hard the Soviet authorities had tried to keep us away.

From Stalingrad the Khrushchev-Tito train was to go to the resort town of Sochi on the Black Sea. Press spokesman Ilyichev told us there was no room for us and that we should return to Moscow. A few of us nevertheless flew to Sochi. Next morning, after breakfast in a seaside hotel, I fainted. I had to be carried aboard a plane back to Moscow, close to unconscious all the way. The American embassy had been advised, and I was met by a consular officer. Back at my hotel I slept for the next twenty-four hours. The embassy's physician said I had experienced a KGB Mickey Finn.

The trip ended better for Tito and Khrushchev than it did for me. Khrushchev's post-Stalin regime had been certified by the most certified foe of Stalin on the block. Tito, a recognized hero of the socialist world, had gained endorsement for his doctrine of "many roads to socialism." Anxious, however, not to lose American friendship, Tito told Ambassador Bohlen during a lavish farewell reception at the Yugoslav embassy that the American press had taken him out of context in quoting him as saying that Yugoslavia was "marching arm in arm" with the Soviet Union.

But Tito was hardly gone before the Khrushchev regime began to feel a backlash from Communist bosses in Eastern and Western Europe who felt their own foundations shaking under the spreading tremors of de-Stalinization. The censors killed my dispatch saying there were widespread reports of a special Central Committee meeting to consider slowing down the de-Stalinization drive. But then delegations of Polish, Hungarian, and French Communists came to Moscow, and the Central Committee came out on July 2 with a seven-thousand-word resolution partially backtracking on the denunciation of Stalin. The new dogma was that his excesses could be understood and the lack of opposition forgiven in the light of imperialist encirclement of the Soviet Union.

The amended dogma had an immediate purpose. The Titoist virus, intensified by the downgrading of Stalin, was spreading among the East European satellites. There had been a violent demonstration in Poznan, Poland, where workers had demanded "bread and freedom." The Soviet papers at first ignored it, then said it was organized by "agents of imperialism." Another official report said that two "spies for imperialist intelligence" had been captured in Hungary. *Imperialist*, a pre-détente word, was apparently being recycled.

"The Soviets are talking of a new American-financed effort to penetrate the Soviet bloc," I said in a broadcast. "Some momentous things must be going on inside the Kremlin."

A chill fell over preparations for the American embassy's Independence Day reception—scheduled to be attended by the Soviet leadership along with a record crowd of five hundred. Irving Levine and I still had the camera crews left over from the Tushino air show, and we were thrilled at the idea of the Moscow July Fourth festivity on television for the first time ever. But, in a meeting with Irv and myself, Chip Bohlen said that he, and especially his wife, Avis, were against having cameras present. The tension over Poland was too great, and he feared that Khrushchev would exploit the occasion to unleash a tirade against the United States. We argued our case strenuously. Finally, Bohlen cut short the discussion. "I don't see why I have to negotiate this with you people," he said. "Look, the British embassy has a queen's birthday reception and never permits cameras."

"Yes, Chip," I said. "And it's because the British act that way that we celebrate this day."

Bohlen cracked up and agreed to the cameras—on our promise that we would not try to provoke Khrushchev. And we didn't. Both he and Premier Bulganin were restrained. Bulganin toasted the health of President Eisenhower. Khrushchev milled around with American tourists on the Spaso House lawn, inspecting Avis Bohlen's corn plants and telling Prof. Philip Mosley of Columbia University that, for the first time, disputes in the eleven-member Communist Presidium were now being settled by majority vote. The Soviet press was charging that day that America was instigating subversion in Eastern Europe, but the hostility did not spill over onto the lawn of Spaso House.

One tourist present, more or less under my wing, was the attractive eighteen-year-old Kate Roosevelt. She was the granddaughter of Franklin D., daughter of James Roosevelt, and her mother, the former Betsy Cushing, was the sister-in-law of CBS chairman William Paley. Kate had been preceded by a letter from Paley asking me to see after his "favorite niece." That was not easy because *Roosevelt* was still a magic name in the Soviet Union, and I had to ward off approaches from Radio Moscow and other propaganda organs seeking to exploit her in interviews to advance the Soviet coexistence line.

She also attracted an amazing variety of fans and would-be suitors among young Russians. I took Kate to watch a parachute-jumping demonstration and came close to a heart attack when I discovered she had gone up in a plane with a pair of parachutists. That was not quite how I wanted to see my CBS career ending. Happily, she did not jump and the rickety plane made it back safely. When I returned to New York at the end of the year, Paley rewarded my guardianship with choice seats to *My Fair Lady*, the musical in which he owned a controlling interest.

The summer of 1956 was a season of foreboding. After the Poznan riots, de-Stalinization and Titoism left Communist regimes edgy about their ability to maintain control. Crisis loomed from another quarter as Egypt's president, Gamal Abdel Nasser, in defiance of the Western powers, moved to nationalize the Suez Canal, previously operated by an international authority. Khrushchev was making speeches to stadium crowds blaming American "imperialists" for the Poznan riots and calling for "vigilance" against them, and warning Britain, France, and Israel to accept the seizure of Suez because "a war is easier to start than to finish."

In the Soviet Union itself the regime seemed to be trying to head off trouble by making life a little easier for its citizens. A new law permitted workers to leave their jobs, and the workweek was cut from forty-eight to forty-six hours. Abortion was legalized. A group of notables petitioned for illegitimate children to be able to take their father's name. There were new rules against "administrative punishment" by the police. Some bribe-taking bureaucrats were demonstratively punished. In gestures toward a more civil society, auto horn-blowing was banned (with little discernible effect) and (with even less effect) a campaign was launched against public profanity.

With two American colleagues I accepted an invitation in August 1956 to join a first-ever press tour of Siberia, involving a five-thousand-mile round-trip flight to the much-talked-about scientific and industrial center of Novosibirsk. We were shown industrial sites, a power project, and a new television tower being built behind barbed wire by what turned out to be prison labor. We were shown the much headlined bumper crop of corn on the "virgin lands" on which Khrushchev was staking so much of his prestige. (But in succeeding years came disaster when the salt table rose to the surface, as some had predicted.)

In the midst of our tour we were suddenly told that several localities on our program had to be dropped. In one case, because a shallow-draft vessel couldn't make it there. In several places hotel rooms were said to be unavailable. Our offer to sleep in haystacks went unheeded. Clearly something had intervened since the foreign press trip to Siberia had been conceived. Much later we would learn that, around that time, preparations were under way for a series of nuclear bomb tests. We may have been thousands of miles away from the test site, but the Soviet bureaucracy was taking no chances and shipped us back to Moscow.

We reflected that this probably made us the first people to be exiled from Siberia.

A note in passing: On the flight from Novosibirsk a young Soviet aeronautical engineer shyly approached me. He wanted to try out the English he had studied at home. He wanted to taste his first chewing gum. And he wanted to look at his first American newspaper—the *New York Times*, which I was carrying. Soon he was back in his seat chewing enthusiastically and glued to one page of the *Times*. Curious about what was holding his rapt attention, I went up the aisle to look. It was the page of stock quotations.

At the end of August I flew to Geneva to celebrate my fortieth birthday (August 31) with Isaac and Vera Stern, who were spending the summer there. We had a great feast with vodka and mounds of caviar. As magnificent a birthday present as I ever hope to receive was being serenaded with the Bach double concerto played by Isaac and the visiting Nathan Milstein in the Sterns' living room.

From Geneva I flew to Berlin, planning to fly back to Moscow with the Bohlens. (By reciprocal agreement, American and Soviet

planes were permitted to fly to each other's capital for the travels of
the ambassador and his family.) However, I had to change my plans
when word came that a trial was opening in Poznan arising out of
the June "bread and freedom" riots. My Soviet visa enabled me to
get a Polish transit visa, permitting me to stop in Poznan and Warsaw and get a sense of the ferment that was raising such hopes
among the Poles and such jitters among their masters.

I found the scene in the Poznan courtroom astonishing—accused
instigators of the June riots, defended by well-known lawyers,
talking back to the prosecutors. Some evidence was excluded by
the judges because it had been obtained under duress. The defendants got off with light sentences. In Warsaw, Party chief Edward
Ochab, a holdover from Stalin days, was on his way out, and Wladyslaw Gomulka, who had been Stalin's prisoner for five years, was
on his way in to preside over that rush of freedom called "the Polish
October."

The Polish press was in the vanguard of liberal reform. "In these
days it is exciting to be a journalist in Poland," said a staff member of a
Communist organ. Another asked how things were in Moscow,
whether I was still subject to censorship. He said, "In Poland, for several
months now the press has been questioning Party policy and demanding economic reform." Journalists found it amusing that Soviet premier Bulganin had been quoted in the Soviet press as saying that some
Polish editors had come under the influence of "hostile elements."

Back in Moscow, I reported on October 2 that Khrushchev was
still on vacation, having spent two weeks with Tito, first in Yugoslavia, now on the Crimean Black Sea coast. They undoubtedly had
problems to discuss about containing the virus of "many roads to
socialism." I added that "a meeting of the Soviet Party Central Committee is due soon."

It was not, in fact, until October 15 that we finally saw Khrushchev
at a reception at the Afghan embassy. He seemed relaxed, but not
exuberant, slower to speak than usual, nursing one glass of champagne. He talked of the record grain harvest and shied away from
foreign affairs. On the pending American election: "That's America's

affair." On what was discussed in his sixteen days with Tito: "I asked Tito every day how he liked Ukrainian borscht, and every day he said he liked it."

I was leading up to trying to learn from Khrushchev what no official would tell us—whether an emergency meeting of the decision-making Central Committee was in the works to deal with an uprising in Hungary and a British-French-Israeli invasion of Suez. I asked Khrushchev how his hunting trip had gone. Although not an enthusiastic hunter, he said he had bagged four deer to Tito's one. Finally I said, "It must be beautiful in the Crimea this time of year. Do you think I could go hunting down there?"

"Pazhalusta!" he exploded. (If you please!)

He motioned to an aide to help make arrangements. I interrupted, saying that first I had to solve a problem for which I needed his help.

"So, tell me your problem, *Gospodin* Schorr."

I said that my bosses in New York would not allow me to leave Moscow because of rumors of a pending Central Committee meeting. He gave a long nod of understanding, leaned over, and spoke in confidential tones:

"When exactly did you want to go on vacation?"

"Tomorrow."

"For how long?"

"Two weeks."

"And you are afraid that during that time you might miss a meeting of the Central Committee?"

"Exactly."

Leaning closer to me he whispered, "You can go on your vacation."

"You mean, there won't be..."

"If absolutely necessary, we will have the meeting without you."

And he poked me in the ribs.

On October 20, five days later, diplomats traveling by train from Moscow to Warsaw were stopped at the Brest Litovsk crossing point and told that the border was closed for five days. The censor would not let me report that—itself a sign of trouble. Then

Pravda came out with an attack of unprecedented fury on the Polish press, accusing it of renouncing socialism and "shaking the very
pillars of the people's democratic system." Next, a brief Tass dispatch announced that Khrushchev had arrived in Warsaw in a delegation that included a moderate, Vice Premier Anastas Mikoyan,
and two hard-liners, former foreign minister Molotov and Lazar
Kaganovich.

They were back before we knew they were gone. My friends in
Warsaw told me Gomulka had stood up to them, demanded that
the menacingly deployed Soviet troops be ordered back to their
encampments, and said he would come to Moscow to negotiate a
friendship treaty, but only as an equal. It was an astonishing display
of courage and boldness by the leader of a country wedged between
the Soviet Union and a still Stalinist East Germany. And the deli-
cately balanced Khrushchev delegation bought it.

In Moscow we thought we had figured out why. Almost simultaneously, a much more direct threat to Communist rule was erupting in
Hungary. We could not reach Budapest from Moscow by telephone.
For three days running the Soviet press repeated that the "counterrevolution" in Hungary had been suppressed. The Soviet regime seemed
to waver, announcing support of the liberal new premier, Imre Nagy.

When *Pravda* printed Nagy's statement about "new democratic
forces," I said in a broadcast, "It now looks as though Russia, having
reluctantly accepted changes in Poland, is getting ready to live with
the more far-reaching changes in Hungary."

At a Turkish embassy reception on October 29, Foreign Minister
Dimitri Shepilov told me that Soviet forces had stopped shooting,
would not fire unless attacked, and would evacuate Budapest "as
soon as the situation is quiet." At the reception, Khrushchev wouldn't
talk about Hungary at all. "Why don't you ask the Hungarian ambassador," he snapped, turned away, then turned back, raised his glass,
and said, "Your health, Mr. Schorr."

At what may have been a crucial moment of Soviet indecision
on Hungary, a British-French-Israeli offensive was launched on
October 31 to seize the Suez Canal. I was standing with Ambas-

sador Bohlen at Vnukovo Airport, awaiting the arrival of Syrian president Shukri al-Kuwatly, when we received word of the Suez offensive.

"This is a historic tragedy," said Chip, shaking his head. "This will let the Russians shift the spotlight away from Hungary. They couldn't have asked for better."

Four days later Soviet tanks were clanking their way back into Budapest for the bloody suppression of the uprising. What the Soviets for a few days hailed as the "democratic forces" had become again "reactionary forces." Premier Nagy, seeking asylum in the Yugoslav embassy in Budapest, was allowed, on Tito's orders, to fall into the hands of the Russians.

In those days a joke was whispered around Moscow that the censor wouldn't let me report. Three Hungarians meet in prison, each asking the others why they were there. One says, "I was pro-Nagy," the second, "I was anti-Nagy," and the third says, "I'm Nagy."

At a reception I heard Ambassador Bohlen, his lips tight with contempt, ask Khrushchev if he thought he had enough troops in Hungary. And with equal anger Khrushchev replied, "I think enough, Mr. Ambassador. And if we don't, we will send more and more." (The censor killed that in my broadcast script.)

I reported that three hundred Russian students had walked out on a Communist Party lecturer at the Lenin Library when he refused to answer questions about what was really going on in Hungary and Poland. I took the chance of not submitting that line to the censor before broadcasting. Or a line saying that the Kremlin, making a big fuss about British and French bombing of Egypt, was "apparently hoping to draw attention from Hungary."

I guess some of us when unengaged reporters in Moscow lost our cool over the brutality in Hungary. Without knowing what sanctions I faced, I several times evaded censorship. It seemed simply impossible to abide by censorship and report what was happening in Moscow. I saw staged demonstrations outside the British, French, and Israeli embassies that the censor wouldn't let me call "staged."

For example, I saw Young Pioneers in red neckerchiefs break into the grounds of the British embassy, then withdraw when their supervisor called on them to "maintain discipline."

The Soviets were going to great lengths to divert attention from Hungary to Suez. On the eve of the American election, Premier Bulganin sent a message to President Eisenhower calling for joint Soviet-American intervention in support of Egypt. Then the Soviet press announced that Soviet volunteers could enroll at the Egyptian embassy. That seemed so patent a propaganda ploy that I went around to the Egyptian embassy to ask how enrollments were going since no lines of applicants were to be seen.

Playing his assigned role, the military attaché said he had two lists of volunteers—individuals and units. The more than fifty thousand "individuals" included tankers and artillerymen, who would presumably be equipped in Russia before going to Egypt. The "volunteer units" included three MiG fighter squadrons. I was prepared to tell America about this propaganda effort in a live broadcast on the CBS "World News Roundup" without showing it to the censor. Unfortunately, he was listening and cut me off in midbroadcast. That created a greater sensation than my broadcast would have. I was told that the San Francisco Chronicle carried a banner headline about a CBS correspondent cut off while revealing Soviet military aid to Egypt.

Ironically, several hours later, the censor approved the script, having presumably been told that he was supposed to go along with the charade.

On a cold, raw November 15 a Polish Communist delegation led by Gomulka arrived at the railway station. The Western ambassadors, who had boycotted events connected with the November 6 anniversary of the Russian Revolution in protest against the bloodbath in Hungary, were on hand—invited by the Polish embassy. Khrushchev stood on the platform, arms outstretched to greet Gomulka and give him a bear hug.

Members of the Polish delegation told us they understood Khrushchev might be on his way out as first secretary of the Party.

The censor wouldn't let me report that. Just as well—it turned out not to be true. It was true that the rumored Central Committee secret session had finally happened in early November. The downgraded Molotov and Malenkov had spoken up in criticism of Khrushchev, Malenkov reportedly accusing the first secretary of performing juggling tricks like an Indian fakir. It had not helped that Tito of Yugoslavia, in whose friendship Khrushchev had invested so much, had made a speech blaming remnants of Stalinism in the Soviet regime for both Poland and Hungary. On top of that, Prime Minister Jawaharlal Nehru of India, which Khrushchev and Bulganin had visited as the first of their sorties outside the Communist world, had also attacked the Soviets for their excesses in Hungary.

Khrushchev managed to hold on to his Party position, but as a concession to his critics, Molotov was brought back into the leadership with the title of "minister of state control"—a title that Stalin himself had once held during his rise to power. Khrushchev was clearly on probation, and patching up relations with Poland was his first test.

That turned out to be not too difficult to do. Both sides were sobered by what had happened in Hungary. Poland, locked between the Soviet Union and East Germany, could not dream of exiting from the Communist camp. Gomulka talked of getting what was "feasible," which had mainly to do with unspecified freedom of action, economic aid, and a promise that Soviet troops in Poland would stay in their encampments.

Without too much difficulty, the Soviets and Poles agreed on a joint declaration. But, under all the pressure, Khrushchev, who in mid-October had seemed so composed, had turned somewhat manic. At a Kremlin reception for Gomulka, the first secretary delivered a violent attack on Britain, France, and Israel over the Suez invasion that caused Western ambassadors to leave the hall. The next night, November 18, at a farewell reception at the Polish embassy, Khrushchev seemed even more out of control.

Khrushchev faced his audience from across a buffet table. Behind him stood Gomulka, impassive, and Molotov and Malenkov, averting their eyes as though in scorn. Banging his fist on the table,

Khrushchev said, "We are Bolsheviks. We stick firmly to Lenin's precepts.... We base ourselves on the premise that we must peacefully coexist. Only a madman would deny this."

He was "very sorry" about the situation in Hungary, but "the counterrevolution must be shattered." He apologized to Gomulka for "making such a speech on the territory of another state." Then he launched an attack on the United States, which he accused of instigating insurrection in Hungary, and on Britain, France, and Israel for going to war over Suez.

Once again the Western ambassadors consulted and, led by Bohlen, trooped out of the room. This time Khrushchev shouted after them, "It doesn't depend on you whether we exist or not. If you don't like us, don't accept our invitations, and don't invite us to come to you. Whether you like it or not, history is on our side. We will bury you!"

The "bury you" expression was deleted from the highly expurgated text published the next day in the Soviet press, but it would come back to haunt Khrushchev when he tried to reestablish relations with the West.

Also born in those days, undoubtedly under the influence of Molotov and other hard-liners, was the doctrine that justified the use of force to keep a member of the Soviet bloc from leaving. *Pravda* asserted that a rebellion against Communist authority had to be crushed even if "large segments of the working people were involved." In such cases, it said, "people must be saved from reaction."

Twelve years later, that would be dusted off as "the Brezhnev Doctrine," justifying the sending of tanks into Czechoslovakia to crush liberal reform. In 1956 I wrote, "It would appear that workers may have to be shot in defense of their interests." The censor, of course, cut that line.

As I prepared to fly home before Christmas, I tried to collect my thoughts about this tumultuous year. It had started with a confident Khrushchev leadership ready to break the Stalinist mold and start a new era. It ended with the leadership running scared at what it had wrought. Tremors from the explosions in Eastern Europe had reached into the Soviet Union itself. Not only were Russian students openly protesting Hungary, but Russian workers were striking in several places for better wages.

A jittery regime raised wages some more, revised the five-year plan to provide more consumer goods, and lashed out at the "imperialist" West. But the genie was out of the bottle, and there was no way back to Stalinist repression. Nor could Khrushchev afford to allow his relations with the West, on which his policy was built, to continue long to lie in ruins. The year that had started so promisingly for him had ended in disaster. And he had to find a way out.

The Murrow "Years of Crisis" program on December 30 proved to be more spirited than the one a year before—perhaps reflecting a violent and ominous year. I reported that from the Party congress until the year's end, the "rosy dream of a Communist future has blurred and turned into a nightmare...the carefully blueprinted transition to a sort of safer and saner Communism after Stalin got out of hand... unexpectedly violent forces threatened the disintegration of this empire that the Russians were trying to turn into a commonwealth."

A couple of unusual clashes between correspondents developed, including one between Dick Hottelet and myself. He said that Poland had achieved a considerable degree of freedom—and "Poland today is a satellite in name only." He proposed that the United States warn the Soviet Union against interfering with Polish freedom and be prepared to use military power. "If that leads to war, then war was inevitable," he said.

There were some heated exchanges between us as I warned that Hottelet's ideas could lead to nuclear war. It was an almost classic hawk-versus-dove argument about the benefits and perils of exploiting the manifest weakness of the Soviet leadership.

I brought the exchange with Hottelet to a close with a crack for which I later apologized: "Gentlemen, I think we have found the mad bomber."

CHAPTER 7

LIFE WITH
KHRUSHCHEV

Nikita Sergeyevich Khrushchev would easily qualify as "the most fascinating person I ever met." Combining qualities of boorish peasant and imaginative statesman, he almost single-handedly wrenched the Soviet Union out of its Stalinist mold. If Mikhail Gorbachev was too late to save Communism by modernizing it, Khrushchev was perhaps too early, and both of them ended up rejected and unappreciated for their titanic efforts.

But I do not know Gorbachev and I did know his forerunner. It is a singular fact that over four years, in colloquies stretching from Moscow to San Francisco, I spent more time with the Kremlin leader than with all the American presidents combined, starting with Eisenhower, whose administrations I have covered.

I saw Khrushchev in many moods—when he was grim and tense over Hungary, when he was puffed with pride over his orbiting Sputniks. Impetuous in manner, he was also cunning and shrewd. He had little formal education, but he had a quick mind, and he knew more associates and subordinates by face and name than anyone else I have ever seen. He was gregarious, but ungraceful. He wore good clothes badly on a stocky frame. Once pushed out on the ballroom floor during a Communist festivity, he danced a few awkward steps and retired quickly.

He said he had no hobbies, and that his idea of a good time was to fly off on an inspection trip. He had little interest in the arts, hated everything nonrepresentational, and issued long doctrinal statements to keep artists and writers from getting too far out of hand in the transition from Stalinist repression.

I returned to Moscow in January 1957, stopping off in Warsaw to cover a Polish election that confirmed Gomulka's popularity. Soviet-Western relations were in the cellar, where Hungary and Suez had plunged them. A whiff of old-time Stalinism was in the air with five American embassy attachés arrested on spying charges and demonstratively expelled. The Soviet press was up in arms about plans to introduce American medium-range missiles into Western Europe. In response to Eisenhower administration statements that tactical nuclear weapons were now considered conventional, Defense Minister Zhukov was saying a new war would be nuclear from the start. Ambassador Bohlen was called home for consultations, and it was announced he would soon be replaced—undoubtedly by someone more acceptable to hard-line Secretary Dulles. Within the Communist camp, Tito was being attacked for propagating "national Communism," and billions of rubles were being earmarked to keep the restless satellite states quiet.

By mid-April it began to look as though Suez and Hungary had delivered lasting blows to Khrushchev's coexistence campaign. The Soviet Union, with whatever consequences for the first secretary's hold on power, was getting ready to draw back into a bellicose shell. Then the wind shifted. At an Albanian embassy reception, of all places, Khrushchev and Bulganin made speeches saying that, with the fighting over in Hungary and Egypt, new opportunities had arisen to resolve international problems by negotiation. I wrote that this looked like the start of a full-scale peace offensive.

Two nights later, at a Syrian embassy reception, Khrushchev sought out the departing Ambassador Bohlen for a farewell chat. He told him he hoped for better relations, said the Soviet government would give sympathetic consideration to the latest American arms control proposal, and noted, "We are ready to agree to everything reasonable." At the same time the Soviet government eased restrictions on travel for foreigners outside Moscow—a sure sign of thaw.

Khrushchev's new peace offensive had a new feature. Talk of four-power meetings was muted in favor of emphasis on direct Soviet-American negotiation. When Khrushchev was asked at receptions, as he often was, whether he would like to visit the United States, his stock answer was that he would be interested in such a trip, but could not go "as a simple tourist." He would have to be invited.

By May one could see the peace offensive rapidly taking shape. Khrushchev talked less of an arms race and more about catching up with the United States in production of milk, butter, and meat. Finland was pressured into inviting Khrushchev and Bulganin for an official visit in June—their first outing in the West since Suez and Hungary. In mid-May Khrushchev gave an interview to Turner Catledge of the *New York Times*, stressing his wish for direct negotiations with the United States. Next it was my turn to play a role in the peace offensive, and time for a television first.

I had routinely been writing letters every three months proposing an interview with Premier Bulganin or Party chief Khrushchev on the CBS *Face the Nation* program. One morning a call came from the Foreign Ministry Press Department asking if CBS was still interested in interviewing the first secretary (no mention of Bulganin). Quickly adjusting myself to the situation, I said yes and next day was at the ministry starting intensive negotiations, with frequent time-outs for telephone consultations with excited, but apprehensive, CBS executives in New York. At upper echelons there was still residual post-McCarthy fear of red-baiters.

The first issue the Soviets raised was a request for questions in advance. I explained that the unrehearsed give-and-take nature of the program precluded that. Eventually we compromised on providing a list of "areas for discussion." When I listed the panelists as Stuart Novins, moderator, B. J. Cutler of the *New York Herald Tribune*, and myself, Soviet officials objected to Cutler, saying their mandate was to arrange an interview with "CBS correspondents." I explained that the format of *Face the Nation* included one newspaper reporter. The negotiations stalled for a day on this issue, CBS unwilling to retreat on Cutler, fearing criticism for letting the Soviets "dictate" our panel. On a telephone I assumed to be monitored, I asked CBS president Frank Stanton to confirm to me that he would not proceed without Cutler. He did. Next day the Soviet officials dropped their objections.

A CBS director and technical personnel arrived with half a ton of equipment (16mm black-and-white film—remember, this was 1957). Cameras, lights, and sound equipment were installed in Khrushchev's Kremlin office, tested, and locked up overnight. On a sunny May 31 I walked with my colleagues from the Hotel Metropol, past children playing in a park under the shadow of Kremlin walls, to the Borovit- sky Gate. I showed my press card to the military guard, was greeted with a present-arms salute, and we were waved through the sally port. We walked across the Kremlin's cobbled courtyard, past the glittering onion-domed churches to the Council of Ministers building. There a colonel met us, then deferentially showed us up a spiral staircase and along a long corridor to an unmarked oaken door that led into the office of the first secretary, Communist Party, USSR.

The enormous office was ringed now with cameras and flood- lights. Soviet television had matched each of our three cameras with one of its own, planning to carry the interview in its entirety on the national network and in theaters. Khrushchev would sit at a small table facing a larger conference table. Around the office were sym- bols Khrushchev held dear—pictures of Lenin and Marx, models of new jet planes, ears of corn, and a sheaf of wheat under glass. We were told Khrushchev was resting in an adjoining room and that there should be no smoking. We were also told that Khrushchev would not allow makeup to be put on him because "he doesn't think of himself as an actor." We pleaded that he at least be asked to put some powder on his shiny bald head. He refused.

At precisely the appointed time, the first secretary entered in well-pressed gray suit and neatly knotted tie, nodded to all in the room, and took his seat, facing the panel. First he wanted to discuss procedure. He listened to Novins's proposed introduction to the program and objected to having his office described as the place where major decisions were made. "We do not have a cult of personality any more," he said.

Then, with cameras ready to roll, Khrushchev sought to put us on the defensive. He said he had agreed to his first-ever TV interview (he had never done one for Soviet television) because he considered improved relations with the United States to be "of primary importance," and he would call the whole thing off unless assured that all questions would serve that end. Working himself up, he pushed his chair back from the table as though ready to walk out. Then he turned off his self-generated anger. An assistant director snapped a clapboard before his face. He said, "Look, they're making an actor of me." And we were off for an interview of a full hour.

He carried it off magnificently—by turns ingratiating, evasive, and stern. He gave short shrift to questions about Hungary, about the jamming of American broadcasts, and kept returning to his theme of wanting peace and good relations with the United States.

Only once did I corner him. The Chinese Communist Party, in a departure from Soviet doctrine, had taken the position that even in a socialist society contradictions could exist between the masses and the leaders. The murky issue appeared to have implications for the legitimacy of a Communist government. I asked Khrushchev what he thought of that, and he went into a long statement to the effect that China, in a different stage of development, was developing its own ideas.

Then I asked, "But are you saying that these contradictions do not exist in the Soviet Union today?"

Khrushchev replied tensely, "We believe we have no contradictions of that nature."

That exchange was excised from the interview as presented on Soviet television and in the text as published in newspapers. Harrison Salisbury wrote in the *New York Times* that we had exposed "a basic doctrinal dispute between Moscow and Peking," and that it was time to reexamine American policy toward China.

For the rest, Khrushchev said mainly what he intended to say about disarmament and cultural and trade relations. He offered to pull Soviet troops out of Eastern Europe if the United States would pull its forces out of West Germany. And he predicted that "your grandchildren will live under socialism."

While the film was being hand-carried to New York (this was before satellite transmission, remember?), CBS asked me to summarize in a cable what news it contained. I replied that most of what Khrushchev said he had said elsewhere, that I did not see any front-page story, but that the novelty of a first-ever program from a Soviet leader's Kremlin office might make it a good television-page story. Too close to the scene, I missed the point. What made front pages around the world was that Khrushchev had appeared in America's living rooms—real, robust, and unthreatening.

The Eisenhower administration reacted with asperity. At a news conference the president said about CBS that "a commercial firm, trying to improve its own commercial standing, went to unusual effort to get someone that really made a unique performance." He added that CBS could do this "because this is a free country." Asked whether he questioned CBS's news judgment in seeking the interview, Eisenhower said, after a moment of thought, "I am not willing to give an opinion on that one."

Khrushchev, on his way to Finland by the time the program aired, was delighted with the reaction. In Helsinki he told me he considered it a good sign that he had been able to speak directly to the American people, "something that would have been impossible a few years ago because of Senator McCarthy." When I told him he had become an instant television star in America, he replied, "If American television depends on me to be its star, it will be bankrupt in a month." (I, incidentally, had also become a recognizable figure on Soviet television, and it was unsettling to find myself stopped on the street in Moscow by Russians to whom I had become an instant celebrity.)

Later, at a diplomatic reception, the first secretary beckoned me forward from a group clustered around him and said, "This is my friend Schorr. They gave a truthful presentation of my interview.

They did it in a correct and straightforward manner." He raised his champagne glass to me and toasted, *"Za pravdu!"* (To truth!)

But he expressed disappointment with President Eisenhower's reaction. "In Geneva [at the 1955 summit] Mr. Eisenhower proposed that we should drink a martini cocktail at every session. So, we drank a martini each time, and we met each other in a better mood. Well, he apparently had no martini before he commented on my interview. He seemed to be somewhat angry. But it doesn't matter."

Khrushchev left little doubt that he regarded his Finnish trip as the first step on the road to the meeting with Eisenhower that Hungary and Suez had so far stymied. At his windup news conference in Helsinki, addressing the inevitable question of a visit to America, he straightened up and spoke carefully. "America is a very interesting country. Good relations throughout the world depend on proper relations between our countries. . . . But no one has invited me to the United States. We have our pride, and we never impose ourselves as guests on anyone."

During the Finnish tour, something seemed to have gone awry between Khrushchev and Bulganin. Bulganin did practically no speaking, but stood by looking gloomy while a statement was read in his name. On our return to Moscow it was announced that a scheduled Khrushchev-Bulganin trip to Czechoslovakia was being postponed, no reason given.

At an Egyptian embassy reception on June 18 I tried some heavy-handed humor to smoke out Khrushchev on the Czechoslovakia trip. As a result of our television interview, I said, I found myself living in his shadow, my plans dependent on his plans, packed to go to Prague, but not knowing when to go. "And thus," I concluded, "I am in a sense a slave of both my capitalist masters and my Communist master."

He closed one eye, cocked his head at me, and said, "I am sure, Mr. Schorr, the time will come when you will be liberated from one of those conditions."

As with the Central Committee meeting a year earlier, I had struck out on finding out what I wanted to know. Three weeks later the mystery of the postponement was solved. On July 3, *Pravda* appeared with a cryptic but ominous front-page editorial stating that the Party Central Committee takes "resolute action" against anyone, no matter how high, who violates the Party line. Next day it was announced that members of an "anti-Party group," Molotov, Malenkov, Lazar Kaganovich, and Dmitri Shepilov, had been ousted from the presidium and from the Central Committee. Molotov was specifically accused of having opposed the liquidation of Stalinism.

What had happened was that while Khrushchev was in Finland, his opponents had banded together to vote him out of power. Bulganin, in Finland with Khrushchev, had apparently known what was going on and taken an ambiguous position. Khrushchev had got Defense Minister Zhukov to send planes to bring members of the Central Committee to Moscow for an emergency meeting that overruled the presidium action and voted instead to oust Khrushchev's opponents.

That accomplished, Khrushchev flew off with a hangdog Bulganin for their postponed trip to Czechoslovakia. Efforts were made by both the Soviet and Czechoslovak governments to discourage Western journalists from covering the trip. Khrushchev flashed a smile of amusement when I caught up with him at a factory visit in Prague, and KGB chief Gen. Ivan Serov shook my hand as though to congratulate me. But Khrushchev's speeches were clearly not meant for American ears.

Having purged the hard-liners from the Kremlin leadership, he had some fence-mending to do with President Antonin Novotny's hard-line Communists. He denounced Tito for accepting American aid, "meant to weaken socialism." He had hard words for President Eisenhower. "He talks about a clean hydrogen bomb. How can there be a clean bomb to do dirty things?" He said America was afraid to disarm because "the big monopolies will have to fire millions of workers," and the Eisenhower administration "is nothing but a stooge of the monopolies."

At the end of July, Moscow was swamped in a great Soviet-sponsored International Youth Festival. It presented the unusual sight of American-style jitterbugging in front of the Lenin-Stalin tomb in Red Square, and young Israelis attracting an emotional crowd of Soviet Jews. There was also a small burst of freedom for Western correspondents. A new radio studio was opened for us, our camera crews were allowed in to film the festival, and censorship was suspended for the duration of the ten-day event.

But other ways were found to keep the pressure on us. I filmed an interview with an American delegate who had met with Russian students and been told that 90 percent of them condemned Soviet brutality in Hungary. A chorus of protests went up from a group of Russians gathered to watch the filming. Other Russians seemed to be assigned to accusing me of intimidating young Americans when I asked them in interviews about their plans to take a trip to China in defiance of a State Department travel ban.

Soviet agents monitored my filmed interviews and radio broadcasts. The Communist youth newspaper, *Komsomolskaya Pravda*, carried two long articles denouncing me. One accused me of being out to "blacken the festival and show Soviet youth through a crooked mirror." The other called me a "provocateur" and an "adventurer" who had abused his journalistic privileges. A cartoon depicted me as carrying a huge smearpot around Moscow.

Such attacks in Communist organs usually have consequences. As soon as the festival folded its tent, censorship was reimposed. In short order I was summoned to the Foreign Ministry Press Department, advised of specific censorship violations, and warned that there would be "serious consequences" in case of repetition. I thereupon introduced a new practice of noting deletions in my broadcasts by saying on the air, "thirteen words deleted here" and "two paragraphs deleted here." I am sure that the censors were irritated, but nothing was said to me about it.

The Soviet authorities had other plans. On August 13, my camera crew and I were working on a feature for television about *Detski Mir* (Children's World), a department store entirely for children. We had done all our filming inside the store and I was standing out in front, my back to the display window, doing the narration on camera. Two people in street clothes came up and denounced us for filming "forbidden objects." Two policemen, conveniently on hand, took cameraman Paul Bruck and me to the police station.

I should explain that the store is across Dzerzhinski Square from the Lubyanka, headquarters of the KGB and its prison. I explained to the police that the confiscated film, when developed, would show nothing but pictures taken in the children's store and myself standing in front of it. The police said they would have the film developed and would advise me further. The two "citizens" who had denounced me meanwhile disappeared after leaving their addresses—in both cases post-office boxes.

Back at the Metropol, I noticed graphite shavings on the desk next to my telephone. That presumably meant maintenance or replacement of the tap on my phone—and that somebody wanted me to be aware of it.

A week later I was called to the police station and handed the film can. What was in it was not the original film, but old film of a non-American make, the emulsion erased so that it had no picture. I wrote to the police asking for the return of our original film and was not surprised to receive no reply. American ambassador Llewellyn K. "Tommy" Thompson told me that, friend of Khrushchev or not, I was clearly marked by the KGB for harassment. The agency was sending a signal that my Soviet career was nearing an end.

If that was so, then I wanted to see what one could still see of this vast territory. When it was announced that four annexed cities on the western rim of the Soviet Union—Riga in Latvia; Lvov, once Polish; Chernovtsy, once Rumanian; and Uzhgorod, once Czechoslovak—were open to foreign travel, my friend Max Frankel of the New York Times and I quickly signed up for a trip to all four places.

I do not know how it would have gone if I were not in the KGB's bad books, but under the circumstances, the trip did not go smoothly. In Riga, we were followed by three cars at a time, leapfrogging each other at intervals. When a young Latvian came up to us in a café to tell us how much he despised the Russians, I said, "If this is some sort of provocation, we could be kicked out." He replied, "You could get kicked out? I could get kicked in."

While Max and I were in Lvov, we were told that Chernovtsy and Uzhgorod, just opened, were closed again. Shortage of hotel space, it was said. On the way back to Moscow we stopped in the Ukrainian capital of Kiev, most of whose Jews had died during the Nazi occupation in what was known as the *Babi Yar* massacre. We were curious about the current situation of the remnant Jews in Kiev. Walking in a park, Max and I saw two elderly men sitting on a bench who, from their beards, seemed to be Jewish.

It was our custom not to accost Soviet citizens, who might get into trouble for contacts with American journalists. So, we strolled back and forth hoping they might address us. Finally, one did, asking in quiet tones, in Yiddish, *"Ir zeit Yidden?"* (Are you Jews?) He was clearly hazarding a guess, probably aware from our dress that we were American.

He asked if we knew a long-departed cousin of his in Philadelphia. Then, hesitantly: "In America, are Jews allowed to leave the country?" This was a poignant reference to Soviet restrictions on Jewish emigration. Max and I agreed not to report this conversation through Soviet censorship.

At the end of August the Soviet regime started a new phase of its peace offensive—an effort to overawe the West, especially the United States, with its military potential. An elaborately underplayed inside-page item announced the successful test of an intercontinental ballistic missile. Also announced was a series of atomic and hydrogen weapons—presumably warheads for a missile that could reach America. And on October 4 came the breathtaking word that the satellite *Sputnik* had been launched and was in orbit around the globe.

At an East German embassy reception, Khrushchev was quick to drive home the propaganda point: "The rocket is an implacable weapon. We don't want to misuse it. . . . It would not be letting out a secret to say that fighters and bombers can now be relegated to museums because they have been replaced by rockets." Then, in the way he had of hamming up his point, he turned to Bulganin and Mikoyan. "I didn't give away secrets, did I?"

Amid the jubilation about the Soviet edge in rocketry came a political bombshell. The first hint of it came from a careful reading of the Soviet press. Two lines on the back page of *Izvestia*, the government organ, reported that "Marshal Zhukov has returned from his trip to Yugoslavia and Albania." When he had left two weeks before it was "the Minister of Defense, Marshal Zhukov." Such a change of description was not happenstance. Next day it was made official—Marshal Zhukov was out as minister of defense, replaced by Marshal Rodion Malinovsky. No explanation.

This was startling. Marshal Zhukov, conqueror of Berlin, was probably better known to the Soviet people than anyone but Stalin. After Stalin's disastrous failure to deal with the oncoming Nazi invasion, Zhukov was credited with having rallied the demoralized army and molded it into a fighting force that stopped the Germans in Stalingrad, then carried the campaign to German soil and a linkup with the Western allies on the Elbe River. In July, Khrushchev had rewarded him for his support against "the anti-Party group" by having him named to the Communist Party presidium—the first professional soldier ever to be so honored. Only a few weeks earlier Khrushchev had criticized President Eisenhower for not inviting Zhukov, his wartime comrade-in-arms, to visit the United States.

At a Turkish national day reception, Khrushchev seemed manic— the way he sometimes was when under great tension. To Ambassador Thompson he raised his glass: "Let's drink to no war between us, and let him be damned who wants war." He told Thompson in a stage whisper a story about Anastas Mikoyan, his loyal deputy, who was standing near him. He said Mikoyan had left the water running in a London hotel during a trade mission in 1936 and flooded the bathroom.

"I was young at the time," said Mikoyan.

"You were never young," joshed Khrushchev.

All this horseplay, and the question of the day hung in the air. I went up to Khrushchev and quietly asked, "How is Marshal Zhukov?"

Khrushchev's eyes narrowed. "I just saw him today. I spoke to him. He was in good health."

"Will he get a new job?"

"We have not yet decided on his new position, but he will have one, in accordance with his experience and qualifications."

And before turning away, Khrushchev said, "In life, one cell must die. Another takes its place. Life goes on."

The Central Committee was still in session, the fate of Zhukov and of his dismissal still to come. Military newspapers paved the way with articles, mentioning no names, but criticizing "swagger and haughtiness" among those who downgraded the role of the Party in the armed forces.

Then, Saturday night, November 2 (taking some of us away from dinner at the American embassy), the second shoe fell. An indictment of Zhukov by the Central Committee, saying he considered himself the exclusive hero of Soviet wartime victories, had fostered his own cult of personality in the armed forces, had tried to "liquidate" Party control, and for good measure, that he had tended toward "adventurism" in foreign policy. Contradicting what Khrushchev had told me, there would be no new job for Zhukov. He was ousted from the Party presidium and the Central Committee, retaining only his Party membership and thus the right to be called "comrade."

At the time, this dismissal was widely regarded as the work of Khrushchev, strengthening his own position, cutting down someone who had traded too much on having saved him from being overthrown. I didn't believe it then and I do not believe it today. Khrushchev struck me as not happy about what was happening to Zhukov. He would not have predicted a new position for the marshal had he thought that it would not happen. In time we learned that the charges against Zhukov were not raised by Khrushchev, but by Mikhail Suslov, the arbiter of ideology. Leninist doctrine stressed Party control, the Communist version of civilian control of the armed forces. In effect, jettisoning Zhukov was not a new extension of his power but the price Khrushchev had to pay for his purge of his hard-line opponents.

The Soviet machinery of character assassination ground on. Zhukov's comrade-in-arms Marshal Ivan Konev wrote in *Pravda* that Zhukov, far from being the architect of victory in Stalingrad and Berlin, had shared responsibility with Stalin for the Soviet Union's unpreparedness. Zhukov was obliged to confess his "errors."

Khrushchev would not join the character-assassination bandwagon. When I asked about Zhukov at an Egyptian embassy reception, Khrushchev said, "He is resting. He asked for leave, and it was granted. He deserved the leave. He did not always turn out to be good in politics, but as a marshal we always valued him and always will." I asked about the new job that Khrushchev had said the marshal would get. His face hardened. "Our business with Zhukov is our business. You must not interfere in our internal affairs."

Early Sunday morning, November 3, we correspondents were still at the Central Telegraph working on the Zhukov story when word came of a new space sensation. *Sputnik II*, much bigger than the first, had been placed in orbit with a dog aboard named Danka (Little Lady), later, for unknown reasons, renamed Laika (Husky, which was her breed).

On the Sunday CBS news roundup I faced a problem—two tremendous stories to cover in one ninety-second spot, and which was the lead? I resolved the problem by starting this way: "The news from here today, very simply, is *Sputnik* No. 2 is up and Zhukov is down."

The last time I saw Khrushchev on his home grounds was on December 6, 1957. At a reception at the Finnish embassy he complained that the rocket carrier of *Sputnik I* had come down in the United States (it wasn't true) and demanded that the Eisenhower administration return it. I told him I was going home for the holidays, and he said, *"Dosvedanye"* (Good-bye). If he knew that, special TV relationship or not, I was not going to be permitted back, he did not let on.

In New York I went through a lot of debriefings on radio and television. In one broadcast I was asked to sum up some of the jokes going around Moscow. This is one of them:

A child in bed asks its mother, "Momma, was Beria [the KGB chief executed in 1954] a good man?"

"No, darling, Beria was a bad man. Now go to sleep."

"Was Stalin a good man?"

"No, darling, Stalin was a bad man. Now go to sleep."

"Is Khrushchev a good man?"

"How do I know, darling? He's still alive. Now go to sleep."

The *Sputniks* and Nikita Khrushchev had seized America's imagination and produced an unaccustomed sense of American scientific and educational inferiority. As an unanticipated consequence, I found myself much in demand on the lecture circuit, and embarked on a jaw-breaking thirty-three lectures in thirty days, coast to coast. Americans seemed awed and mystified that a regimented society could achieve results we normally associated with free inquiry. I explained at length that the requirements of the modern age had dictated the need for de-Stalinization and an end to terror. I said that Khrushchev was having trouble keeping control of the artists, writers, musicians, and scientists. In a flight of hyperbole, I suggested that the Soviet Union would one day face the revolt of the Sputnik-makers against rigid bureaucratic controls.

By the thirty-third, jet-lagged appearance, which was in Cleveland, I was pretty well worn-out responding to questions about *Sputniks* and Khrushchev. When a woman in the audience asked "What is Khrushchev really like?" something snapped and I said, "Lady, I answered that question in Des Moines last night." Then, feeling foolish, I apologized and explained about combat fatigue on the lecture front.

By April 1958, it was clear that my return visa to Moscow would not be forthcoming. I asked Paul Niven, my "temporary" replacement, to pack and ship my effects, to arrive in two months. My tennis racquet I needed soon, and I asked E. J. Kahn of *The New Yorker*, going to Moscow on a brief assignment, to bring it back with him. He wrote amusingly about that. (A year later, at a Central Park South café in New York, a waiter handed me a note: "Could you bring my golf clubs from Havana?" I looked around to see a smiling E. J. Kahn.)

A few months later the CBS bureau in Moscow was shut down and Paul Niven expelled. Not for anything he had done, but because CBS had presented, in its *Playhouse 90* series, a docudrama called "The Plot to Kill Stalin." It told an apocryphal story of Khrushchev as an accomplice in Stalin's death. We were told that Khrushchev hit the ceiling when he learned of the program. (Marvin Kalb would reopen the CBS Moscow bureau in 1960.)

I was sent to open a bureau in Warsaw so that we would have some East European dateline. And I was there to greet Khrushchev when he came on a tour of Poland in July 1959. It was Premier Khrushchev now, as well as First Secretary. Bulganin had finally been retired. On his first evening in Warsaw, at a crowded Polish-government reception, Khrushchev, going down a receiving line of diplomats, turned and caught sight of me in the crowd of onlookers. He walked up to me, mouth dropping open, hands turned up as though to say, "Where have you been?" He shook my hand and said deadpan, "It seems to me we have met before."

The eighteen-month lapse gave me a fresh impression of the survivor of storms and a short-lived collective leadership, now alone at the top and looking for clear water. The wisps of hair on the back of his bald head were whiter and sparser. His clothes were better tailored—in Italy, I was told. A gray silk shirt with gold cuff links and a most un-Russian spread collar. No more rows of decorations, but just two gold stars of the Order of Socialist Labor and the Lenin Peace Prize. The Bolshevik agitator had molted into the statesman with a pink glow on his face and a measured walk.

He spouted less and read prepared speeches more, sounding bored as he read them. Occasionally, before workers, he showed a spark of the old spontaneity:

"Bureaucrats are the chicken pox on the face of our system. . . . The capitalists will be afraid to show their people our country. . . . The time will come when only the bones of capitalism will be left, like a prehistoric monster."

He had also begun to create a persona for himself, Western style, having his wife listed as accompanying him and telling stories of his childhood.

"My father sent me to school, but when I came home one day and said I could count to thirty, he said that was enough schooling.

'You will never have more than thirty rubles.' Later I went to a church school and got a prize because I knew the gospel by heart."

Khrushchev had toured Poland with a secret. Within an hour of his return to Moscow, he would be meeting with Vice President Nixon, coming to open an American exhibition of household appliances. The unreconstructed anticommunist said he was not coming to negotiate, but the Soviet leader had reason to believe that Nixon was bringing a long-yearned-for invitation from President Eisenhower to come to the United States. So, in a speech in the Polish provinces, Khrushchev casually announced that he was canceling a scheduled official visit to Denmark and Norway. His stated reason was that he was being attacked in the press of those countries— something that had never stopped him before. His real reason was that he expected to be going to America and no longer felt a need for tiresome preliminary visits to other Western countries.

In Moscow, an American visit was discussed at a dinner for Nixon and Khrushchev at Spaso House, the American embassy residence. Jane Thompson, the ambassador's irrepressible wife, told Khrushchev she wished he could come to America not as an official guest, but incognito, so he could learn what Americans are really like. That must have puzzled him.

"Would you suggest that I put on a beard for the purpose?" asked the premier with heavy-handed irony.

Not to be put down, Mrs. Thompson replied, "No, a wig would be enough."

For Khrushchev the prospect of an American trip soothed the sting of the famous "kitchen debate," in which he realized he had been put at a disadvantage by an ambitious politician. Khrushchev turned down Nixon's request to fly home by way of Siberia and the Pacific, saying to reporters, "Beyond the Urals we have certain things which we would not like to show to strangers. Nobody lets another willingly peep into his bedroom." Nixon, instead, made a hastily arranged visit to Poland on his way home, getting a warmer reception than Khrushchev had gotten a week earlier. All things considered, the Soviet boss would have been well advised to let the vice president exit across Siberia.

Khrushchev's American trip was soon announced, and I flew from Warsaw to be on hand for his arrival in Washington on September 15. Along his tumultuous way across America, we talked several times. He soon took umbrage at the way Ambassador Henry Cabot Lodge was following him around, contradicting him, performing a sort of "truth squad" function. That was not, to his mind, how one treats guests. He was furious when he learned that Radio Free Europe anticommunist commercials were shown during a television interview with him. By the time he reached Los Angeles, needled on arrival by Mayor Norris Poulson, he was ready for a showdown.

He told me he thought he was being deliberately heckled and being kept from contact with ordinary American people. The last straw was word that he would not be allowed to visit Disneyland. (That was an ill-conceived State Department ploy to protest against off-limits areas in the Soviet Union with an overlay map that arbitrarily put large regions of the United States off limits to Russians. Including Disneyland, as it happened.)

Khrushchev said, "Some people do not seem to understand the reason for my coming here." He recalled the CBS interview two years earlier and how he had emphasized the interests of world peace. But, he said, he was not being allowed to convey that message. A few hours later, at a civic dinner at the Ambassador Hotel, Khrushchev dramatically threatened to fly home. There was a stunned silence in the ballroom and visions of a possible nuclear war.

It reminded me of the scare tactic Khrushchev had tried before the CBS interview, pushing back from the table and threatening to walk out if the questions weren't to his liking. With American officialdom, this piece of Stanislavsky theater worked. Ambassador Lodge was pulled off his "truth squad" assignment. (Khrushchev later chortled to Ambassador Thompson, "Your Mr. Lodge tried to fart and ended up shitting in his pants.") Next day the Khrushchev special train to San Francisco made an unscheduled stop in Santa Barbara so that he could mingle with mainly friendly crowds.

Back on board, he came walking through the train in exuberant spirits. "I have been released from house arrest," he gurgled. I remarked that he seemed to be in better humor than the night before.

"You know, Mr. Schorr, when they stick pins in you, you have to retaliate." He illustrated with a right jab toward my stomach that made me instinctively step back. I asked if he had been serious in his threat to fly home. He chose, as he often did, to evade the question.

"Why should I go? Did you see that crowd at the station? Did you see that little girl waving at me? No? Well, there was a little girl, maybe three or four years old, in her mother's arms. Probably her mother told her I am a Communist. But she was waving at me. She was waving at Communism!"

He stopped and laughed at himself. "Oh, well, she probably didn't even know who I am. But she knew that I am one of the men who can bring world peace."

Next day, on the deck of a Coast Guard cutter touring San Francisco Bay, Khrushchev for the first time discussed Communist ideology with me. He said that the concept of proletarian dictatorship was being abandoned because "we no longer have antagonistic classes and there is no great external threat." That put him at odds with the dogma of Mao Tse-tung in Red China—where he would be flying on an unsuccessful fence-mending trip soon after his return from the United States.

Khrushchev was pleased with his conversations at Camp David with President Eisenhower that concluded his stay. He had gotten the president to agree that the situation of Berlin divided among the Soviet Union, the United States, Britain, and France so long after the war was "abnormal." Khrushchev took that to mean that the Eisenhower administration was ready to negotiate a new status for Berlin. He would soon find out that President Eisenhower did not attach the same significance to the word *abnormal* and had no intention of leaving Berlin.

But, as he finished his tour, the premier and first secretary was a happy man. At his final news conference, at the National Press Club, I asked him how he now regarded the attempts to heckle him.

"Of course," he said, "there were people—and rather influential people, I suppose—who did not like this visit. But I believe that their plans failed."

Looking forward to an Eisenhower trip to the Soviet Union that would follow the scheduled Paris four-power summit in May, I asked Khrushchev to have me allowed back into his country. He said, *"Kharosho!"* (Good), and we shook hands on it. Soon thereafter I asked the Soviet press attaché in Washington whether my KGB file would bar my return, even aboard a White House press plane. Next day he called to say, "You should have no trouble. It appears that your KGB file has been lost."

But, before the prestige-conscious President de Gaulle would host the four-power summit, he insisted that the Soviet leader first make an official visit to France—as he had done to Britain and the United States. So, in March 1960, I was dispatched from New York to Paris, as CBS's resident Khrushchev-watcher, to reinforce David Schoenbrun's Paris bureau, with the expectation that I would come up with something exclusive.

Under de Gaulle's tightly stage-managed program, an interview with Khrushchev would not be easy. From the moment of the French president's typically magisterial airport greeting, *"Enfin voilà!"* (Finally you are here!) it was clear that de Gaulle was calling the tune. The microphone at plane-side was positioned so that the Soviet leader had to speak with his back to the cameras. Khrushchev had planned to make a scorching anti-German speech at the World War I battleground of Verdun, but was told that speeches were not allowed on this hallowed ground. So, in Bordeaux, he wildly attacked West German chancellor Konrad Adenauer as promoting a new Nazi master-race idea. And in Reims he urged the revival of the Russo-French alliance. De Gaulle, remaining in Paris, brushed off Khrushchev's sallies.

The eleven-day tour was nearing an end, and there had been no opportunity for a Khrushchev "exclusive." That I finally managed—or rather my good friend Michel Gordey of the newspaper *France-Soir* managed for me—on the Khrushchev special train between Lille and Rouen on the way back to Paris. Recalling that Khrushchev had visited the press car on the American trip the previous year, Michel suggested that we occupy a table, hold an aisle seat vacant with the microphone on the table, and position our camera in the aisle facing that seat.

It worked like a charm. Within an hour Khrushchev entered the car, sat down in his designated seat, recognizing Michel and myself, and said, "Just came to see how you are all holding up." For the next half hour he responded discursively to questions from Gordey and myself and the dozens of reporters crowded behind the CBS camera. It was vintage Khrushchev. As he had learned a few words of English for his American trip ("Okay" and "Goodbye, good luck"), so now he tried out his first French words, *"Vive la paix!"*

He attacked the Western position on arms control requiring on-site inspection (foreshadowing a deadlock at the Geneva disarmament conference). He talked ominously of a showdown on Berlin at the Paris summit. Discussing East-West tensions, he gave his own version of Scripture: "If someone strikes my left cheek, I will hit his right cheek so hard it will knock his head off."

This curtain-raiser for the Paris summit made international headlines, but only we had Khrushchev on film saying it. CBS was a very happy network. And, in truth, I, uneasy about having had no steady assignment since my exclusion from Russia, felt immensely relieved at having justified myself and the expense of the trip.

The four-power summit in May would be the first such East-West meeting since the original one in 1955, whose "Spirit of Geneva" promise of an era of good feeling had long since evaporated under the pressures of East European repression, arms control stalemate, and crisis over Berlin. But the Paris summit was not to be, nor the ensuing Eisenhower trip to the Soviet Union, for which a golf course had already been built near Moscow.

On May 1 the Soviets shot down a high-flying American U-2 spy plane and captured its pilot, Gary Powers. Khrushchev arrived in Paris—on May 14, a day early—saying he was ready, despite the U-2, to negotiate about Berlin and disarmament.

But first, he demanded that President Eisenhower apologize for the U-2 incursion and punish those responsible. Eisenhower, instead, assumed full responsibility for having sent the plane. The proper response of a commander, but in the circumstances, a cardinal mistake that left Khrushchev with no dignified exit.

On May 16, President de Gaulle called the meeting to order, asking uncertainly if anyone had anything to say. Khrushchev announced, "I have something to say," and launched into a half-hour tirade against President Eisenhower. The president replied by reading a prepared statement, saying reconnaissance flights over the Soviet Union had been canceled, but offering no apology. Khrushchev said his conditions had not been met and rebuffed the appeals of de Gaulle and British prime minister Harold Macmillan for a day's delay to reconsider. And it was over. Khrushchev stormed out of the Élysées Palace in a towering rage and held a two-hour news conference to denounce President Eisenhower in vitriolic terms, then flew off to East Berlin to rattle some sabers.

Before he left, a member of his delegation told me, "Eisenhower is persona non grata to the first secretary, and there will be no summit as long as he is in office."

I believe that the rage was partly theater to cover other reasons to abort a meeting that promised to be a disaster for Khrushchev. A preparatory meeting in Geneva on disarmament had bogged down in stalemate. The Berlin issue was similarly deadlocked. A summit meeting would have exposed Khrushchev's illusion that, at Camp David, he had talked Eisenhower into a more accommodating stand on giving up the Western enclave 110 miles inside the Iron Curtain that gnawed at the Communist vitals like an ulcer.

On an official visit to Austria in July 1960, his first venture outside the Soviet orbit since the summit breakup, Khrushchev seemed to be under stress. Not only was his coexistence policy at a dead end for the second time, but, as predicted by experts, his massive gamble on sowing the "virgin lands" of Siberia and Kazakhstan had come a cropper (pun intended) with the rise of the salt table under the inhospitable soil. His characteristic reaction was to appease his hard-line critics at home by talking tough to the West.

Cautioned about respecting Austria's neutrality, he first limited himself to denouncing "aggressive forces" and "certain Western countries." Then, at a rally in Vienna of the Austrian-Soviet Society, he abandoned caution to make a slashing attack on the Eisenhower administration for "the piratical U-2 flights," for approaching the Soviet Union "with drawn pistols," and for torpedoing the Paris summit. He warned that unless the West agreed to leave Berlin, he would force the issue by signing a separate peace treaty with East Germany. He suggested that he was ready to resume summitry in 1961—after Eisenhower was gone.

I caught up with Khrushchev at a spectacular hydroelectric dam a mile high in the Austrian Alps. He was in one of his manic moods, clutching a bottle of vodka from an open-air buffet and chortling, "This is my portion." He eyed an abstract sculpture symbolizing the rushing torrent and said, "This looks like nothing at all," only to be told the sculptor was standing next to him.

To an Austrian reporter's question about the secret of his vitality, he replied that his elixir was the fight for Communism and the hope that the red flag would be unfurled over the globe. Then, espying me in the cluster of reporters, he said, "There is Mr. Schorr. We have already converted him, but he has to go on writing nasty things about us or his capitalist bosses won't pay him."

I said I would be glad to debate him—but not on neutral Austrian soil. "I was only joking," he replied with unusual meekness.

In September I flew to New York, where Khrushchev was arriving by ship with a covey of East European Communist leaders for a summit session of the U.N. General Assembly. He had clearly come to make trouble, and he acted like a Bolshevik trying to break up a parliament meeting. He urged the resignation of Secretary-General Dag Hammarskjöld, demanded immediate freedom for all colonial countries, denounced lynching in the United States, and called President Eisenhower "perfidious." Demanding the admission of Red China into the United Nations, he pounded the table and took off his shoe and brandished it. At one point, he mounted the podium, interrupted a speaker, and forced the first-ever recess of the Assembly because of disorder.

Later, unrepentant, he gloated, "This is the beginning of the end. It shows how shaky the United Nations is."

His mood was no better for what turned out to be our last conversation, at a reception at the Soviet U.N. mission. He had talked at various times of possibly staying until New Year's, although I didn't think he was serious. But I, preparing to return to my post in Germany, needed once again to know his plans.

I asked, "Is this your farewell—are you leaving soon?"

With a steely look he replied, "Mr. Schorr, what is your advice? Would you like me to leave?"

"Well, you are a guest in my home..."

"No, you are a guest in my home."

Feeling uncomfortable, I reverted to my old joke, not improved with age, about being a slave both to my capitalist bosses and a Communist's schedule.

"You had better get used to being a slave of Communism," he said unsmilingly. "It's growing and there will be more of it."

"But not in America, I think," I responded.

And on that dismal note ended a remarkable five-year association across the barricades. I would be in Vienna in July 1961 for the summit meeting with a new president. Instead of making a new start, Khrushchev tried to bully the young John F. Kennedy out of Berlin. In an atmosphere Kennedy later described as "somber," there was no general reception or opportunity to speak with the Soviet leader.

Thereafter, I observed only from afar what appeared to be Khrushchev's increasingly frantic efforts to keep his grip on power— building up a Berlin crisis and a wall across the divided city in 1961, placing missiles in Cuba in 1962 in an ill-conceived shortcut to nuclear superiority that brought him close to a nuclear confrontation.

In October 1964, for the second time, a faction in the presidium moved to drive Khrushchev from office. Joining against him was his protégé, Leonid Brezhnev, who would succeed him. They accused Khrushchev of "harebrained" initiatives in domestic and foreign policy. Khrushchev was called back from vacation, and this time was made to resign before any rescue could be mounted. His policies, from raising farm production to driving the West out of Berlin, lay in tatters, and in Cuba he had come perilously close to nuclear war.

Khrushchev went into retirement and died in 1971. From the United States, now occupied with other assignments, I watched the Soviet regime slip back into orthodoxy under Brezhnev, Andropov, and Chernenko. Then Gorbachev arrived on the scene with a reformist boldness that reminded me of my friend Khrushchev— whom Gorbachev praised in a major speech.

In 1988 I returned to Moscow for the first time in thirty-one years, to cover the Reagan-Gorbachev summit and see what the Soviet Union was like under *Glasnost* and *Perestroika*.

After three decades there were still long lines outside retail shops—but now those in line openly complained. And antiregime jokes were no longer whispered. One story going the rounds was of a Russian standing for hours on line outside a vodka shop, suddenly exploding, "I'm not taking this anymore—I'm going to go and kill Gorbachev." Returning to the line two hours later, he was asked what had happened to his idea of killing Gorbachev. "Oh, that line was much longer," he said.

I was struck by what a communications revolution had done in thirty years. On a television monitor at press headquarters in a hotel ballroom, I watched Reagan and Gorbachev in Red Square, talking to Soviet citizens. The scene was two miles away, not carried live by Soviet television, but the picture had traveled ten thousand miles— by satellite to Atlanta and back on another CNN satellite to our press headquarters. I thought back to my 1957 Khrushchev interview that CBS had to wait twenty-four hours to see until the film arrived in New York and was processed.

In Red Square, President Reagan asserted that he had changed his mind about the Soviet Union's being an "evil empire."

I took time out to visit Khrushchev's grave in the famous Novidevichi cemetery. His tombstone is a startling cubistic black and white—intended, it is said, to symbolize the good and bad parts of him.

I remained at the grave for several minutes, then heard myself saying, "So, Nikita Sergeyevich, in the end they buried you."

CHAPTER 8

KNOCKING AROUND
THE WORLD

The two years from the spring of 1958, when CBS gave up trying to get me back into the Soviet Union, until the spring of 1960, when I finally alit in Germany, were like a kaleidoscope. Without a permanent address, living in hotels or the homes of friends in Washington and New York, I served as a CBS utility infielder, available as an extra hand for whatever foreign crisis or domestic situation presented itself.

My principal domestic assignment, in Little Rock, Arkansas, in late August and early September 1958, brought home to me how expatriated I had become. A year earlier the city's Central High School had been integrated with the aid of federal marshals in the face of angry demonstrations. I had reported from Moscow what a field day the Soviet press enjoyed with pictures and reports of racial oppression in the bastion of the "free world." Now I mingled with segregationists and civil rights workers, spending much time with Harry Ashmore, the courageous editor of the *Arkansas Gazette*. I was almost unable to comprehend how such an issue could divide Americans so sharply and hold us up to foreign ridicule.

I was in Little Rock because Gov. Orval Faubus was trying to reimpose segregation by legislative ruses. The schools remained closed while the U.S. Supreme Court considered the issue. President Eisenhower demanded that the schools be opened, but Faubus replied that they were being kept shut in the interests of law and order.

During the tense standoff, I moderated a *Face the Nation* interview with the governor, who talked of reopening Central High School as a private facility. We got into an argument when I asked him whether he thought he had the right to interpret Supreme Court decisions as he pleased. He snapped back, "Mr. Schorr, do you mean to say that all citizens no longer have the right to an opinion or viewpoint of their own?"

In the end, I thanked Governor Faubus for his appearance and said it was time to "segregate you now from this panel." He didn't even laugh.

I had left Little Rock, figuratively shaking my head all the way, by the time the Supreme Court on September 12, in a unanimous decision read by Chief Justice Earl Warren, ordered resumption of racial integration in Central High School.

The experience made me feel like a foreign correspondent in my own country. I realized that I was more at home abroad than at home.

My longest sojourns during this period were eight months in New York as United Nations correspondent and seven months in Poland. There was also a trip to Havana to interview Fidel Castro and a visiting Soviet leader. There were, as already noted, trips with Nikita Khrushchev in the United States, Austria, and France, leading to the aborted Paris summit. But there were also trips with President Eisenhower to Asia and South America, in competition with Khrushchev as traveling salesman for an ideology and a way of life.

This enabled me to compare the contrasting styles of the leaders of a bifurcated world. President Eisenhower was clearly a less engaged barnstormer than the rambunctious Soviet leader, who once said, "Life is short. Live it up. See all you can; hear all you can; go all you can." Khrushchev had already made twenty-two foreign trips before Eisenhower, in his second term, announced that he would go anywhere if it would serve the cause of peace. But he clearly had less zest for crowds and for the rigors of travel in third world countries.

Much less the agitator and crowd pleaser, the American president tended to play his role straight, waving genially but impersonally from an open car and refraining from mugging, baby kissing, or donning of local headgear. He seldom deviated from his set itinerary, unlike Khrushchev, who would stop a motorcade to plunge into the crowd or would cancel museum or opera visits that bored him.

The Eisenhower trip to India in December 1959, part of an extensive Asian tour, was meant to overcome a period of chilly relations, with India tilting toward the Soviet Union because of American disapproval of India's neutralism. Now Eisenhower sought to reassure Prime Minister Jawaharlal Nehru of American support against the pressure of an aggressive, revolutionary China.

In New Delhi, treated more as potentate than president, Eisenhower slept in a ten-by-ten-foot, super-Hollywood-style bed in the ornate presidential palace. His suite also had a bathroom with three spigots, running cold, hot, and—apparently very important at the time—COLORED water. The suite also boasted one of the first television sets in New Delhi.

Television in India was in its infancy. With virtually no experience, New Delhi television committed itself to live coverage of the president's arrival and motorcade. Watching from the control room, I heard the director interrupted by a telephone call from a viewer asking how to turn on his TV set. The minute-by-minute coverage plan was disrupted by a thirty-two-minute delay in the arrival of Air Force One from Rome. At plane-side Eisenhower said simply, "I'm sorry I was late. I couldn't help it."

I had arrived in New Delhi a week earlier to make arrangements for CBS coverage. My friend Eugene Rosenfeld, the American embassy public affairs officer, introduced me to a taste of postcolonial living at the Gym Khana tennis club, where one didn't have to be a tournament player to have the services of a ball boy. I also had to deal with the rigid Indian bureaucracy inherited from the British.

Indian officialdom remains in my memory symbolized by a sign on an elevator that read, "Available for upward journey only."

But I also encountered American bureaucracy. A few days before the president's arrival, I entered my room in the dowdy Ashoka Hotel and noticed an unfamiliar white telephone. I picked it up and was surprised to find myself talking to a White House operator, who was genially willing to connect me with my mother in New York and, in fact, any number I wished to call anywhere. For a Canadian colleague, I arranged a call to his ailing wife in Montreal. Also, I found slipped under my door a "welcome packet" from the American embassy, including a PX card. Alas, after several days it was discovered that my room had erroneously been included in a list of the White House advance party, and I had to surrender my PX card and magical white telephone.

Eisenhower, often accompanied by Prime Minister Nehru, followed his program determinedly, facing blinding sun and vast multitudes of flower-pelting Indians. Generally he stuck closely to his prepared speeches. At the New Delhi fair ground, speaking to a million or more people stretched out farther than the eye could see, the president began by saying he had not realized "how impressive and moving and inspiring the sight of you would really be. Now I know." But those words were in the text of his speech, distributed hours earlier to Indian as well as American reporters.

Eisenhower ad-libs were sometimes unfortunate. I walked alongside as Nehru guided him on a tour of the Taj Mahal. The president remarked that he had always dreamed of seeing this architectural jewel, then pointed to the graceful minarets and asked whether they were watchtowers. Gently Nehru explained that their purpose was religious, not military.

In impromptu remarks to the American colony at the U.S. embassy, Eisenhower said that peace would be made by peoples talking with peoples, not by "two or three persons sitting at something called a summit." Press Secretary James Hagerty had trouble explaining why the president was discounting summits only three months after his meeting with Khrushchev at Camp David and five months before the planned four-power summit in Paris.

Yet, the trip was counted a success. Nehru, interviewed for the CBS *Face the Nation* program after the president's departure, spoke warmly of a new relationship that acknowledged India's peacemaking role as a neutral power. Perhaps the best sign of Eisenhower's success was the bad temper of Khrushchev on a visit a few months later. He lashed out at India for accepting "the American dole."

The poor of India had one concrete benefit from the Eisenhower visit. After his departure some ten thousand forty-nine-star American flags made for the event were dyed a neutral color and turned into clothes for some of the ragged.

In 1996, when India blocked an international treaty banning nuclear testing, I thought back to all the nuclear disarmament speeches I had heard in India in 1959. But that was before India started developing its own nuclear weapons.

In February 1960, in South America, as in Asia, the Eisenhower "soft sell" proved effective. In his traveling-salesman role the president seemed more comfortable in a Latin than in a Hindu environment. In Buenos Aires, with a rare display of temper in public, he waved away the mounted grenadier guards who stood between his open limousine and the crowds on the street, and a cheer went up from the multitude.

In Montevideo, Uruguay, he was met by a student demonstration—perhaps the first hostile civilian manifestation he had ever faced. With unperturbed dignity, he sat back in his bubble-top car to wipe his eyes, reddened by a whiff of misfired tear gas. Then he rose to his feet again, waving as though oblivious to the protesters. A changed itinerary took him through narrow back streets where his unexpected appearance brought enthusiastic vivas from windows and doorways.

But I also witnessed off-key moments, such as the visit to a low-income housing project in San Gregorio, near Santiago, Chile. A poorly dressed woman thrust her paralyzed and weeping five-year-old daughter toward Eisenhower, imploring him to take the child to the United States for polio treatment. Eisenhower, nonplussed, edged away, saying, "I am sorry...I am very sorry."

As I look back on these Asian and South American trips, I realize how much we reporters were focused on Eisenhower, how little on the alien peoples and cultures that passed in array before us. In South America, we spent less than a day in each country. Life in those days, before live satellite coverage, was a nightmare of completing narrations for film packages and shipping the product by plane to New York, then getting on the press plane to the next stop. In Buenos Aires I found a few minutes to buy a pair of shoes of famous Argentine leather. But I misunderstood the Argentine system of sizes. The shoes didn't fit.

My other Latin American foray—into Cuba—came about by happenstance. On a plane from Washington to New York in February 1960, after another nationwide round of lectures, I ran into James "Scotty" Reston and his wife, Sally. They said they were on their way to Havana and suggested that I come along. Scotty noted that Fidel Castro, having no formal diplomatic relations with the Soviet Union, was about to play host to his first important Soviet visitor, Vice Premier Anastas Mikoyan. That might be a good story for an old Soviet hand like me, Reston observed.

CBS, having nothing better for me to do at the moment, agreed that I should team up with cameraman Wendell Hoffman, and we would see what we could come up with. Postrevolutionary Cuba was in a strange twilight state of relations with the United States. A year later it would become known that the Eisenhower administration had decided on the overthrow of the Castro regime. In February 1960, exiles were already in training in Central America for the Bay of Pigs invasion that President Kennedy would inherit.

There were few Americans in Havana. The pianist Eugene Istomin was on hand to play a concert, and we became friends. The Havana Libre (formerly Havana Hilton) Hotel was almost deserted. To provide a semblance of activity, the casino croupiers provided me with a supply of free chips.

I was on hand the next day when Castro went out to the José Martí International Airport, where soldiers armed with machine guns watched from the terminal roof, to welcome Vice Premier Mikoyan.

We were acquainted from many Moscow receptions. The only Armenian in the top Soviet echelon, he was a loyal Khrushchev lieutenant (as he had been a loyal Stalin lieutenant). His forte was trade, and he was credited with having introduced ice cream to the Soviet Union after tasting it on a trade mission to New York in the 1930s.

The Cuban hosts made no effort to accommodate the small American press contingent. We were told that they would discuss the sale of Cuban sugar and establishment of diplomatic relations. We were not invited to join their tour of the island. When Mikoyan placed a wreath at the statue of José Martí, the Cuban patriot, some students erupted into an anticommunist demonstration, shouting, "Viva Fidel! Down with Communism!" The police fired on the demonstrators, wounding three and arresting seventeen. I reported that on radio, but, alas, we had not gotten there in time to get pictures.

As the weeklong Mikoyan tour of schools and sugar plants drew toward a close, I worried about coming up with a television story that would justify my trip. As so many times in the past, I felt the twinge of insecurity of the stringer, only as safe as his latest big success. My editors in New York reminded me that the big question remained: Did the Mikoyan trip mean that Castro was moving into the Soviet orbit and establishing a Communist foothold ninety miles from Florida?

I had an invitation, "personal and nontransferrable," from the Cuban Association of Industries for the farewell reception to Mikoyan in the Havana Riviera Hotel. This would clearly be my last chance. Arriving early, I managed to get Wendell Hoffman and his camera into the reception ballroom. Perhaps the Cuban security people thought we were Russians, but no one interfered as Wendell set up his camera where Castro and Mikoyan would have to pass between the camera and me. Wendell handed me a microphone at the end of a long line. They walked in together, Castro towering over the diminutive Armenian. Stopping them, I asked whether I could put a few questions about the trip. Castro, remembering me from an interview in New York during the U.N. summit the previous year, readily assented.

In heavily accented but serviceable English, the Cuban premier confirmed that agreement had been reached on opening diplomatic relations and on trade and cultural exchanges. Then I asked Castro if it was true, as rumored, that he had discussed with Mikoyan the purchase of Soviet MiG fighters. Castro spread his arms wide and exclaimed, "But this is a secret!" I turned to Mikoyan, who reminded me that his brother was the designer of the MiG. (The *Mi* in *MiG* is for Artem Mikoyan. The "G" is for codesigner Mikhail Gurevich.) Smoothly, the Soviet official said that Cuba would not need military planes were it not for fear of American aggression.

When I asked Castro to confirm that he was acquiring Soviet warplanes out of fear of the United States, he said, "I don't hear very well," and he began to guide his guest away. But then an amazing thing happened. Mikoyan's eyes widened with recognition. Turning his back to the camera, he shook his finger at me and said, "Didn't we have trouble with you in Moscow?" Castro, meanwhile, ignoring or not understanding Mikoyan, congratulated me on my interview. "I'm going to tell you something. This has been a privilege for you, CBS, to be able to make this program. You asked many questions that our reporters would like to ask." I agreed that this was probably true.

The interview had lasted eight minutes, and Wendell chortled, "Got it all!" It ran on the *CBS Evening News* next day—every last frame of it, I was told. Anchorman Charles Collingwood, substituting for Walter Cronkite, called to say, "Dan, that was the damnedest interview I ever saw!" My interview was quoted on the wires and in the newspapers.

I had once again justified myself and once again I felt secure for the moment.

One of the longer assignments of my two globe-trotting years was eight months at the United Nations in New York. It was, for the most part, a leisurely assignment where much business was transacted in cocktail lounges, in restaurants, and at mission parties. As anchor of the regular Saturday television program *U.N. in Action*, I was much in demand among delegates and U.N. bureaucrats. There was something surreal about covering the United Nations, and seeing not nations and their problems but abstractions of nations and problems mouthed by professional diplomats remote from what they represented.

The constructive work of the United Nations—in health and child care—rarely received media attention. The skyscraper on the East River served as a stage where controversies and crises could be debated and perhaps resolved when it suited the purposes of the government impresarios to play out a settlement there. So, for example, in 1949, when Stalin tired of his fruitless blockade of Berlin, he arranged for the first backstage negotiation to take place at the United Nations.

I got to cover one such crisis. In July 1958, the Egyptian-Syrian United Arab Republic, led by the expansionist-minded Gamal Abdel Nasser, made menacing moves toward Lebanon and Jordan. The collapse of these two buffer states would have brought hostile Arab forces right up to the border of Israel, almost guaranteeing a renewed conflict so soon after the 1956 Suez war.

In addition, the monarchy in Iraq was overthrown in a revolutionary coup, and Premier Nuri Pasha as-Said was assassinated. Clearly, the Eisenhower administration had made a tremendous mistake two years earlier in forcing Britain, France, and Israel back from their invasion of Egypt to secure the Suez Canal. Now, with the United States and Britain reunited in the face of a threatened Middle East conflagration, President Eisenhower ordered five thousand marines to land in Lebanon, and Britain sent a military force into Jordan.

The two governments had acted on their own, asserting that there had been no time to consult the United Nations. Most third world countries supported the Soviet Union in resolutions demanding the withdrawal of American and British forces.

With the U.N. Security Council in emergency session, I received word of a high-level CBS decision to go "live" with coverage of the deliberations. I was astonished. Had I been consulted, I would have pointed out that the Security Council generally got involved in long procedural wrangles before getting to the point. Further, that the required consecutive interpretation in three languages (English, French, and Russian) meant that two-thirds of the time we would have to "fill" with analysis or interviews.

But, mine was not to reason why CBS was willing to preempt lucrative prime-time programming for long sessions that might bog down in technicalities. Eventually I came to understand what lay behind the quixotic, if public-spirited, decision. On a Saturday morning during a recess I ran into CBS president Frank Stanton in the elevator at 485 Madison Avenue, CBS headquarters. When I complimented him on his willingness to sacrifice commercial time to public interest, he replied frigidly, "That was not my decision; that was Lou Cowan."

This was my first clue to the gathering conflict in the upper echelons of CBS, rivaling any Middle East crisis. Cowan, on the strength of the successful quiz shows he had introduced, such as *The $64,000 Question*, had been catapulted to the head of CBS television—just one rung below William S. Paley's heir presumptive, Dr. Stanton. Cowan was also allied with Edward R. Murrow, who was feuding with Stanton over the allocation of airtime for public affairs programs.

The gavel-to-gavel coverage of the Security Council, a ratings disaster despite my learned and long commentaries, was soon canceled. But Cowan's ill-considered decision would come back to haunt him a few months later when the scandal of the manipulated quiz shows erupted. There was no evidence that Cowan had played any part, or even knew of the deception, but a disenchanted Paley left it to Stanton to ask for Cowan's resignation.

But before Cowan's departure, I had the benefit of another of his Tiffany network preemptions. The Middle East crisis had been disposed of in a long session of the U.N. General Assembly in August, addressed by President Eisenhower and Soviet foreign minister Andrey Gromyko. The danger in the Middle East having settled down, the United States and Britain agreed to a resolution under which their forces would be withdrawn in favor of a U.N. monitoring contingent. The United Nations, restored to its cocktail-lounge placidity, worked on plans for a celebration of its thirteenth anniversary on October 26.

The centerpiece would be an afternoon concert featuring the famous Spanish cellist Pablo Casals. He was living in Puerto Rico, having vowed never to set foot on the soil of the continental United States because of its failure to support the Loyalists during the Spanish civil war. But Casals agreed to make an exception for the extraterritorial ground of the United Nations. I was asked to anchor the event on television and to record an interview with Casals in advance to be aired during the intermission.

This was the fulfillment of a youthful dream. How many times, in my living room during opera and New York Philharmonic broadcasts, had I mimicked the sonorities of the famous Milton J. Cross: "Good evening, ladies and gentlemen, we are speaking to you from box forty-four of the Metropolitan Opera in New York, where we are about to present Verdi's immortal opera *Aida*, in four acts." And now I was to do it for real!

One question I asked during our seated interview has stayed with me through these years. "Maestro, why is it that you play Bach so much?" Beaming and spreading his hands, he replied, "Because he is my best friend."

Later, because Murrow knew that I liked music and he claimed to be tone-deaf, I would substitute for him as host on his program *Small World*. In these presatellite days, three guests conversed from different places over audio circuits, each being simultaneously filmed, the film then to be edited into a half-hour program. On this occasion the guests were Casals in Puerto Rico, Isaac Stern in Vancouver, and the Swiss conductor Ernest Ansermet in Geneva. It was a lovely, civilized conversation about music and its charms, of which I remember little detail. What I do remember is that, in my earpiece during the filming, I heard producer Fred W. Friendly tell me to ask Casals and Stern to pick up cello and violin and spontaneously play something. I pretended not to hear.

During that period I also spent many pleasurable moments— nay, weeks—in Geneva, the site of so many international broken dreams. Between 1959 and 1962 I covered three lengthy conferences—on Berlin, on disarmament, and on Laos—all of them unsuccessful. Unsuccessful, that is, for the participants and perhaps for the world, but not for the little corps of correspondents—such as Ned Russell of the *New York Herald Tribune,* Sydney Gruson and later A. M. Rosenthal of the *New York Times,* Arnaud de Borchgrave of *Newsweek,* and among the few Europeans allowed into our inner sanctum, Michel Gordey of the Paris newspaper *France-Soir.*

What made this lakeside paradise of fine hotels and restaurants so enjoyable a stint was the leisurely pace of diplomacy. (One American diplomat, sent on a one-week temporary assignment to the disarmament conference, remained for two years, retaining the per diem advantages of temporary assignment.) The pattern of all the conferences was much the same—a closed-door session during the morning, enabling the reporters to play tennis, and a noontime briefing, enabling me to report on the CBS "World News Roundup" before joining colleagues or delegates for lunch. In the early evening came the diplomatic cocktail parties, and soon it was time for dinner.

To the narrow and snobbish Geneva gentry, who fancied themselves as speaking better French than the French, the conference crowd were like aliens from another planet, tolerated as a source of revenue for the city. So, the journalists, more often than not, dined together at one or another of the restaurants overlooking the lovely Lac Leman and its geyser spurting up from the center of the lake.

One evening, with fourteen of us around a table at Le Globe restaurant, Syd Gruson made a great production of choosing the wine. I, suffering from a chronic duodenal ulcer, was impatient for food and not interested in a long wine ceremony. Syd consulted endlessly with the *sommelier,* agreed to try his suggestion, but warned that he would send back the wine if not satisfied. Then Syd postured at length, chewing loudly on a piece of bread to clear his palate, taking a large sip of wine and sloshing it around in his mouth as though uncertain. Finally, unable to abide the production any longer, I said from across the table, "Sydney, why don't you send back the bread?" That became a durable anecdote to be recalled when we met years later.

Another cherished anecdote grew out of lunch with Abe Rosenthal, who had replaced Gruson in Geneva in 1961. I had invited Abe to lunch to celebrate his birthday. That morning word came that he had won the Pulitzer Prize for the reporting from Poland that had led to his expulsion. At one point at lunch Abe whispered that an American family in the adjoining booth had been looking our way and were about to come over to congratulate him. A moment later, the American (a physician from Long Island) walked over to us, ignored Rosenthal, and said he had seen me many times on television and was thrilled to meet me. I tried, in vain, to call his attention to my prize-winning companion.

Abe, never an admirer of television anyway, was furious. He told me, "That is the last time I will ever have lunch with anybody from television on the day I win the Pulitzer Prize." Then, after a pause: "Do you think I can win it again?"

Not likely for covering the exercises in futility in Geneva's Palace of Nations.

In May 1959, Secretary of State Christian Herter, replacing John Foster Dulles, who was dying of cancer, arrived for a conference with Soviet foreign minister Andrey Gromyko and the ministers of Britain and France on the future of divided Berlin. The first days were occupied with arguing about the shape of the table (round, in the end); the next several days, about where West Germany and unrecognized East Germany would be seated (at separate side tables); then, whether Poland and Czechoslovakia, as victims of the Germans, should be added (no).

Eventually, proposals were exchanged, from Gromyko a demand that the Western powers give up their rights in Berlin, and from the West a demand for reaffirmation of Allied rights in Berlin. Various versions of these hopelessly incompatible proposals went back and forth. On June 2, four weeks into the parley, Gromyko expressed exasperation: "It is necessary to stop these hopeless efforts to submit drafts deliberately made unacceptable."

A few days later Gromyko said that a hundred Western speeches wouldn't change his mind. British foreign secretary Selwyn Lloyd said that a hundred Gromyko speeches would not change his mind. Diplomacy languished while journalistic tennis flourished. My final broadcast on June 9 on the Berlin conference noted that hostility had become so great that East-West cocktail parties had been suspended.

In March 1960, I was back in Geneva ready for more tennis, gas-
tronomy, and conviviality as delegates of ten countries of East and
West gathered, seeking a way out of the arms control deadlock in
time for the scheduled four-power East-West summit in Paris in
June. The Soviets wanted more sweeping disarmament and less
intrusive inspection. The West wanted more inspection and less
reduction in nuclear arms. The delegates sat facing each other at two
long tables, ranged alphabetically from Bulgaria to the United States,
meeting day after day and getting nowhere.

I was reduced to broadcasting a short history of disarmament,
dating back to the ninth century B.C., when the authorities in Shang-
hai tried (unsuccessfully) to negotiate an agreement with Chinese
river pirates. Efforts at nuclear disarmament dated back to 1946,
when the United States, then the sole possessor of nuclear weapons,
offered to put them under international control if Stalin agreed to
a foolproof inspection system to insure that the Soviets were not
developing their own weapon. For reasons subsequently apparent,
Stalin said *nyet* to that. Now, fourteen years later, Nikita Khrushchev
seemed no more willing than Stalin to allow foreign inspectors to
run around his country.

After seven weeks and thirty-two negotiation sessions, I reported
that "every issue that comes to Geneva seems to settle down and
join the scenery." The delegates eventually gave up, approving a
report expressing hope that after the Paris summit there would be
more fruitful negotiations. But after the Paris summit had broken up
in a spasm of acrimony over the U-2 spy plane, there was no return
to Geneva. East-West relations went into deep freeze awaiting the
appearance of the next American president.

A new East-West issue had, meanwhile, arisen in Laos concern-
ing the offensive of the Communist-supported Pathet Lao rebels to
drive out the neutralist government of Prince Souvanna Phouma. As
a gesture to the new president, John F. Kennedy, the Soviets agreed
to a conference in Geneva aiming at an agreement that would end
the fighting, neutralize Laos, and keep it from being swept up in the
war in Vietnam. The conference opened in Geneva in May 1961,

recessed for the Vienna summit in June, and then resumed. I shuttled back and forth between Geneva and Vienna.

In protracted futility, the Laos conference surpassed any of the others. Secretary of State Dean Rusk, continuing the policy of John Foster Dulles, refused to meet with the Chinese Communist delegation. Eventually, Rusk returned to Washington, leaving special ambassador W. Averell Harriman in charge of the American delegation.

As the days drifted on, I invited Harriman to lunch on a Sunday afternoon, hoping to get some idea where this negotiation was heading. On the terrace of the lakeside restaurant Perle du Lac, we sipped Scotch and soda while I probed whether he would meet with the delegation of the unrecognized Chinese Communist government.

He was about to tell me, I thought, when he suddenly stopped and said, "Dan, tell me, who is paying for this lunch—you or Bill Paley?" I admitted that this would be a CBS expense-account item. "In that case," he said, "do you think I could have another Scotch and soda?"

He told me that he had been authorized by President Kennedy to talk to the Chinese. The negotiations picked up, but after three more weeks had reached no conclusion. CBS ordered me to give up my sybaritic existence and return to Germany. (In the end an agreement to neutralize Laos was reached, which the Pathet Lao promptly broke.)

In the fall of 1958, CBS had sent me to Warsaw on an assignment of indefinite duration. I had been in Poland on reporting trips several times in 1956 and 1957, but now CBS wanted me to establish an outpost from which to report on the Soviet Union and Eastern Europe. This was because, as noted, our Moscow Bureau had been shut down in reprisal for the airing of a controversial docudrama on Stalin's death. CBS felt that, in Warsaw, we would at least have a dateline from behind the Iron Curtain. Poland had been known for its rampant anti-Semitism even before Hitler, and memories of the Auschwitz death camp and the Warsaw ghetto uprising lingered. But some of the few remaining Jewish intellectuals found themselves at home in the liberal post-Stalin regime.

Poland excited a strong sympathy among the handful of Western correspondents stationed there. The country had lost a third of its population—10 million people—to German and Soviet invasion and occupation. After the war it lost a piece of its eastern territory to the Soviets, being compensated with a piece of German Silesia— almost literally being moved westward. Poland's whole history was a saga of futile gallantry against invaders. A Polish intellectual said, "I would gladly trade our great history for some better geography."

The Polish intellectuals we mostly dealt with were infectiously charming and hopelessly romantic, dreaming centuries-old dreams of one day no longer being squeezed between powerful neighbors.

It was in Poznan on June 28, 1956, that the standard of insurrection was raised against the Communist empire. Some sixteen thousand workers in this industrial city marched to the city's central square, carrying banners that demanded "bread and freedom." Hungary would follow, and later Czechoslovakia, but Poznan was first.

In October 1956—the "Polish October" as it was fondly called— Polish Communist leader Wladyslaw Gomulka, who had been a prisoner in Stalin times, faced up to the threats of Khrushchev and his Politburo. They stormed into Warsaw threatening invasion unless anti-communist heresies were stamped out. Undoubtedly because they considered they had all they could handle in Hungary, the Soviets backed off from their threats to Gomulka.

In January 1957, I had covered the election—free by East European standards, meaning no organized opposition party—in which 94 percent of eligible voters turned out for a rousing endorsement of their simple, uncharismatic, but courageous Gomulka. Khrushchev, it turned out, had made only a tactical retreat. Once Hungary had been brought under control, the pressures on Gomulka were gradually ratcheted up, and the exuberance of the Polish October began to be choked off. Anti-Semitism returned. One week the impudent weekly *Po Prostu* failed to appear. Censorship was reimposed on the rest of the press. The Polish jamming station started up again, drowning out even the popular jazz programs on the Voice of America shortwave transmitter.

So, in the fall of 1958, when I moved into the ancient Hotel Bristol and hired a Polish secretary-translator, the chill in the air was more than the chill of autumn. The question of whether the Polish October of two years earlier was dead and gone became a subject for debate when *New York Times* correspondent A. M. Rosenthal, a no-nonsense anticommunist, arrived shortly afterward to replace Sydney Gruson. Sydney and his wife, Flora Lewis, who wrote for British newspapers, were among the most sentimental fans of Poland. At a welcoming party at the Bristol, he tried to convey to Rosenthal his enthusiasm for the band of reformist intellectuals who had made the Polish October.

While Sydney, drink in hand, was in midflight, Abe suddenly exploded. As I remember it (and after forty-odd years, I do remember it), it went something like this: "Enough of that horseshit! All you know about Poland is what you get from a self-deluded bunch of intellectuals, most of them Jewish. Poland isn't free and won't be free as long as Soviet troops are stationed all over the country. Poland doesn't have freedom of speech. Poland has freedom of talking. You say what you want on a street corner, but try saying it in a hall or on the radio, and you'll see how much freedom of speech there is."

None of our little group of journalists would openly agree with him, although he gave us pause. Flora, who would write an admiring book about Poland titled *A Case History of Hope*, tried to dispute him. But I sensed that all of us wondered whether we had been carried away by irrational hopes for a country locked in the Soviet grip. And the only Pulitzer Prize to come out of Poland was won by Abe Rosenthal, expelled for his hard-nosed reporting.

My efforts to cover Communist Europe from Warsaw met with indifferent success and brought admonitions from the Polish Foreign Ministry that, much as the presence of CBS in Warsaw was appreciated, reporting from there on other socialist countries might disturb Poland's relations with these countries. When Sen. Hubert Humphrey visited Moscow, I was able to reach him on the telephone to get his exuberant report on his six-hour meeting with Khrushchev, featuring a discussion of disarmament. I keenly regretted not being in Moscow for Vice President Nixon's famous July 26, 1959, "kitchen debate" with Khrushchev, a spirited argument about competing values and economies that happened while the two were touring an exhibition of American products featuring a model kitchen.

But then it was announced, on short notice, that Nixon would visit Warsaw on his way home from Moscow—the highest American official to date to visit any Soviet satellite.

The Polish government was both delighted and nervous about a Nixon visit—fearful that a too enthusiastic popular welcome would compare invidiously with the lukewarm reception for Khrushchev three weeks earlier. It was only a few months since Willis Conover, who conducted a jazz program on Voice of America, had been mobbed by young Poles on a brief visit to Warsaw.

Nixon arrived late in the afternoon of August 2. Abe Rosenthal and I drove out to the airport in my Mercedes to meet him and found ourselves in his motorcade driving into the city. Although the government had withheld the time of arrival and the route, an estimated one hundred thousand Poles were on hand.

They cheered. They threw flowers. They shouted, "Long live Nixon." Some kissed his car. They swept past the police and sometimes blocked the motorcade. This was unlike anything I had ever seen in the well-policed Soviet satellite world. Another crowd was waiting when the Nixons arrived at the beautiful Myslewicki Palace, where Napoleon had once stayed. Nixon handed roses to women in the throng and shouted Polish words he had learned for the occasion, *"Niech zyje Polska!"* (Long live Poland!) And the crowd went wild again.

Receiving American correspondents at the palace for a background briefing, the vice president was elated, saying he had seen many crowds on many continents, "but nothing has ever exceeded this."

This was my first experience with Nixon. I was impressed with his professionally analytical talent. He told us that the meeting with Khrushchev in Moscow had started badly, the Soviet premier in a rage about the American "Captive Nations Week," but then had settled down to more friendly conversations, anticipating president Eisenhower's invitation to come to the United States. Nixon felt pleased about how he had handled the "kitchen debate," standing up to Khrushchev's bluster.

As to Poland, Nixon was fully aware of the delicacy of his position—the government trying to turn his presence into an endorsement of the Communist regime, he determined to tell the Poles they had a friend in America. His schedule had been packed with meetings and ceremonies, but he found ways of meeting the public. When he laid a wreath on the tomb of the Unknown Soldier, a crowd appeared, shouting, "Long live Nixon! Long live America!" Nixon also made a point of laying a wreath at the site of the destroyed Jewish ghetto. I don't know why we American correspondents didn't ask if he was starting his campaign for president.

We wondered how Nixon would handle the touchy question of the Church in this most ardently Catholic country in Eastern Europe. To meet with the embattled Stefan Cardinal Wyszynski would offend his Communist hosts. What Nixon did was to stop, during a tour of Warsaw, at the famous Cathedral of St. John in the reconstructed Old City, aware that the cardinal was out of town. A crowd quickly formed, and the vice president was photographed paying his respects to the Catholics who formed 90 percent of the Polish population—many of whom had voting relatives in America.

My last major assignment in Poland was to produce, in 1959, an hour-long documentary, "Poland—Country on a Tightrope," for Ed Murrow's *CBS Reports* series. This gave me a production team and the time and resources for a deeper look at Poland—its people, its schools, its fast-decollectivizing farms.

And Oswiecim . . . Auschwitz.

In 1959 not many from the West had visited Auschwitz, and I was not prepared for what I would see and try to capture on film. I have always tried to separate my Jewish heritage from my reporting, but keeping emotion under control in Auschwitz, where members of my family may have died, was not easy.

I had to read parts of my script several times, trying to control a catch in my throat and sound detached as I reported, "Here was the greatest death factory ever devised...where a million died... pushed through these gas chambers at a rate of sixty thousand a day...their bodies efficiently moved out and lifted mechanically into brick ovens...after their clothes and hair and gold teeth had been removed.... For many, there was no room in the ovens, and they were buried in open pits...now these stagnant ponds. If you run your hand along the bottom, you will pick up human ashes and fragments of bone."

I interviewed a guide, Tadeusz Szymanski, who had Auschwitz number 200,314 tattooed on his forearm, asking whether he found it painful to be working there. He said, "When some of my friends were carried off to be executed, they shouted, 'Remember us and avenge us!' So I am here to see that they are remembered."

As we talked, a group of young Poles passed, ushered along by a woman who also had an Auschwitz tattoo. She sounded so remarkably matter-of-fact: "Here stood a crematorium.... Here was where people were pushed into a room, and then the doors were sealed, and the gas—so-called Cyclon B—was released. In most cases they died in ten minutes."

A young Polish girl gulped. Mostly they just stood and stared, and no one asked any questions.

While working on this Polish documentary, I ran into what may have been the greatest ethical dilemma of my career. Our little CBS cavalcade of three rented cars, carrying the camera crew, the producer, and a Polish interpreter, was driving through a small town in eastern Poland, not far from the Soviet border, when we espied a strange sight. It was a caravan of about ten horse-drawn wagons, carrying a few dozen people and piled high with their possessions. Stopping to talk to them, I discovered that they were Polish Jews and that I could converse with them in the Yiddish that I had hardly used since childhood.

They had come from across the border in the Soviet Union and were on their way to a railway station, bound for Vienna and from there to Israel. Our camera was soon set up in the muddy road, and I interviewed them in Yiddish. They could not tell me, however, how it was that they were permitted to travel to Israel. Out of consideration for Arab opinion, Russia and its satellites officially banned emigration to Israel.

Back in Warsaw the next day I consulted the Israeli minister, Shimon Amir, a chess-playing friend of mine.

"They told you they were on their way to Israel, and you have that on film?" he asked.

"Yes," I said. "But how is it possible?"

"All right, since you know this much, I will tell you the rest, and then you will decide what you will do."

He explained that the Jews came from a part of Poland that had been annexed by the Soviet Union, that there were several thousand more caught on the Soviet side who had survived the war and the Holocaust and were desperately anxious to leave. Israel had negotiated a delicate secret arrangement with the Soviet and Polish governments. The Jews would be "repatriated" to Poland with the understanding that they would almost immediately leave the country—bound for Israel.

"But there was one condition attached to the agreement," said Amir. "The arrangement must remain a secret. If any word becomes public, the Soviets will immediately cancel the arrangement.

"So," my friend concluded, "you can decide, Mr. Schorr. Put this on television, and you condemn some thousands of Jews to remaining in the Soviet Union."

Each evening, my cameraman would pack the cans of film we had shot that day and ship them by air to New York, later to be assembled with narration for our documentary. But I held back the reel with the Jewish interviews. It stayed on my desk in the hotel next day, and the next day and the next. I would have liked to have consulted Murrow, but could not do so over an open telephone. I never decided, exactly, that for humanitarian reasons I would practice self-censorship. I simply kept postponing the decision until it was too late. After a while, my camera crew stopped asking about it.

This was a profound violation of my journalistic ethic that a reporter has no right to interpose himself between information legitimately acquired and the public he serves. Once before I had done so—in the case of the Dutch queen. This seemed even tougher.

My *CBS Reports* program, "Poland—Country on a Tightrope," went on the air, documenting the political chill settling over Poland as Gomulka came to terms with his Soviet bosses. Auschwitz was in my film. But not the caravan of Jews making their way to Israel.

When next I was in New York, I brought the reel of film with me and went to see Murrow. He had strong pro-Israel sympathies himself. When he was sick, my Zionist mother had a tree planted in Israel in his name as a prayer for his recovery. His first question to me was, "How is my tree doing?"

I then produced the can of film and explained how, against all my principles, I had withheld it. All he said was, "I understand."

After the Khrushchev tour of the United States in September 1959, I returned to Poland to find the country in the midst of a political and economic crackdown. The most maverick country in the socialist camp had become a lot less maverick. Tough ex-Stalinists were returning to government. Gomulka was seldom seen in public and was reported to be variously in a constant rage or depression. Diplomats believed that the spontaneous demonstrations for Nixon in August had given the regime a scare. It became harder to see Polish journalists and intellectual friends. Then Abe Rosenthal was expelled—a warning to the rest of us Western correspondents.

I ran into one Polish friend in a café in the reconstructed Old City of Warsaw. He declined the invitation to sit down at my table, but leaned over and whispered, "I think I'll go to Moscow, where I can breathe the air of freedom."

It became more and more difficult to work in Poland. The Foreign Ministry became increasingly insistent that I not report from Warsaw about other socialist countries. On occasion I would drive to Berlin to sum up the situation in Eastern Europe. I also had a romantic interest in Berlin—a woman in the U.S. Mission whom I had known since my Moscow days.

I had, by now, become weary of knocking around the world on short-term assignments and wanted to have some assignment where I could unpack for a while. When CBS offered me the choice between the United Nations, in New York, and Germany, I quickly chose Germany for reasons professional and personal—namely my woman friend in the foreign service.

After the summit conference scheduled in Paris for May 1960, I was to proceed to Bonn to replace bureau chief Ernest Leiser. I would also be available to cover the Eisenhower trip to Russia, a trip that would never happen.

Smiling for the folks back home. Reluctant
soldier Schorr spent most of his wartime
service as an intelligence sergeant in Army
headquarters in San Antonio, Texas.

Joining CBS News in 1953, Schorr
learned about retouched publicity
pictures. CBS

AUTHOR'S COLLECTION

First assignment—keeping track of Sen. Joe McCarthy and his Red Hunt.

AUTHOR'S COLLECTION

Assigned to Moscow in 1955, Schorr records his impressions in Red Square.
LIFE MAGAZINE

Schorr doubles as a TV cameraman while a KGB officer keeps watch over him. AUTHOR'S COLLECTION

A TV feature in the making. . . . *LIFE* MAGAZINE

Many late hours are spent working at the Central Telegraph office, where radio scripts must be submitted for censorship. *LIFE* MAGAZINE

For Schorr, the routine of correspondent-cameraman-radio technician is more exhausting than glorious. *LIFE* MAGAZINE

In 1957, a historic coup: Schorr arranges for Communist chief Nikita Khrushchev to appear on *Face the Nation* from his Kremlin office. Schorr is joined by anchorman Stuart Novins and *New York Herald Tribune* correspondent B. J. Cutler. AUTHOR'S COLLECTION

Khrushchev calls Schorr, ever nearby, his "sputnik" in orbit around him. Here a stop to meet members of Congress on Capitol Hill during Khrushchev's 1959 American tour, with Sen. Lyndon Johnson behind. AUTHOR'S COLLECTION

An encounter on the "Khrushchev Express"—the special train taking the Soviet leader from Los Angeles to San Francisco. AUTHOR'S COLLECTION

Barred from the Soviet Union for defying censorship, Schorr is assigned to the United Nations. At the UN, a rare interview with Pablo Casals, who says he likes to play Bach "because Bach is my friend." UNITED NATIONS

After the 1961 *Years of Crisis* roundtable with Edward R. Murrow (to Schorr's right), a visit to the Chicago Council on Foreign Affairs. AUTHOR'S COLLECTION

Assigned to Germany, Schorr covers the building of the Berlin Wall. Here an interview with the beleaguered mayor of West Berlin, Willy Brandt. AUTHOR'S COLLECTION

And a new friend—Shirley MacLaine, who has come for the Berlin Film Festival.

Sen. Barry Goldwater, nominated for President by the Republicans in San Francisco in 1964, is angered by Schorr's report on his plan to visit Germany for a vacation in Berchtesgaden, once Hitler's favorite retreat. When Goldwater, after losing the election, makes his delayed trip to Germany, Schorr is on hand, but not many words pass between them.

Having hung up his foreign correspondent's trench coat, Schorr is back on the domestic beat. In 1967, he covers a visit by Sen. Robert Kennedy to the poverty-stricken Mississippi delta country.

Reporting from the floor of the tumultuous 1968 Democratic convention in Chicago.

At the 1973 Senate Watergate hearings—Sam Donaldson of ABC, Schorr, and Douglas Kiker of NBC broadcasting live outside the Senate Caucus Room. There Schorr read from the Nixon "enemies list" on-air and found that it contained his own name.

Former CIA Director Richard Helms, angered by Schorr's 1975 revelation of assassination plots, denounced him in unprintable language after testifying before an investigating committee headed by Vice President Nelson Rockefeller. UNITED PRESS INTERNATIONAL

A conversation with CIA Director George Bush leads to a front-page photo in the *Washington Evening Star*, speculating about a quarrel with a new CIA chief.

WASHINGTON EVENING STAR

VOICE *EXCLUSIVE*

24-Page Supplement

THE REPORT ON THE CIA THAT PRESIDENT FORD DOESN'T WANT YOU TO READ

TEXT HIGHLIGHTS FROM THE SUPPRESSED HOUSE INTELLIGENCE COMMITTEE REPORT (P. 69)

The U.S. House, yielding to President Gerald Ford, voted to suppress the final report of its committee that investigated the CIA. Schorr obtained a copy, reported on it for CBS, and gave it to the *Village Voice*. THE VILLAGE VOICE

The House Ethics Committee, investigating the leak, demands that Schorr name his source on pain of a prison sentence. He refuses, and cartoonists give their impression of the confrontation.

'The charge against you, Mr. Schorr, is assault with intent to commit truth.'

TONY AUTH, *PHILADELPHIA ENQUIRER*

DANIEL IN THE HOUSE ETHICS COMMITTEE

'We Can Make Things Hot For You'

PAUL CONRAD, *LOS ANGELES TIMES*

ENGELHARDT, *ST. LOUIS POST-DISPATCH*

Dan and his wife, Lisbeth, enjoy some good wishes as favorable mail begins to outnumber denunciatory letters. DIANA H. WALKER

Schorr's lawyer, Joseph Califano, coaches him on how to stand firm without sounding defiant —a whole new skill.

DIANA H. WALKER

Schorr with Lisbeth and Califano, waiting for the gavel to fall. DIANA H. WALKER

Schorr taking the oath before the House Ethics Committee. Publisher Clay Felker sits behind. DIANA H. WALKER

Three times Schorr is threatened with being cited for contempt, and three times he refuses to name his source. The committee eventually voted not to cite him. Seated next to him is Califano. DIANA H. WALKER

After 23 years, Schorr leaves CBS "with sadness, but without rancor."

DIRCK HALSTEAD

. . . and has time to reflect in Lafayette Park.   DIRCK HALSTEAD

In 1979, a new career opens. Ted Turner asks Schorr to help him launch the Cable News Network, the first 24-hour-a-day television news service.   AUTHOR'S COLLECTION

Many times a day there are dialogues with anchorman Bernard Shaw. AUTHOR'S COLLECTION

Henry Kissinger is one of the many notables Schorr interviewed as CNN strained to fill its round-the-clock mandate. AUTHOR'S COLLECTION

After six years, a parting of ways over Schorr's refusal to team up with former Gov. John Connally, whom Turner wooed to help raise money for a buyout of CBS.
AUTHOR'S COLLECTION

President Clinton changed the time of his Saturday radio address when Schorr told him that it conflicted with NPR's *Weekend Edition*.

THE WHITE HOUSE

Since 1985, Schorr has been Senior News Analyst for National Public Radio. He is able to do some of his work at home—on a typewriter.

PAULA DARTE, WASHINGTON, D. C., 1998

Every week, Schorr reviews the week's news on NPR's *Weekend Edition* with program host and friend Scott Simon. "The most enjoyable thing I do at NPR," says Schorr. NPR

Octogenarian Schorr is the oldest broadcaster at NPR, an organization of young people. "Trying to keep up with them keeps me young," he says.

NPR

Schorr enjoys the luxury of visiting places without the tension he had once known—like Berlin's Brandenburg Gate, where the Wall is only a memory. CHARLES WILLIAM MAYNES

Of his many awards, Schorr particularly prizes one: the 1999 award of the Massachusetts Society for the Prevention of Cruelty to Children. It is for the whole family (Schorr, Lisa, Lisbeth, and Jonathan) for "contributions to child, family, and community well-being." AUTHOR'S COLLECTION

CHAPTER 9

ADENAUER'S GERMANY

On May 22, 1960, leaving behind in Paris the debris of the summit, I boarded the night train for Bonn, which was now facing new tensions. Khrushchev had held a news conference at which he made a saber-rattling speech, a uniformed general by his side for effect, aimed at President Eisenhower, then flown off to East Berlin to start a new phase of the Cold War.

In Cologne next morning I was joined in my otherwise empty compartment by a commuter carrying four morning newspapers, which he held neatly folded on his lap. Eager for the latest news, I waited for him to finish one paper and put it by his side, then leaned forward and said, *"Darf ich?"* (May I?) With a look of alarm he snatched up his paper, saying, *"Die sind meine!"* (These are mine!) I began having misgivings about working in Germany.

The "federal village" of Bonn, as it was scornfully called by Germans from elsewhere, is a damp and misty Rhine-side town, known as the birthplace of Beethoven and not much else. A standing joke had a visitor asking a bartender, "Where's the action in this town?" He replies, "Oh, she's gone home to Cologne."

Why this sleepy town was chosen over Frankfurt and Hamburg to be the "provisional" capital had to do with West Germany's authoritative, if not authoritarian, head of government. The eighty-

147

four-year-old federal chancellor, Konrad Adenauer, had been the pre-war mayor of Cologne, ousted by the Nazis for refusing to fly the swastika. Arrested, he made it out of the hands of the Nazis to refuge in a monastery. After Germany's defeat he came out of retirement, founded the Christian Democratic Union, won the first free election, and established a stable government that led West Germany into the European Community, the North Atlantic alliance, and a remarkable reconciliation with President de Gaulle of France.

A capital in the Rhineland not only suited Adenauer's personal convenience—he could commute by ferry across the Rhine to his hilltop home in Rhoendorf—but it expressed Adenauer's conception of a westward-looking Germany in a Europe with a Catholic bloc in its center. Government and parliament buildings seemed built to last. I think that Adenauer doubted that Berlin would once again be the capital of a united Germany—not in the twentieth century anyway. Bonn seemed to exemplify the French saying "There is nothing more permanent than the temporary."

My first home in Germany was the dowdy Hotel Koenigshof, built to spartan postwar specifications, with a showy lobby and restaurant, but tiny bedrooms. A few months later I was rescued from there by Arthur Olsen of the New York Times, who was being transferred to Warsaw and offered me his rented house in suburban Bad Godesberg, complete with a cheerful, solidly-built German housekeeper whose husband was happy to help around the house.

The unprepossessing two-story house at Heerstrasse 102 (funny the things one remembers after four decades) was a short distance from the American embassy. Also conveniently nearby was the American Club, where correspondents gathered for lunch around the Stammtisch (communal table) to exchange gossip and play the match game. (That involves guessing the total number of matches in a closed fist.) Nearby, built with occupation money, was the American housing development called Plittersdorf, generally known as "the golden ghetto," where diplomatic personnel could enjoy commissary duty-free lives amid the drabness of defeated Germany. It was a day of wailing and hand-ringing, in December 1960, when the State

Department, needing funds for new embassies in Africa, announced that the German service staff would be cut in half, meaning that embassy wives (at a time when diplomats were all men) would have to carry out the trash.

My departing predecessor, Ernest Leiser, introduced me to the modest CBS News office in the Reuters news agency building on the Koenigsallee (later to become Adenauerallee). My combined office manager, bookkeeper, researcher, was Frau Ursula Schultz, a mature, intelligent woman, willing to work all hours and exhibiting a loyalty that neither CBS nor I merited. Ursula steered me through the shoals of a German bureaucratic culture more alien than I had expected. (She taught me to address someone with two degrees as "Herr Doktor Doktor.")

Our camera crew, quartered in Frankfurt, was headed by Gerhard "Jerry" Schwartzkopff, who had grown up under the American occupation and spoke a totally American idiom. (He often referred to Germans as "they.") We developed a warm relationship, covering stories together not only all over Germany, but everywhere from a Polish election to a Macedonian earthquake.

For a television reporter, rapport with his cameraman is indispensable. Our communication was so deep that a telephone conversation would be enough to send him and his soundman to the scene to shoot the "silent" material. I would arrive hours or a day later, and after a briefing on what he had "in the can," I would tap out my script, do whatever interviews were needed, shoot the "stand-up" narration, and finish the story with minimal delay or fuss. Jerry would then ship the film and advise CBS in New York by cable of the flight and waybill number. In Berlin we had a cheerful and indefatigable young cameraman, a born Berliner, Hans-Juergen Neumann, whose feeling for his city would serve us in good stead.

On my second day in Bonn, May 24, 1960, I witnessed in action the man who would come to exemplify Germany for me as Khrushchev had exemplified the Soviet Union. Chancellor Konrad Adenauer addressed the lower house of Parliament, the Bundestag, on the collapse of the East-West summit. There was no real debate.

Adenauer put the blame for the breakup on Khrushchev, whom he called "irresponsible." If anyone in the Social Democratic opposition thought it might have been irresponsible for President Eisenhower to send a spy plane over the Soviet Union and then dissemble about it, he did not rise to say so. It was remarkable how this aging ex-mayor, exuding self-confidence, dominated a parliament still too new to democracy to go in for fractious debate.

Adenauer then left for his customary monthlong vacation in Cadenabbia on Italy's Lake Como. It occurred to me that this might be a good time to renew our brief acquaintanceship of five years earlier in Moscow. Through the federal chancery, he indicated that he was amenable to my coming down to Lake Como for a get-acquainted chat without camera or microphone.

Stern of demeanor in Bonn, *der Alte* (the old man)proved to be a smiling and relaxed host in sunny Italy. From the hilltop promontory of his rented house, Villa Collina, he pointed out the islands in the lake that marked the farthest westward spread of the Byzantine empire into the Roman world. "The iron curtain of that time," he called it. He showed me where the Italian dictator Benito Mussolini had passed on his futile dash for the Swiss border. He believed that Mussolini, who was executed by Italian partisans, would have done better to have waited in Rome to be captured by the advancing Americans.

The chancellor introduced me to his favorite pastime, the Italian bowling game of *boccie*, a form of bowling in which a ball is used to hit other balls. The way he played the game—utter concentration, keen competitiveness, and turning his hand as though trying to control the path of the rolling ball—seemed to reflect his nature as a politician.

It was hard to relate the leader of a truncated country on the front line of the Cold War with this elderly gentleman who enjoyed lunch with wine on the sunny terrace or conversation in the evening with a recorded violin concerto playing softly in the background. He talked discursively of his view of the East-West conflict. He foresaw mounting Soviet pressure over Berlin during America's presidential election season. But then, assuming that President Eisenhower would be succeeded by someone equally willing to stand up to the Russians (he didn't mention Vice President Nixon by name), there would be a period of "clearer sailing for the West."

In 1955, said Adenauer, Khrushchev had hinted to him of trouble with Red China and a coming split in the Communist camp. Adenauer was convinced that, in the end, Khrushchev would back off on Berlin and seek support from the West against a Chinese menace.

As to whether Adenauer had any thought of retiring, he responded with a twinkle, "Khrushchev might like to see me retire, but for the time being I do not intend to satisfy his wishes."

In a calculated, almost malicious put-down of Economics Minister Ludwig Erhard, his heir presumptive, Adenauer said that he had not yet found anyone with the necessary political skills to replace him and so would have to stay on at least until the West German election eighteen months off (when he would be eighty-five) and possibly longer.

As the American primary contest wore on, the chancellor viewed with increasing apprehension the emergence of the young Sen. John F. Kennedy, seeing him as representing a new generation of American politician less wedded to Cold War rigidities than the Eisenhower-Nixon-Dulles administration. This although Kennedy, at least for campaign purposes, assumed a hard-line posture of his own with the fictitious charge that the administration had permitted a missile gap with the Soviet Union to develop and was losing the confidence of America's allies.

I played a cameo role in the campaign. During one of the Kennedy-Nixon televised debates, the senator referred to a "prestige poll" indicating waning European confidence in America's military superiority. This poll was apparently one of a periodic series measuring the standing of America around the world. On television Nixon denied the existence of such a poll. In fact, as a friend in the American embassy told me, such a poll had been conducted by the United States Information Agency and suppressed because it reflected poorly on the administration. I arranged for CBS to broadcast the story, without attribution to me or to Bonn, to safeguard my source. The ensuing headlines in America embarrassed Nixon. The administration launched an investigation of the leak, which, like most such investigations, got nowhere.

When Kennedy won the election, Chancellor Adenauer was, at least outwardly, unfazed. He told correspondents that he planned to visit the new president in February—just days after the inauguration—to brief him on the German situation. The White House, unenchanted by the casual self-invitation, stated that Adenauer would be invited at a time "convenient to both parties." Thus started a rocky relationship between the senior statesman of the West and a president he regarded as a young whippersnapper.

To make sure Adenauer knew he was being rebuked, Kennedy first invited West Berlin mayor Willy Brandt, Adenauer's election opponent, and then Adenauer, in April 1961—the chancellor's ninth visit to Washington in little more than a decade.

As Adenauer prepared for his trip, a new concern about German-American relations arose. The trial of Adolph Eichmann, who had helped organize the Holocaust, was about to begin in Jerusalem, where he had been brought after being abducted in Argentina. Adenauer had presided over a massive payment of reparations to Israel and international Jewish organizations in an effort to promote reconciliation. He feared the Eichmann trial would negate his efforts and produce a resurgence of anti-German feeling in the United States.

I asked Adenauer whether he thought his government should have demanded that Eichmann be tried in Germany. The chancellor said he was quite content to see Israel try him. "We have no special feeling for this murderer," he said.

More than anything else in my six years in Germany it was having to report German reaction to the Eichmann trial that made me conscious of being a Jew. I studied German television coverage of the trial and found it exemplary. On the opening day of the trial the principal network aired a hard-hitting documentary about the Auschwitz gas chambers. I was less satisfied with my "man in the street" interviews, a typical reaction being, "What's the use of making such a sensation? It was all so long ago." I found, however, that young Germans tended to be more sensitive to Nazi crimes than their elders, still wrestling with their generation's shame.

There had been a few Jewish cemetery desecrations in Cologne and elsewhere, and American Jewish organizations sent a delegation to Bonn to inquire whether this was part of a Nazi resurgence in Germany. I had reported that the isolated desecrations looked like a minor manifestation. At dinner with the Jewish leaders, one of them asked whether I saw much anti-Semitism in Germany. Perversely I replied, "Some. Not as much as in the United States, but some." That turned out to be a conversation stopper. In fact, with so few Jews left, there were few signs of anti-Semitism.

The Holocaust was on Adenauer's mind as he flew to Washington to meet a young president still living down his own father's support of appeasement of Hitler while serving as ambassador to Britain. Adenauer returned from Washington enormously relieved, saying that American reaction to the Eichmann trial seemed less vehement than he had feared, and that the subject had not arisen in his talks with the president.

What they did discuss, aside from the ritual reaffirmation of American support for West Germany and Berlin, was the road ahead. Khrushchev's constant saber-rattling about the status of West Berlin was spurring an increasing exodus of East Germans. Kennedy was thinking of an early meeting with Khrushchev, who had made a gesture to the new administration by releasing the two American fliers whose reconnaissance plane had come down in Soviet territory.

From "diplomatic sources" in Bonn I learned that Kennedy had sent Ambassador Llewellyn K. "Tommy" Thompson to catch up with Khrushchev, who was on a tour of Siberia, and sound him out on Berlin and the possibility of a meeting. Thompson's dispatch to Washington, a copy of which I read, confirmed that both sides were deadlocked on Berlin, and that diplomatic exchanges should precede a summit session to be held in some neutral capital. (Thompson protested angrily to Washington about the leaking of his secret dispatch.)

The summit was scheduled for June 1961 in Vienna. Because this would be, for the first time, a summit of the two superpowers alone, without Britain and France, a hectic series of Western consultations got under way in advance of the Vienna meeting. President de Gaulle came to Bonn to meet with Adenauer, with a remarkable relationship developing between them. Then, in May, there was a NATO summit in Oslo. All this was intended to coach President Kennedy for his first outing as leader of the free world.

Adenauer, familiar with Khrushchev's bluster and having experienced Kennedy's understated manner, feared—as he always did when Americans and Russians got together—that the unpracticed president would give up the store, the store being Berlin.

What was, for those days, a huge media corps of several hundred, a dozen of them from CBS News, collected in Vienna at the end of May. Khrushchev, coming by train, could be seen on Czechoslovakian television stopping for pep rallies along the way.

Kennedy made the gesture of stopping off in Paris to meet with President de Gaulle. (David Schoenbrun, longtime CBS correspondent in Paris, wanted to accompany Kennedy to Vienna for the sole reason of being able to sign off a report, "This is David Schoenbrun, CBS News, at Schoenbrunn Palace." His request was turned down by CBS.)

The two-day summit, with sessions alternating between the American and Soviet embassies, turned out to be grim. Khrushchev used threatening words about Berlin. Kennedy warned him not to underestimate American resolve. As we were told in a briefing, the president said that America had fought two wars to keep Western Europe from being overrun, and "that goes for Berlin, too." Khrushchev warned that, unless the Western powers yielded on their rights in West Berlin, the Soviets would sign a separate peace treaty giving East Germany control over access to Berlin.

At their final lunch, Khrushchev, apparently aware that positions were hardening more than he wanted them to, invited Kennedy to come to Moscow. The president did not respond.

I returned to Bonn to find that in the week after the Vienna summit a record number of forty-six hundred East Germans had fled westward, obviously in fear that the boom would soon be coming down. And the growing exodus seemed to insure that the Communist authorities would have to take action to stop it.

Events began moving rapidly. Khrushchev proposed to make West Berlin a demilitarized "free city." President Kennedy called up the reserves. On June 21, the anniversary of the German invasion of the Soviet Union, Khrushchev made a Kremlin speech setting a year-end deadline for an East German peace treaty. On June 23, the White House announced that American troops in Berlin were being reinforced. On July 4, President Kennedy sent Khrushchev a message rejecting his proposals for a peace treaty and calling, instead, for "self-determination" for the East Germans.

By July 11, a thousand East Germans a day were streaming into West Berlin, swamping the reception center. They told of fear back home of an imminent war. From the Marienfelde reception center I reported that East Germany could not long survive this emptying of its population.

By this time the CBS bureau had, for all practical purposes, moved from Bonn to Berlin. We opened an office in a building near my friend Arthur Olson of the *New York Times*. Our stay was enlivened by increasingly frequent Soviet scare tactics such as MiGs flying close to commercial planes in the air corridor to Berlin or creating sonic booms over a nervous city.

August brought what looked like an orchestrated series of moves in the Communist bloc headed toward some kind of showdown. East German Communist boss Walter Ulbricht flew to Moscow for an emergency meeting with Khrushchev. On his return, he called his rubber-stamp parliament into session for Friday, August 11, to approve some plan that was not immediately disclosed.

At the reception center, now receiving twenty-five hundred East Germans a day, American GIs began distributing C rations to people waiting in long lines for processing.

Sunday, August 13, 1961, about 4 A.M., I was awakened in my room at the Kempinski Hotel by a call from Hans-Juergen Neumann, our Berlin cameraman. He had been up all night patrolling the crossing points between East and West Berlin. He told me to come to Pots-dammer Platz (Potsdam Square) to see the amazing things going on. I said I would come as soon as I had some coffee. Getting no response from room service, I called the reception desk, where I was told that, for unknown reasons, none of the East Berlin help had shown up for the midnight shift. That was enough to rouse me without coffee, and soon I was at the Potsdammer Platz where, indeed, an amazing thing was going on. Under garish floodlights, East German police, guarded by troops, were unrolling bales of barbed wire, sinking posts to con-nect them, and tearing up cobblestones to bar the road.

We ascertained that something like this was going on at sixty-seven of the eighty crossing points. Someone brought us a copy of the East German Communist organ *Neues Deutschland*, which con-tained the decree severing the city. Twelve crossing points would remain open for supervised entry of West Germans (not West Berliners). One crossing point on the Friedrichstrasse would be for non-Germans. Soon the U.S. army, which took up positions on the western side, would designate this Checkpoint C for Charlie.

As I reported in a narration on film, "I toured East Berlin and found it an occupied city, police and troops everywhere to hold back the sullen population... Russian and East German tanks held in reserve... my cameraman and I arrested and held in a police station for ninety minutes, our film confiscated."

On the western side, Berliners gathered from the early morning at the checkpoints being abolished. They hooted and shouted at the Communists building a barricade that would divide families. West Berlin police, fearing violent clashes, tried to hold the West Berliners back from the border.

Neumann got an unforgettable shot of a helmeted soldier, rifle swinging from his shoulder, vaulting over the barbed wire into the welcoming hands of the West Berlin police. Juergen never told me how he happened to be standing there at the Bernauerstrasse in the French sector, some distance from the city center. I suspected that the defection had been prearranged and that Juergen had been tipped off by friends in the West Berlin police.

Because of the early start, we had a completed film report that made a flight to Frankfurt and a connection to New York in time to be aired the same evening. That was, incidentally, a moment of media history—the first time in the presatellite era that a film report from Europe was aired on the same calendar day. I heard later that President Kennedy expressed concern about not having enough time for a considered reaction to this dramatic event. This was a small foretaste of what the age of live-from-everywhere satellite television would bring.

As the day wore on, the mood in West Berlin turned nasty. Citizens demanded to know why Allied tanks did not mow down the barbed-wire barricades. President Kennedy had undoubtedly signaled to Khrushchev that, while he would defend West Berlin by force of arms if necessary, he was less concerned about what East Germany did to seal itself off. That night, fearful of a repetition of the 1953 uprising in East Germany, Mayor Brandt broadcast an appeal to the East Germans: "Despite the provocation, do not let yourselves be provoked."

By next day, Monday, East Berliners were making desperate efforts to escape—swimming across a canal, burrowing through the barbed wire, leaping from windows of houses located on the dividing line. The windows were soon bricked up.

On Tuesday, the third day, I reported seeing slabs of concrete being moved into place "as though to build a wall." This was the first indication that the East Germans planned a permanent structure of masonry. The three Western commandants sent protests to the Soviet commandant against the violation of four-power agreements, but made no move to impede the building of the wall.

"Another protest, " said one West Berliner. "Ulbricht must have his office papered with them."

Some day President Reagan would demand of Mikhail Gorbachev, "Tear down that Wall!" Someday I would walk through the Brandenburg Gate for the thrill of being able to do so again. But that would be twenty-eight years later. For now, during those first weeks, the Wall would be my life.

Each day brought its desperate escapes that we covered as best we could. Each day brought its tearful demonstrations by West Berliners gathering at the Wall, in some cases to wave to relatives on the other side. One day Ed Murrow, who had become director of the United States Information Agency, startled me by showing up to watch me film a narration at the Wall. I had not known that he was in Berlin on an inspection trip for President Kennedy.

I remembered his dramatic reporting from an airlift plane during the 1948 Berlin blockade and suggested that, for old times' sake, he might want to take my place in front of the camera.

"Carry on, Brother Schorr, you're doing fine," said Murrow. Afterward we chatted for a few minutes. He deplored the passive response of the West to the closing of the border. "We've lost our nerve," he said, not yet bureaucrat enough to add, "off the record." The next time I saw Ed, three years later in his New York apartment, he was very ill and still smoking.

As the first week of the Berlin Wall dragged on, the rage of the citizens began to take on an anti-American tone in what had probably been the most America-worshiping city in the world. A rally of a quarter million citizens featured placards like "Munich 1938, Berlin 1961." Mayor Brandt drew cheers when he told the crowd that he had written President Kennedy asserting that Berlin "needs something more than protests."

The "something more" turned out to be a fifteen-hundred-man U.S. army battle group that barreled across East Germany into West Berlin. And, as a further morale-raising move, Vice President Lyndon Johnson flew in on August 19. In a hectic day, Johnson led a motorcade through streets lined with cheering citizens. In rapid succession he made three speeches, the last of them to a crowd of two hundred thousand in City Hall square. Somehow the vice president also found time for an unpublicized visit to the army PX, where duty-free bargains were to be had.

On the way to Berlin, Johnson had stopped off in Bonn for a courtesy call on Chancellor Adenauer, but had declined the chancellor's request to take him along to Berlin. The Kennedy administration had no intention of aiding Adenauer in his election contest with Willy Brandt. The chancellor followed three days later, receiving a conspicuously cool reception in the mainly Social Democratic city. Berlin, officially under occupation, did not vote in federal elections—one of the many oddities of an unresolved war.

The campaign was particularly nasty. Adenauer questioned the patriotism of Brandt, who had fled from Germany during Hitler's time and had returned to Berlin in Norwegian uniform. Brandt wrapped himself in the cloak of the Kennedy New Frontier and presented himself as the symbol of a beleaguered Berlin. In the September election, Adenauer's Christian Democratic Union came out ahead, but for the first time without an absolute majority, making it necessary for Adenauer to bring the small Free Democratic Party into a coalition government.

At a news conference after a sleepless night, the eighty-five-year-old Adenauer, starting his third term amid a crisis over Berlin, airily dismissed the handicap of dealing with an American president half his age.

"There is no substitute for experience," Adenauer drawled, "and the young have much to learn from the old."

October brought an episode at the Wall that, for the first time, threatened to drag America and the Soviet Union into a confrontation. Allen Lightner Jr., U.S. mission chief, and his wife were stopped seeking to drive into East Berlin at Checkpoint Charlie. East German border guards asked to see identity cards. Under the prevailing American policy of not dealing with the East Germans, the pair refused to produce them. Lightner radioed for help. American tanks came rolling up to the checkpoint. Military police escorted the Lightners through—and then three more times back and forth to emphasize the point.

When the East German government then announced that henceforth American officials not in uniform would have to identify themselves, American soldiers in jeeps with fixed bayonets began escorting civilian officials through the checkpoint.

It seemed a small point to make a big fuss about. It was orchestrated by retired general Lucius Clay, hero of the 1948 airlift that had sustained Berlin during fifteen months of a menacing Soviet blockade. Clay had returned to Berlin as President Kennedy's "special representative" to help raise Berlin's morale. He had no intention of making any concessions to an unrecognized East German government.

The situation moved, step by step, toward a showdown. On October 26, American Patton tanks rolled up to the checkpoint and, after several hours, withdrew. Then, suddenly, Soviet tanks appeared on the other side. American tanks rushed back to find the Soviet tanks gone. Then, on October 27, the American tanks arrived at the checkpoint to find themselves confronting ten Soviet tanks. And there they all stood for the next sixteen hours, their big guns pointed at each other.

Never before had there been a face-to-face confrontation of Soviet and American armor. It looked like a visual representation of how World War III might start. Yet somehow the scene looked unwarlike. GIs sat atop their tank turrets, eating dinner out of mess kits. West Berliners bought pretzel sticks from street vendors and presented them to the American tank crews. Not to be outdone, the East Germans sent children with flowers for the crews on their side.

The Soviet-made tanks bore no markings and could have been manned by East Germans, which would have made the situation more serious. I strolled through the checkpoint and addressed one of the black-garbed crew members sitting atop his turret. I greeted him in Russian, *"Zdrasvitye"* (Hello), and he responded in Russian. We exchanged a few more words and I reported back to my colleagues that these appeared to be Soviet-manned tanks.

"So here," I reported on CBS radio, "is this incredible picture of these war machines pointing flower-festooned guns at each other while cameras grind and Berliners eat pretzels."

Was this really how World War III would start? We sensed that this surreal scene was some new kind of Cold War charade. After a night and a day, the Russians suddenly started up their motors, wheeled around, and cranked away. A few minutes later the American tanks withdrew. In time, we would learn that President Kennedy, who thoroughly disapproved of General Clay's war games, had contacted Khrushchev, giving his word that if the Soviet tanks withdrew, the Pattons would do likewise.

Then, to preclude further identity-card standoffs, American ambassador Thompson in Moscow worked out an arrangement with Foreign Minister Andrey Gromyko. American civilian officials entering East Berlin would show identity cards from behind closed car windows—as the British had long done. We learned from the checkpoint episode that the Berlin Wall situation was a lot less volatile than appeared on the surface.

Among the many plans the building of the Wall disrupted was a CBS project for an East German documentary. Fred Friendly had proposed it to me in July. I had scoffed at the notion that we could get into East Germany, one of the more closed Communist societies. On Fred's insistence I made a pro forma proposal by telex to the East German Foreign Ministry; I was surprised to receive a favorable response. The date for entry into East Germany, with camera crew and truck, was set for August 15. The closing of the border on August 13 ended that plan—presumably forever.

But, in October, again to my amazement, the East German Foreign Ministry asked by telex whether I was interested in reinstating our project. There were conditions. We would have an East German chaperon. We would work in one city—Rostock, a showplace port city on the Baltic.

It dawned on me that Ulbricht's regime, expecting that Khrushchev would soon sign a peace treaty conferring statehood on East Germany, was interested in achieving some measure of recognition in the West and believed that exposure on television might help. Friendly thought—after the Wall more than ever—that America was curious to see this unknown piece of Germany.

And so, in November, I stood atop our camera truck, narrating what it was like to be snaking our way through the barriers at Checkpoint Charlie to explore this forbidden country. For the next three weeks we filmed what we could of life in Rostock. Even in this showcase city, life was pretty grim. Butter was rationed, fresh vegetables almost unavailable except for cabbage. People told us that fear of war had led to hoarding. The rector of Rostock University told me in a filmed interview, "Since the Wall went up we can, for the first time, maintain discipline among our students. Before then the university was losing its students in large numbers in flight to the West." There was no pretense that the Wall, as claimed by the Communist regime, was meant to keep people out rather than in.

East Germany, with possibly the most Stalinist regime in Eastern Europe, was also having trouble coming to terms with the de-Stalinization drive that Khrushchev had launched five years earlier. We filmed the street sign, UNIVERSITY SQUARE, which had a day before been STALIN SQUARE. We also filmed a spot where, until recently, a statue of Stalin had stood.

Our work in Rostock was almost completed when our escort officer asked if we would like to climax our stay with a first-ever interview with the Communist chief, Walter Ulbricht. I doubted the value of letting him spout Communist clichés, but Friendly sent instructions to go for it. As with the Khrushchev interview in 1957, it was first necessary to negotiate terms. Our East German liaison insisted on having questions submitted in advance. I insisted on being able to ask follow-up questions. After getting a haircut in East Berlin, which, I am convinced, was intended to make me look worse than the balding, spade-bearded Ulbricht, our crew showed up at Communist Party headquarters for our interview.

I asked my first question, and Ulbricht gave a fifteen-minute lecture in response. I interrupted to ask about the pace of de-Stalinization. He denied that Stalinism had ever existed in the German Democratic Republic. I noted that we had actually seen and filmed the removal of Stalin symbols. Apparently unprepared for my follow-up questions, he twitched nervously as my remark was translated for him. He began muttering, *"Bitte...bitte...bitte!"* (please...please...please!) Then he rose from his desk, pointed an accusatory finger, denounced me for "provocation," and shouted,

"Schluss! Es ist beendet." (Finished, the interview is over.) With that he stalked out of the room while the camera rolled.

Not in a million years could we have conceived of a more emphatic conclusion to our tale of this Communist state that survived on Soviet bayonets. "East Germany—Land Beyond the Wall" aired in January 1962 to good reviews. On German television the sequence with the unnerved Ulbricht played hundreds of times. A West Berlin paper spread a frame from the interview across its front page under the streamer headline "America Laughs at Ulbricht."

A reaction I found interesting came a few weeks later at lunch with Chairman Paley for his European correspondents at the Ritz Hotel in Paris. Paley said that what impressed him most about the East German show was the serene way I had nodded back at Ulbricht while he was storming at me.

"Thank you, Mr. Paley," I said, "but surely you understand that my reactions were filmed after Ulbricht had left the room and were spliced in for editing purposes."

The chairman, apparently unaware of the inserted "reverse shots" routinely used in television news, said, "But, is that honest?"

"Well, not exactly, if you put it that way. But it is what they taught me when I went to work for CBS."

Paley cabled New York ordering immediate abolition of all reaction shots that were not contemporaneous. The ban lasted about twenty-four hours. What Paley apparently did not understand is that television relies on its small deceptions.

By early 1962, the Wall began to look like a permanent fixture. In February, Attorney General Robert Kennedy received a thunderous ovation in City Hall square, speaking with a frankness that Berliners seemed to appreciate. He said that the Wall was an atrocity, but he could promise no miracle to bring it down. As he spoke, balloons from East Berlin released red flags that floated down on small parachutes. To cheers, Kennedy ad-libbed, "The Communists will let out their balloons, but not their people."

In Berlin, Robert Kennedy was joined by his brother, Ted, who had come to celebrate his thirtieth birthday. As the youngest of the

Kennedys arrived at the snow-swept Tempelhof airport, I was on hand to ask the mandatory question relayed from New York: This being the first day he was constitutionally eligible to run for senator, would he?

"You want me to announce in Germany, do you?" he said laughing.

With the support of Mayor Brandt and the visits of the vice president and the attorney general, the administration managed to retain the support of most Berliners. But another story was the relationship between Adenauer in Bonn and President Kennedy, which never really stabilized. Reassurances had to be sent constantly, through visitors such as Defense Secretary Robert McNamara, that overtures to the Russians for an easing of tensions did not signify an abandonment of West Germany.

I was constantly receiving—and reporting to America—leaks from Adenauer cabinet meetings and party caucuses underscoring the chancellor's baleful suspicions about the president. On May 9, 1962, I reported on the CBS "Radio World News Roundup" that Adenauer had said, in one caucus, that relations with the United States were "worse than at any time during my thirteen years in office." He added, "I sometimes wonder whether the Kennedy administration considers the Federal Republic as America's ally against the Soviet Union, or vice versa."

That day I was having lunch with the president's press secretary, Pierre Salinger, who was on his way to Moscow, trying to arrange an exchange of television addresses between Kennedy and Khrushchev. (The project died when the Russians resumed nuclear testing.) During lunch Salinger was called away to the telephone. Returning, he said, "You may be interested in knowing who that was. That was the leader of the free world, and he said he was listening to you while shaving. And he asked, since I seemed to be doing such a great public relations job for him in Germany, where was I going next?"

Salinger said that the president had a news conference scheduled that day and was in a mood, after my broadcast, to let Adenauer have it. Germany was not raised at the news conference and Kennedy held his piece, to the immense relief of the State Department and Ambassador Walter Dowling in Bonn.

The West German government's rigidity about any change in Berlin's status was a constant source of irritation in Washington. When the State Department came up with an idea for a compromise on the status of Berlin, it was promptly leaked in Bonn. Secretary Dean Rusk, furious, accused the Adenauer government of "a breach of confidence." Adenauer told Ambassador Dowling that he had never been so insulted in his whole career. And the feud bubbled on.

As the one reporting German perceptions, I was not popular in the administration. CBS News director Blair Clark, friend and Harvard classmate of Kennedy's, told me of attending a White House dinner. The president, leaning over the woman seated between them, said, "Blair, that Dan Schorr in Germany is a pain in the ass. Why don't you pull him out of there?" Blair said he was immensely amused.

But the Kennedy administration did succeed in getting Clark to veto one Berlin project I was planning. August 13, the first anniversary of the Wall, had brought new tensions. A nineteen-year-old building worker, Peter Fechter, had been shot trying to scale the Wall and was left to bleed to death. That set off four days of riots, aimed partly at a passive United States. For the first time in Berlin I heard the shouts of "Ami go home!"

I reported, "Peter Fechter's body has become a symbol of East-West conflict as John Brown's body came to symbolize North-South conflict."

A few East Berliners managed to get out by digging tunnels under the Wall from basements. One group of young West Berliners offered to let CBS film the digging of a tunnel and the escape for what would surely be a dramatic documentary. Our foreign news desk in New York gave a green light.

A few days later Clark called me after midnight in my hotel room and told me to go immediately to the U.S. mission so that he could speak to me on a secure telephone. The military police on duty at the mission seemed prepared for my visit and showed me into a small office, pointed to a telephone, and closed the door behind them.

On the phone was Blair Clark, speaking, he said, from the office of Secretary Dean Rusk and in his presence. Blair said that the State Department, fearing that the tunnel was "compromised" (that is, known to the Communist authorities), was concerned it would be denounced as an American provocation. Over my protests, Clark ordered me to desist. A few months later we saw a gripping NBC documentary, "The Tunnel." Our rivals had been less squeamish than CBS about the State Department's concerns.

Under a pall of tension, West Berlin, a metropolis without a hinterland, seemed in danger of dying on the vine. To maintain morale, Mayor Brandt strove to attract international conferences and festivals. One such event was a film festival that brought several stars to the city, including Shirley MacLaine. On the way to address a rally of Berliners, she asked me how to say "I love you" and wowed her audience with a heartfelt *"Ich liebe dich."*

I found myself spending more time with the charming and outgoing actress than was journalistically required. One evening I arrived at the Berlin Hilton Hotel to pick her up for dinner in a nearby restaurant. A swarm of young fans awaited her in the lobby. She jovially signed a few dozen autographs and finally said, "Okay, kids, that's it!" and we started walking to the restaurant. We found ourselves being pursued by what began to seem like a menacing throng and arrived at the restaurant panting. I asked her whether she found this fan frenzy hard to take.

"It gets pretty bad at times," she said, "but it will be a lot worse when it stops."

After dinner I took Shirley for a sight-seeing drive, ending up at a park on the picturesque Wannsee Lake. Trying to get close to the water, I found my rented car up to its hubcaps in wet sand. Abandoning the car, we walked a half hour before we found a taxi. Shirley took it all in good spirit, but that was not how I had intended that evening should end.

Miss MacLaine was leaving the next day and, on the telephone, proposed that I go to Rome with her. I told her that was one of the best invitations I had ever had, but I could not, on such short notice, leave my post in Germany. "Earthbound!" she exclaimed. And that was the end of that rendezvous in Berlin.

Berlin occupied most of my attention in the post-Wall period, but occasionally a story took me back to West Germany. Word reached me that Major General Edwin A. Walker, commander of the Twenty-fourth Infantry Division, was indoctrinating his troops with ultranationalist messages drawn from John Birch Society literature. My broadcast report led to his being recalled to Texas. He eventually retired and became a spokesman for the John Birch Society in Dallas. When I came to Dallas to lecture with other CBS correspondents, Walker issued a press statement denouncing me.

If the name Edwin Walker sounds vaguely familiar to you, it is because he was the target of a Lee Harvey Oswald assassination attempt. In April 1963, seven months before Oswald shot President Kennedy, he fired a shot into the window of Walker's home. That time he missed.

Another story that engaged my attention concerned a pharmaceutical firm in northern Germany that became associated with a generation of deformed children. *Chemie Gruenenthal* had marketed a new sedative, especially effective in relieving morning sickness in pregnant women. Its original name was Contergan. In Britain and elsewhere it was called thalidomide. That it might have a terrible side effect became clear when five thousand children in Germany and hundreds in Britain, all of whose mothers had used the sedative, were born horribly deformed, often with flippers for arms.

Thanks to a wary Food and Drug Administration employee, Frances Kelsey, the drug had not yet been licensed in the United States. Sherry Finkbine of Phoenix, who had used thalidomide while abroad, became a subject of controversy when, unable to obtain an abortion in the United States, she flew to Stockholm. That helped to stir a controversy in the United States about state laws banning abortion.

Visiting the *Chemie Gruenenthal* plant, I was shown where the drug had been tested on monkeys—but not on pregnant monkeys. Dr. Werner von Schrade, head of the firm, agreed to sit for a filmed interview, in which he staunchly defended his drug.

"Would you give Contergan to a woman in your own family?" I asked.

"Absolutely!" he said. "However, as of now, I would not give it to my wife if she was pregnant."

I still have the package of Contergan I was given as a souvenir. It has been interesting to watch the recent comeback of thalidomide as a promising treatment for leprosy.

But inevitably my journalistic pendulum would swing back to Berlin, fulcrum of the Cold War and, as far as we German hands were concerned, the center of the universe. It was with mystification that we viewed what appeared to be a Kennedy obsession with Cuba, which not only diverted energy and resources from the confrontation over Berlin, but established a kind of linkage between the two issues.

The disastrous Bay of Pigs invasion in April 1961 left not only Chancellor Adenauer but Americans in Germany shaking their heads. During the Vienna summit in June, we learned belatedly, Khrushchev had referred to the Bay of Pigs and asserted the right to take any measures necessary to protect Cuba from another invasion.

In retrospect, one can see the link between the Cuban and Berlin crises. In 1962, Khrushchev would try to smuggle nuclear missiles into Cuba, ostensibly to guard the island against another invasion. If he succeeded in deploying the missiles, he would be in a position to use them for pressure against the United States to get out of Berlin. When the missiles were discovered in October and President Kennedy announced a blockade of Cuba until the weapons were pulled out, White House reporters were alerted to the chance that Khrushchev might retaliate with a new Berlin blockade. CBS instructed me to fly to Berlin immediately, rent a car, and lay in supplies for the contingency that I might be broadcasting from a city under Soviet blockade.

In the first of several special broadcasts, I reported that Berlin seemed almost weirdly calm—with none of the Soviet pinpricks or harassment of ground and air traffic to Berlin that might foreshadow more drastic action. In the end, Berlin remained the eye of the hurricane. Khrushchev, it soon appeared, had no intention of adding a Berlin crisis to a Cuban crisis.

Much though he was part of my professional life, I had never met President Kennedy. So I was excited at the announcement that he would visit West Germany and West Berlin in June 1963. This would also be the biggest television production in which I had ever been involved. CBS News producers and technicians came over in droves to survey the sites in Bonn, Berlin, and Frankfurt where Kennedy would appear.

President Kennedy had chosen a particularly delicate moment in Europe to make this trip. Not only was there tension between East and West, but tension within the East and within the West. In the Communist community, Khrushchev was trying to fend off an ideological challenge from China's Mao Tse-tung, aimed in part against the Soviet leader's efforts at détente with the West. In the Western community, President de Gaulle was mounting a challenge to Anglo-Saxon leadership, with Germany caught in the middle. In Berlin, the president faced the problem of rallying the citizens of the Western sectors without inciting an uprising in East Berlin or an effort by the West Berliners to tear down the Wall.

One of Kennedy's first events in Germany was a news conference in Bonn, timed so that it could be transmitted live to the United States by Telstar satellite, which was available only during specified hours. Seeking to get a sense of how he viewed his delicate mission of making friends on this side without making trouble on the other side, I rose to ask whether, while in West Berlin, he would exercise his right, under four-power agreements, to visit East Berlin, as well. With a look of cool asperity, he replied that entering East Berlin might be a spectacular gesture, but he didn't think it would help the people very much.

I reported back to America that thus Kennedy signaled to Khrushchev that he had not come to Germany to make trouble.

At an official reception that evening, Chancellor Adenauer, standing with Kennedy, stopped me on the receiving line to introduce me to the president as "an esteemed American correspondent, well informed of German views." Kennedy, all too familiar with my reporting of German views, gave a thin smile of amusement and said, "Oh, yes, I know Mr. Schorr very well. I listen to him all the time."

With memories of how he had tried to get me moved out of Germany, I tried to respond in the same tone of banter. "Thank you, Mr. President," I said. "I listen to you a lot, too."

Had I known that, with Kennedy having five more months to live, this would be last time I would speak to him, I might have found something less inane to say.

In his tumultuous tour of West Berlin I never came close to him. That was because of the burgeoning live coverage by satellite, which required me to operate from the studio of the Berlin television station, *Sender Freies Berlin*, narrating events as I saw them on a TV monitor. I described the tumultuous motorcade and the almost hysterical reception from a half million citizens when he stepped out on the City Hall balcony.

Kennedy used cautious language, describing the Wall as a symptom of Communism's failure, but without suggesting that it should be brought down. The climax of his appearance, of course, was the line that did not appear in his prepared text, his saying that, as a lover of freedom, *"Ich bin ein Berliner."*

Those historic words appear to have been his own idea. I learned later that as he'd mounted the stairs to the City Hall balcony, the president had turned to his interpreter, an American foreign service officer, and asked, "How do I say in German 'I am a Berliner?'" He had then repeated the words several times as he went up the steps.

Not wanting to stir up people in East Berlin, still Kennedy could not leave without seeing the Wall. He drove up to Checkpoint Charlie, accompanied by Chancellor Adenauer and Mayor Brandt. Here is an excerpt of my ad-lib narration:

"You can hear the roar of the crowd, chanting, 'Ken-ne-dy...Ken-ne-dy.' That chant has swept through Germany wherever he has been. Now the president is getting an explanation from American officers of what Checkpoint Charlie represents—the crossing point for non-Germans.... There are barriers that force a car to weave back and forth in a kind of slalom. That's because too many people have crashed through the barrier and escaped....

"The president mounts a platform for a better look into East Berlin. Now that he can be better seen, the cheering on this side increases. On the other side you can see the Vopos, the East German police, watching through their binoculars. And some East Berliners are gathered on a street corner."

"The president stands there and just stares. It is an amazing sight!"

Kennedy had done what he had come to do—give West Berlin a big lift without stirring up trouble in East Berlin. Two days later Khrushchev paid a visit to East Berlin that seemed almost a parody of the Kennedy tour. Four days later President de Gaulle arrived in Bonn and, brushing aside the memory of three wars, addressed a crowd in German—a lot more fluently than Kennedy...but less electrifyingly.

All this came back to me with a surge five months later, on November 22. Perhaps nowhere outside the United States were the shock and the grief greater than among the Germans, who had so recently taken him to their bosom.

Mayor Brandt, who had just returned from Washington, one of the last foreign statesmen to see the president, flew back for the funeral. He returned to Berlin to address a mournful rally in the City Hall square (renamed John F. Kennedyplatz). He said that Mrs. Jacqueline Kennedy had told him, "Jack loved Berlin." The recently installed chancellor Ludwig Erhard also flew to Washington for the funeral and was delighted to be invited to spend Christmas with the Johnsons at the LBJ ranch.

Interesting was the reaction to the assassination from behind the Iron Curtain. Communist functionaries must have wondered whether Oswald, a known Communist sympathizer, may also have been a Communist murder agent. In East Germany and elsewhere in the Soviet orbit, newspapers cautiously speculated about a right-wing conspiracy. That there had been some kind of conspiracy seemed to be taken almost for granted. In that part of the world murder plots, intrigue, and espionage were in the air one breathed.

In West Germany there was also a real espionage problem of huge proportions. A divided country made West Germany a happy hunting ground for agents who could blend in easily with the West German population. One woman spy managed to become Willy Brandt's confidential secretary and almost destroyed his career. Another was elected to the Bundestag, the West German parliament. In a decade, some thirty thousand spies were uncovered.

I produced a CBS documentary on German espionage with a considerable assist from the CIA, which was anxious to shake the West Germans out of their complacency about Communist infiltration. The agency arranged entrée for me to West German counterintelligence and provided the highlight of my film—an interview, in a CIA safe house near Frankfurt, with a defector from the East German intelligence service. Lt. Guenter Maennel said that of the fifteen thousand East Germans who went west in a year, a full one-third had accepted some espionage assignment from the Stasi, the East German security agency. Maennel's particular speciality was targeting Americans—members of the armed forces and embassy personnel. He identified by name an American air force captain who, he said, was a Stasi paid agent.

The CIA's Bonn station chief, Henry Pleasants (in his spare time a jazz critic for the *New York Times*), told me that Langley (CIA headquarters) had been well pleased with my documentary. So was CBS, and so was I.

My collaboration with the CIA may raise eyebrows among those who know of my later run-ins with the agency. In the field, a correspondent's relations with the CIA follow a certain code. In Berlin, Prague, and Budapest I would exchange observations with CIA officers, it being understood that anything I told them might be, or already had been, included in my news reports. Often they would help to fill out my impressions, it being understood that I would not identify them as sources.

There were other CIA contacts. In the 1950s, CBS made it a practice to arrange a dinner of top CIA people and CBS correspondents home for our year-end televised roundtable, "Years of Crisis." If anything of great significance was said at these dinners, it has eluded my memory. I do remember, though, that in 1958, having been excluded from the Soviet Union, I was invited to a private lunch with CIA director Allen Dulles. After some general conversation, he led me into an adjoining room, where, to my surprise, I found a dozen CIA desk officers and other officials waiting with notepads and clipboards to debrief me. Uncomfortable about the position I was put in, I responded to questions in general terms and balked completely when asked my views about my Moscow journalistic colleagues and certain ones that the agency suspected to be under Soviet influence.

Years later, through a Freedom of Information application, I received my own CIA file with copies of envelopes I had sent. I also learned that when Dulles had invited me to lunch, he was considering recruiting me as a Soviet analyst. The CIA went so far as to ask the FBI to run a security check on me. The Bureau reported that it could not vouch for my loyalty because, in the 1930s, I had been a member of the "Communist-influenced" New York Newspaper Guild. Ironic, then, that the Soviet organ *Pravda* should later accuse me of being a CIA agent. I had managed to come under suspicion from both sides.

There is nothing like the quadrennial presidential election to give a foreign correspondent a sense of expatriation. In 1964 it struck me that this would be the fifth consecutive campaign year to find me outside the United States, an absentee voter. We had a mini-campaign in Germany because of the votes of several hundred thousand servicemen and their families. In June, Att. Gen. Robert F. Kennedy came to Berlin and attacked Sen. Barry Goldwater, the odds-on Republican candidate, as someone who would use the atomic bomb as a way of displaying American courage.

Among Germans, a certain polarization was developing over the American election. President Johnson had strong support from Chancellor Ludwig Erhard, who had enjoyed his Christmas visit to the LBJ ranch. Goldwater had a special appeal for right-wing Germans, who saw in him someone who shared their ideas of standing

up to the Soviets, promoting German unification, and perhaps helping Germany recover the territory it had lost to Poland.

CBS cabled me asking for a filmed report analyzing German
views on the election, to be aired the evening before the opening of
the Republican convention in San Francisco. In my research, I
learned a singular thing—that Goldwater had plans, as yet unannounced, to leave directly after the convention for a vacation in
Germany as guest of his bridge-playing friend Lt. Gen. William
Quinn, commander of the Seventh Army. They would spend their
time mainly at an American army recreation center in Berchtesgaden in the Bavarian Alps. Berchtesgaden was famous as Hitler's
favorite retreat. Apparently no thought had been given to the sym-
bolism of an American politician spending his first days as a presidential nominee at Hitler's hideaway.

This, along with the obvious enthusiasm of right-wing Germans
for Goldwater, I reported from Munich in my analysis, which ran on
the CBS news on the eve of the convention.

Supporters of Pennsylvania governor William Scranton, fighting
an all-but-lost battle against Goldwater, transcribed my report, I
later learned, and put copies under the doors of the delegates. Next
morning brought an explosion from Goldwater. He called a news
conference to excoriate CBS and announce the cancellation of a
scheduled CBS interview, as well as his vacation in Germany.

"I'll never forgive them," he said. "I don't think these people
should even be allowed to broadcast."

Fred Friendly, the newly minted president of CBS News, tracking me down in Vienna by telephone, was obviously greatly agitated.
"This is my first big operation, and you've given me a clubfoot!" he
shouted. He demanded that I make an immediate retraction on
radio. But, retraction of what? Goldwater had acknowledged the
planned trip to Germany.

In the end I broadcast that, in reporting that right-wing German
groups were rallying to Goldwater, I had not intended to suggest
that he was cultivating ties with them. That seemed to satisfy
nobody. Chairman Paley demanded that Friendly immediately fire

me. I was later told that Friendly was only dissuaded from doing so by other CBS News executives, arguing that this would make CBS look cowardly.

Later I learned of the land mine that my report had tripped. Paley was friends with ex-president Eisenhower, who was supporting Scranton. Paley had gone to San Francisco against the advice of CBS president Stanton precisely because of the fear of Paley's becoming involved in the nomination fight. Goldwater was already angry at CBS because of the way he had been depicted in a CBS documentary, "Thunder on the Right," and because Walter Cronkite had made a point of saying on the *CBS Evening News* that Goldwater had missed the funeral of President Kennedy, neglecting to add that Goldwater was attending the funeral of his own mother.

Thus, Goldwater saw my report as the third in a series of attacks on him orchestrated by Paley in the interest of his opponent—a veritable conspiracy, of which, Goldwater assumed, I was a part.

In April 1965, the defeated candidate finally made his trip to Germany, and I was on hand at the Stuttgart airport for his arrival. We exchanged no words. *Newsweek* reported that this was the delayed Goldwater trip that had been loused up, "and the louser-upper was present."

General Quinn's daughter, Sally, subsequently wrote that President Johnson denied her father a promotion, and he retired in bitterness from the army. Goldwater, in his own book *The Conscience of a Conservative*, devoted many pages to reviewing what he called "a deliberate tampering by a major network." As late as 1977, appearing on Dinah Shore's television show, Goldwater was still denouncing me for "the damnest lie."

In 1980, when Ted Turner hired me as the first editorial employee of his new Cable News Network, he told me that Senator Goldwater—important to him as chairman of the Senate communications subcommittee—had expressed objections to me, which Turner said he had ignored.

Eventually wounds heal. In 1990 I met General Quinn at a reception and we exchanged letters, his ending, "Let's forget it." In

1996 I ran into Goldwater at the National Press Club, and we exchanged friendly words. Both have since died.

In 1965, my sixth year in Germany, the character of my work began to change with changing technology. Fred Friendly was fascinated with the Early Bird satellite, which had replaced the original Telstar satellite. Instead of produced film reports, shipped by plane, he demanded more live reports directly on the *Evening News*. It took some ingenuity to figure out what to cover live at midnight European time. One night I reported from the Brandenburg Gate, a part of the Berlin Wall, not far from the bunker where Hitler had died. My script started, "It is just before midnight and history walks here."

Another night I appeared from the Frankfurt courtroom where Nazi Auschwitz guards were being tried. I interviewed the prosecutor, who was good enough to show up for the purpose. I reported, "Today started the summation against Wilhelm Boger, the inventor of the so-called Boger seesaw, of which this is a model. On this seesaw prisoners were hung up and beaten."

The easing of tension in Berlin also enabled me to spend more time working on documentaries. One of these was "The Plots against Hitler," telling of the small but courageous group of Germans who tried to kill Hitler.

The plot that came closest to succeeding involved the planting of a bomb concealed in a suitcase at a table in a field headquarters in East Prussia where Hitler was scheduled to receive a briefing. It was planted by a general staff colonel, Count Klaus von Stauffenberg, leader of a group of disaffected army officers who had been plotting for five years to kill the Führer, sue for peace, and bring democracy to Germany. By happenstance someone moved the suitcase behind a table leg, deflecting the force of the explosion. Hitler was injured, but not seriously.

I interviewed the widow, Countess von Stauffenberg. She recalled how, one day, her husband, in the hospital after being wounded in Tunisia, had said, "I think it is time for me to save Germany." She found comfort now in that "at least it is clear today that there really existed in Germany people willing to give their lives to oppose power." Most of the plotters were rounded up, executed, and hung from meat hooks in Berlin.

One who survived, Axel von dem Bussche, became a close friend of mine. As a twenty-four-year-old infantry captain, wounded on the Russian front, he devised a plan to kill Hitler with hand grenades in his pockets while modeling a new uniform for the Führer. The display of uniforms was canceled at the last moment. Some twenty years later, I asked Axel on camera what it takes to perform such a suicidal act.

"It's like steeplechase, horse-jumping," he said. "You throw your heart over the hurdle, and the horse will follow."

I was able to roam to other parts of my East European "domain" to cover an earthquake in Skopje, capital of Macedonia, or to film a feature on an American independent movie company shooting a cowboy picture in Bulgaria, where cowboys came cheaper than in Hollywood. Indeed, I worked in every East European country except Albania, hermetically sealed in those days.

My most interesting project in this period was an examination of two Communist satellites beginning to pull in different directions as the Soviets, preoccupied with their ideological war with the Chinese Communists, loosened their hold. Romania and Czechoslovakia offered an arresting contrast. Romania remained severely repressive at home, but flaunted an independent foreign policy and friendship with China. Czechoslovakia, on the other hand, was easing its internal controls, but remained slavishly supportive of Moscow in foreign policy and opposition to China.

Both governments, when we approached them, seemed nervous about opening their doors to American television, yet eager for exposure in America. That our program, "Satellites out of Orbit," would be a contrast between the two we kept secret from them, knowing that would be anathema to both of them.

In Romania, our host was Silviu Brucan, head of the state television committee, to whose sardonic humor I became attached. When I asked him, over dinner at a lakeside resort, to explain to me why there was so much tension between Romania and Hungary, he responded with a riddle: "How do you tell the difference between a Hungarian and a Romanian? Answer—each would sell you his mother, but the Romanian would deliver."

My stay in Bucharest started with a peculiar experience. Remembering the Bronx delicatessen stores of my youth that advertised "genuine Romanian pastrami," I looked forward to tasting *really* genuine Romanian pastrami. I found no pastrami on our hotel restaurant menu, and when I asked a waiter, he gave me a funny look and walked away. Something of the sort happened in several other restaurants.

Finally, my friend Brucan explained that pastrami was a Romanian Jewish delicacy that had disappeared with the destruction of the Jewish community during the war. Romania had been allied with Germany and had its own fascist Iron Guard regime. To ask for pastrami now was taken by waiters as a rebuke for what had happened to the Jewish population.

After much negotiation, a first-ever filmed interview was arranged with Romania's dictator, Gheorghe Gheorghiu-Dej. I told him he was the fourth Communist leader I had interviewed after Nikita Khrushchev, Wladyslaw Gomulka of Poland, and Walter Ulbricht of East Germany. Ruefully, he remarked that he understood that Khrushchev was very good on television. The interview turned out to be one string of clichés. When we finished, the dreaded dictator put a friendly arm on my shoulder and said, "I hope you will not unleash any sensations as a result of our talk." I told him he need not fear.

Neither in Romania nor Czechoslovakia was it easy to interview unofficial people. Our biggest coup in Romania was making contact with a group of young dissidents, one of them, an artist, painting in a forbidden abstract style. His paintings were all in gleaming enamel because the only paint he had was Duco stolen from the auto assembly plant where he worked.

This, in the midsixties, was the stuff of high adventure, exploring seldom-seen countries under Communist control, feeling the first tremors of the forces that would, twenty years later, shake the Soviet empire. As expected, "Satellites out of Orbit" caused some commotion in both capitals. I was thereafter barred from Czechoslovakia as I had been barred from Hungary in 1961 after doing a program commemorating the fifth anniversary of the suppression of the anticommunist revolution, including a sequence in a Budapest cemetery where family members laid flowers on the graves of some of the victims of the Soviet tanks.

I was also persona non grata in Romania for four years—until assigned to cover the visit in 1969 of President Nixon. This was the first state visit of an American president to a Communist satellite country, and he was elated by the large crowds turned out by the new dictator, President Nicolae Ceausescu. Several hundred Chinese students in Bucharest were taken out of town for fear that they would demonstrate against the "imperialist" from America. This was ironic because, through Ceausescu, Nixon sent what was probably the first message to Mao Tse-tung that eventuated in the "breakthrough" to China in 1972. Ceausescu apparently also helped to pave the way with North Vietnam for the Kissinger secret negotiations in Paris that started in August 1969.

In Germany, my last big project was a *CBS Reports* documentary on Adenauer and his era. It was called "Germany after Hitler—Adenauer Sums Up." It was produced by the talented Bill McClure, who had worked with me on several documentaries, including Romania-Czechoslovakia.

The eighty-nine-year-old retired chancellor sat before the hot lights for eight hours of filmed interviews spread over five months. I knew that he hated bright lights. Once, on a visit to Japan, he had created consternation by walking out of a live telecast, returning only when the lights were dimmed.

"When are you people going to invent cold lights?" he asked me. But, once started, he was patient and cooperative, saying, "Now that we are doing this, let us do it right."

The result was a unique documentary about a municipal official in Cologne who had emerged after the war to create a party, found the West German state, and lead it, rearmed, into the North Atlantic alliance and the European Common Market. He made no apologies for loving the exercise of power, expressing contempt for those who had failed to act to stop the Nazi takeover.

"If those who had power in their hands had used it, there would have been no Hitler regime," he said.

He had no problem taking credit for the German comeback. "I did not do it alone, but I did contribute much," he said. But he was also willing to take some of the blame for German materialism. "We would ask the voters, 'Do you want a new sofa or a good book?' And when the voter chose the sofa, he got it."

Of the three American presidents he had known, the one who had won his greatest respect was Truman, "who will rank in history as one of your greatest presidents." As to Kennedy, he acknowledged a generational strain, saying that only in their second meeting, in two long sessions in November 1961, did they make contact. "The conversations were so personal in nature that we had the interpreters tear up the notes," said the old man.

As we stood beside his rose garden in Rhoendorf, looking across the Rhine, he told me how, in the last days of the war, he had just missed being killed by the advancing Americans. He pointed to where he had seen American soldiers reach an intact bridge at Remagen. "The Americans, across the Rhine, saw me and fired at me. I realized the shell was coming at me and threw myself flat on the ground."

Adenauer's vividly told and fervently believed story of outracing a mortar shell turned out to be the hit of the program when shown in Germany, producing great hilarity. But Der Alte still insisted it was true when I, preparing to leave Germany for a new Washington assignment, visited him to say farewell.

My final farewell came a year later. Adenauer died on April 19, 1967, at the age of ninety-one. His last reported words were *"Kein Grund zu weinen."* (No reason for tears.) His death found me in my new role of domestic correspondent, covering a United Auto Workers convention in Detroit. Orders came from my bosses to drop the convention and fly to Cologne for Adenauer's funeral.

With the presence of Presidents Johnson and de Gaulle and other world dignitaries, most of whom had last seen each other at the Kennedy funeral, CBS elected to cover the ceremonies live—one of those ad-lib situations where a knowledge of faces and history came in handy.

I noted the contrast between Kennedy, cut off in his youth, and Adenauer, who had outlived his era. I said, "Der Alte—the Old Man—ruled with an iron hand, not even permitting his ministers to smoke at cabinet meetings. If Bismarck gave Germany a Prussian accent, Adenauer provided the accent of the Rhineland. He enjoyed Rhenish wines and a Rhineland capital for West Germany."

My six years in Germany had all been tied up with him, and perhaps I yielded a little to sentiment when I said, "You will not see much grief here. But there is no reason for grief. These prosperous Germans have come to do honor to the father of postwar Germany."

CHAPTER 10

GOING HOME

Let me back up a bit and tell how it was that, after twenty years, I hung up my foreign correspondent's trench coat and came home—a professional and personal watershed in my life.

By October 1965, the German situation was quiet enough to allow me to range widely to cover stories in Athens, Budapest, Vienna, and Yugoslavia. I could also take time from my post for an extensive and lucrative coast-to-coast U.S. lecture tour, covering ten cities in less than two weeks. I could also go on vacation to São Paulo, Brazil, where the foreign service woman with whom I had conducted a decade-long love affair in Moscow, Warsaw, Berlin, Munich, and Budapest was stationed, for the first time, out of my European territory.

It did not go unnoticed by my bosses that things had quieted down in Germany and Central Europe. And so, in a meeting in New York, Fred Friendly said it was time to come back to the United States, where something like a revolution was going on. He proposed an assignment as New York correspondent, covering "everything from Carnegie Hall to Wall Street." While agreeing that it was time to come home, I said I would prefer Washington to New York.

"Why not New York?" Fred asked.

"Because I had an unhappy childhood in New York and don't like it very much. And, frankly, I have always enjoyed keeping some distance between my boss and myself."

Friendly finally agreed that I would return to Washington, where my CBS career had started in 1953 as State Department correspondent. But he made clear that the diplomatic beat (capably covered by my friend Marvin Kalb) was not open. I perceived that I would be putting behind my twenty years of foreign experience and plunging into the turbulent domestic arena. We agreed that I would have a few months to wind up affairs in Germany, and then I would make the move to Washington.

But first, Friendly had a request to make—that I fly to Rhodesia to spell the correspondent covering the crisis over Prime Minister Ian Smith's effort to perpetuate white rule. The correspondent, whose name I no longer remember, wanted to come home for Christmas. I agreed, unenthusiastically, to the two-week assignment on a continent I had until then successfully avoided.

Before going, I would need to replenish three ulcer medications. The pharmacist in the CBS building said he would be glad to oblige, but required prescriptions. Having no physician in New York, I asked Nathan Bienstock, my agent, to recommend one and soon found myself in the office of Dr. Aronson on Fifty-seventh Street. He said he could not prescribe without a physical examination, including an X ray. Grumbling about medical red tape, I submitted to the examination and then paced the waiting room, muttering about what one had to go through just to get refills for a few medications.

Eventually Dr. Aronson emerged, bearing the X ray pictures. I had told him I was planning to leave for Africa the next day. He said, "I see an ulcer about to perforate, and I would suggest you not go to Rhodesia, but to the hospital for a possible operation."

Next day I was in New York Hospital near the East River as an emergency patient. After a second opinion, on December 16, 1965, I underwent a "subtotal gastrectomy." That meant excising about two-thirds of my stomach and ridding me of my ulcer.

As I progressed from intravenous feeding to liquid by mouth to solids by mouth, I began to perceive how the ulcer had dominated my life, sometimes subconsciously. It had made me often irritable. During ulcer attacks I had contrived to avoid assignments involving travel. At times I would cancel appointments with last-minute excuses that must have appeared strange. Often I had felt a malaise that simply robbed me of initiative—or drove me into initiatives to take my mind off the ulcer. The ulcer had also profoundly affected my social life. I found myself tending to delay making social engagements until I was reasonably sure I would not have an ulcer attack. I was fully aware that a woman did not appreciate being called on a few hours' notice to be asked if she was free for dinner.

Now, with a new sense of being able to plan ahead, I looked forward to meeting Bill Small to discuss my Washington assignment. I was recuperating at the home of my brother and sister-in-law, Alvin and Ann, in suburban Alexandria, Virginia. Together we watched President Johnson's State of the Union address on January 12, 1966. Alvin, who worked for the new federal antipoverty agency, noted that the CBS correspondents, in their "instant analysis" of the speech, all said, one way or another, that they could find nothing new on Vietnam policy in the president's address. None of them dealt with the news in the speech, which was all on the domestic side.

Johnson made a ringing pledge to pursue the building of a Great Society, to wage "our war on poverty," to rebuild slum areas, enforce civil rights, and prohibit housing discrimination. He unveiled two initiatives—a new cabinet Department of Transportation and a proposal to extend the term of representatives to four years, "concurrent with the president."

Perceiving the gap in CBS's coverage helped me to decide what I would propose as my Washington assignment. When I met three days later with Bill Small, he was quick to point out that all the "regular" posts were filled—Dan Rather at the White House, Roger Mudd on Capitol Hill, Marvin Kalb at the State Department, and Bob Schieffer at the Pentagon. I said that I was aware of that, and I was volunteering to cover some of the less glamorous and undercovered areas—Health, Education and Welfare; Housing and Urban Development; the newly created Transportation Department; plus the environment and civil rights—indeed everything that the president included in his Great Society.

Clearly relieved that I was not seeking to replace one of his stars, Small said he doubted that I would get on television very often with these "soft subjects," but agreed to let me try. Once again, although now a CBS correspondent for more than twelve years, I felt I was having to prove myself.

But first, in February 1966, back to Bonn to wind up my European assignment, with farewell visits to some of the countries in my "domain." In Hungary I reported on the long-overdue departure of Jozef Cardinal Mindszenty, the staunch anticommunist who had taken refuge in the American legation during the 1956 revolution and had refused to budge for ten years. Legation officials had regaled me with stories of the cardinal, stalking the halls by night, poring over books and documents to improve his English, leaving cigar butts on the officers' desks.

I went to Amsterdam to cover the marriage of Crown Princess Beatrix to a German diplomat whom I had known in Bonn, Claus von Amsberg. Amsterdammers, furious over the marriage of the future queen to a German army veteran and onetime member of the Hitler Youth, marred the wedding procession with demonstrations.

On a trip to Warsaw, I managed permission to film one of the odd periodic meetings of the Chinese and American ambassadors that had been going on for ten years in a Polish palace. Ambassador John Gronouski told me that these meetings, the only official contact between two adversary governments, featured stiff formal statements of position and apparently accomplished nothing. But, in these days before Ping-Pong diplomacy, Washington and Beijing found some reason to maintain this contact, and the Polish government enjoyed playing host.

As I learned on that trip, Poland had also tried to broker a cease-fire in the Vietnam War. In January, Ambassador Averell Harriman had flown to Warsaw on a secret mission for President Johnson to arrange for a Polish envoy to fly to Hanoi to sound out possibilities for a truce preliminary to peace negotiations.

The envoy was Jerzy Michalowski, a senior diplomat with good Chinese connections—and a friend of mine from the days when we had both served at the United Nations. Stopping first in Moscow and Beijing to get concurrence with his mission, Michalowski had then flown on to Hanoi for three weeks of talks with Ho Chi Minh and other officials—in vain. The North Vietnamese made clear that they had no intention of giving up at the conference table what they thought they were winning in the field. Shortly after Michalowski's return to Warsaw, President Johnson ordered resumption of bombing of North Vietnam. Nothing of the Polish mediation effort had been known before I reported it.

(Ironically, as though to show that no good deed goes unpunished, in April the Polish government protested to Ambassador Gronouski that a Polish motor ship had been damaged in an American bombing raid on Haiphong harbor.)

In April came my last story from Berlin. An advanced Soviet MiG-19 jet fighter had crashed in flames into the Havel River in the British sector. Standing up to the rage of the Soviet command, the British insisted on salvaging—and inspecting—the wreckage before allowing the Russians to take possession. Four busloads of Soviet troops, commanded by a general, were turned back by the intrepid British in the weeklong standoff.

This Berlin trip also allowed me to do a long-planned film report on Spandau prison, where seven of the Nazi war criminals sentenced in the Nuremberg trials served their terms. Only three now remained—Rudolf Hess, Hitler's deputy, serving a life sentence; and Baldur von Schirach, head of the Hitler Youth, and Albert Speer, Hitler's armaments chief, both serving twenty-year terms.

The four powers rotated each month in guarding the prison. The day I was there, the Russians were taking their turn. The Western powers had, for many months, sought to have Spandau closed as an unnecessary expense and to transfer the remaining three inmates to other prisons. But, for the Russians, Spandau represented a toehold in West Berlin that they would not give up.

I asked the Russians, in vain, to let me interview the prisoners. From outside the prison, we could see the guards, but little of the prisoners. I learned from American sources that Hess, famous for his zany flight to England during the war, was now, at seventy-one, emotionally unstable, groaning in his cell and expressing fears of attempts to poison him.

My last visit to Frankfurt, on April 20, was to report on the first Jewish school to be opened in Germany since Hitler. Under the new Germany's antidiscrimination laws, the school, connected with the Frankfurt synagogue, was not allowed to bar non-Jewish pupils. So, two of the thirty children I heard singing a Hebrew song were Christians, whose parents wanted to make a gesture of reconciliation.

My departure from Germany was attended by some of the same sense of weirdness that had attended my arrival six years earlier, when a petty bureaucrat had turned frantic at my effort to borrow his newspaper. I was invited to lunch by an official of the Government Information Service, Baron von Schweinitz, who said he was on a delicate mission. He said that my work in Germany—especially the East German and Adenauer documentaries—had been much appreciated and that I was in line for a presidential decoration. However, the government had recently had an unpleasant experience with someone who had publicly rejected a German honor. So, the baron's task was to ascertain whether I would accept a decoration if offered. He was aware, he said, that some (he did not mention Jews) had qualms about being honored by Germany.

I replied that I found the question weird. I had one other foreign decoration—from the queen of the Netherlands—and the question of whether I would accept it had never come up.

"Isn't it time," I asked, "that this prosperous, democratic Germany begin acting like a normal country? You act normally, and so will I."

"Can I take that as a positive response?" he asked.

"You'll have to figure it out for yourself."

In the next few days an article by me appeared in the liberal Munich newspaper *Süd-Deutsche Zeitung*, which had asked me to sum up my impressions of Germany after six years. Along with admiration for the economic comeback and burgeoning democracy, the article expressed my reservations about the Germans.

I pulled no punches, saying that I had friendly professional relations with Germans, but had made few German friends. I quoted Chancellor Erhard saying that, for Germany, "the postwar era is over" and commented that he was premature, that "the past is everywhere in Germany," often expressed in silence. I wrote that Germany had not yet succeeded in becoming "a nation like other nations." It had foresworn nuclear arms. It had put its army under NATO command because it didn't trust itself.

The day after the article appeared I was a guest at a long-scheduled farewell luncheon given by Günther von Hase, director of the Government Information Service. My assistant, Frau Schultz, told me that I could expect to learn at this lunch of the decoration being conferred on me. After wine and champagne, von Hase rose for a lengthy toast to my journalistic accomplishments and presented me with a hand-tooled leather box. In that box I found no medal, but a silver ashtray with a German coin at its center.

Returning to my office, I found Frau Schultz excitedly waiting to hear of the medal presentation. When I showed her the ashtray, she was nonplussed. "Such a thing has never happened before. Perhaps some technical problem in getting all the necessary clearances. I cannot imagine that there would be a political problem."

At a dinner that night, I was seated with Jürgen Rufhüs, head of the Foreign Ministry Press Department (later to become ambassador to Washington). I told him of the mystery of the vanishing decoration, and he offered, with great gusto, to explain. (The Government Information Service and Foreign Ministry Press Department were frequently at sword's point.)

"It was all settled," he said, "and then your article in the *Süd-Deutsche* appeared—some people in the federal chancery took exception. The bureaucrats would rather cancel your decoration than risk being criticized themselves. Enjoy your ashtray!"

Next morning I was having breakfast with Konrad Ahlers, an editor of the widely circulated newsmagazine *Der Spiegel*, which was generally critical of the government. He found my story hilarious and promptly phoned his office in Hamburg to insert a fat paragraph in the personalities column.

Almost as soon as the magazine hit the stands, I had a telephone call from an anguished-sounding Günther von Hase.

"My dear Dan! There has been a terrible mix-up. Of course you will receive your well-merited decoration. I didn't mention it at lunch only because there were a few formalities to complete. It will not be ready before you leave Germany, but it will be presented to you in Washington."

I put down the phone, shaking my head at this latest evidence of a neurotic bureaucracy, veering back and forth as it strained to do the "correct" thing.

The saga of the medal was far from over. At the end of April I packed up and flew to Washington, putting my furniture in storage. In Washington, I took up quarters in the comfortable Jefferson Hotel while prospecting for permanent lodgings. Eventually, prodded by my sister-in-law, who had determined that it was time for me to settle down, I bought a newly built house on R Street in the Georgetown area, planning to move in over the July Fourth weekend.

The intended bachelor pad was not destined long so to remain. On June 20, at a dinner party at the Georgetown home of Rep. James Scheuer (Dem., N.Y.), I met an attractive young woman, Lisbeth Bamberger. She was poised and knowledgeable. She worked on health ventures for the poor in the Office of Economic Opportunity, which, as I brightly observed, put her on my beat. By Independence Day, when I moved into my new digs, we had dated. Ulcer-free, I found myself able to pursue a promising romance.

One Saturday evening, we were dining at my home (a meal prepared by Li, an excellent cook among other attributes) when a telephone call came from the West German embassy—a surprising time for a diplomatic call, suggesting some degree of urgency.

The counselor brought breathless word that the decoration, which I had by now forgotten, was being brought to Washington the following week by Chancellor Ludwig Erhard. The plan was that, before a White House dinner, to which I was also invited, there would be a presentation ceremony by the chancellor himself at the Blair House guest residence.

As the diplomat rattled on excitedly, Li began shaking her head vigorously, whispering, "No German medals!" Caught between the woman I love, a German refugee with some bitter memories whose father had spent a month in Dachau, and my implied promise not to turn down a German decoration, I desperately tried to figure a way out. I heard the counselor explain that the medal was the Cross of Merit, First Class. He went on to say that, alas, it was not the Grand Cross, which the embassy had recommended.

"Very unfortunate," I lied. "CBS does not allow its correspondents to accept inferior awards. Please advise Bonn I was honored to be considered, but I cannot accept the award. No hard feelings."

The diplomat, sounding shattered, said he would transmit my message to Bonn. I put down the phone, asking Li to admire my finesse.

Next morning, early, the German embassy was on the line again. "Very good news, Mr. Schorr. The government has reconsidered and decided to award you the Grand Cross of Merit. So the chancellor looks forward to seeing you on Tuesday, September twenty-sixth, at seven P.M. at Blair House. Black tie, of course, since you will be proceeding directly to the White House. There will be champagne."

Perhaps I should have guessed that the Germans would take a rejection as pressure for a concession. It had not occurred to me that a powerful government would cave so abjectly.

In any event, Li agreed that I had no way out, and she would make her peace with my presence on the German honors list.

On September 26, I was working on a complicated story for the Cronkite show. President Johnson's bill to continue the war on poverty for a third year was stalled in Congress. Rep. Adam Clayton Powell Jr., chairman of the House Education and Labor Committee, was, in effect, holding the bill hostage to fend off an investigation of him for corruption. As luck would have it, late developments obliged me to update the story for the "second feed" of the *Evening News*. That left me with no time, after changing into formal clothes, to get to Blair House before the White House dinner.

The decoration jinx had reared its head again. I called Blair House with apologies. The German who took my call said, "A great shame. We have already uncorked the champagne."

I made my apologies again to Chancellor Erhard as he stood in the receiving line with President Johnson. The president was curious to know what we were talking about in German.

To the president's great amusement, I explained that, working on his antipoverty bill, I had missed a Blair House reception to present me with a German honor. The chancellor seemed not quite ready to accept my apology. "It would have given me great pleasure had it been possible for me to make this presentation to you." The German subjunctive has many uses.

In May, I was invited to the West German embassy for a luncheon, and the gaudy enamel cross, pendant from a broad red-and-black ribbon, was draped around my neck.

Since then I have worn the rather ostentatious medal in public only once. It was at the 1982 dinner of the Gridiron Club, a white-tie affair calling for "full decorations." The cross dangling from my neck proved to be so eye-catching that it brought Vice President Bush clear across a crowded reception to ask what was this handsome thing I was wearing. I explained. Then he turned to his wife and, in somewhat plaintive tones, asked, "Barbara, why don't I have any of those?"

To break the embarrassed silence that ensued, I said I thought I remembered something in the Constitution that forbade federal officials to accept foreign decorations. He said he was not aware of that, and I promised to look it up.

To my great relief, my memory turned out to be correct, and the next day I sent the vice president, who might have been expected to know the Constitution he had sworn to uphold, an excerpt from Article I, Section 9, which forbids officers of the United States to accept "any present, Emolument, Office, or Title, of any kind whatever, from any King, Prince, or foreign State."

The vice president's handwritten acknowledgment thanked me profusely and said that knowing of the prohibition had eased his mind.

CHAPTER 11

THE NOT SO
GREAT SOCIETY

My first years back in Washington moved swiftly, in both personal and professional terms. Not long after meeting Li Bamberger on June 20, 1966, I felt my long-standing aversion to commitment crumbling. First, we had to overcome my maladroitness.

At the dinner at the Scheuers' home, I had asked Li if she would be free for lunch sometime. She responded that because of the press of business at the Office of Economic Opportunity, the antipoverty agency, in the last days of the fiscal year, she was not going out to lunch. Showing I knew when the fiscal year ended, I asked if she would be free on July 1. A few days later it dawned on me that on July 1 I would have to be in Baltimore reporting on the launching of Medicare. I called to ask whether she could change our appointment to dinner.

A day later, I realized that on the evening of July 1 my mother would be arriving from New York to stay with my brother in Alexandria, and I was expected there for dinner. In some embarrassment, I called Li again to ask if she minded going to dinner at my brother's home—and meeting my mother on our first date. She was a great sport about my confusion, which, she said, had caused multiple visits to the dressmaker, to change a hemline with each change in venue.

No thanks to me, the relationship survived and blossomed and we were married in January 1967. The wedding was in Li's rented house in Georgetown, a few blocks from my new house, conducted by a rabbi chosen by my mother because he was a good Zionist. At our wedding reception, my friend Abe Rosenthal of the *New York Times* approached my mother to say what a wonderful woman her son was marrying. She replied, "Believe me, Abe, I would have settled for a lot less." My mother's relief that her son was finally marrying at fifty was paralleled by the relief of Li's parents that their only daughter was finally marrying at thirty-five. (Both our brothers were long since married with children.)

We left next day for a honeymoon on the Caribbean island of Antigua. Nine months later, almost to the day, Jonathan was born, and two and a half years later, Lisa.

In 1970, when I wrote a book on health insurance, *Don't Get Sick in America*, based on research for a *CBS Reports* documentary, I observed that my first five years back in Washington had produced a series of firsts—a house of my own, a wife, a son, a daughter, a book.

Not bad!

In the CBS News building on M Street in Washington, I occupied one of a row of windowless cubicles looking out over the newsroom. The arrangement, I was told, was originally meant to allow cameras to wheel up so correspondents could report from their desks. To my knowledge, that never happened. Producers put considerable emphasis on doing "stand-ups" outdoors—anywhere outdoors—to add an element of activity to an otherwise static picture.

I found my jurisdiction broader than I had expected. It ranged from the introduction of mandatory seat belts in cars to antismoking and antialcoholism programs. I worked with the talented Los Angeles producer Jack Beck on an hour-long documentary, *The Poisoned Air,* which won a Peabody Award. Another documentary examined the menace of mercury in the water.

Having worked for most of the previous two decades abroad, I found myself plunged into what seemed like another foreign country—the turbulent America of the sixties. I had missed the all-too-short Kennedy era and the launching of President Johnson's broad program of social renewal.

I had missed most of the civil rights revolution and all the "long, hot summer" of 1965, the summer of urban riots that started in the Watts district of Los Angeles. I had missed the launching of the "war on poverty" and the escalation of American involvement in the war in Vietnam, which ended up with the one being shortchanged to wage the other.

I had a new language to learn—the language of fighting words such as *white backlash, black power,* and *forced busing.* There were new personalities to get to know—such as OEO director Sargent Shriver, who, as Peace Corps director, had tried to recruit me in Germany to teach journalism in Ethiopia. Joseph A. Califano, President Johnson's domestic affairs adviser, who briefed me on the programs the administration was trying to save from the budget ax. The Reverend Adam Clayton Powell, the flamboyant chairman of the House Education and Labor Committee, who greeted me as "the new cat from CBS," presumably a friendly appellation.

In an initial radio broadcast on May 19, 1966, I acknowledged feeling lost in "the land of VISTA, Head Start, CAP, and Medicare, all these uncharted on the map of America I had left behind in the Eisenhower days." (VISTA was the domestic Peace Corps program. Head Start, of which more later, was the innovative program for preschool children. CAP was the Community Action Program, which opened the door to activists such as Marion Barry, later to be mayor of Washington. I interviewed him about the rat extermination campaign being conducted by his community action group, called Pride.)

During the first week on my beat, I was asked to participate, with Roger Mudd and Harry Reasoner, in a television special titled "Vietnam and the Elections." This was an early effort to assess the impact of the war on the coming congressional elections. My segment included interviews with the vice president, Hubert Humphrey, who loyally defended the need for budgetary constraint, and Sen. Robert Kennedy, who charged that programs for the poor were being "stultified." This was a harbinger of the hawk-dove struggle that would soon rend the heart of America.

I found much of my time taken up with routine assignments from the newsdesk, covering congressional hearings and conferences that rarely produced airworthy stories. The chances of "making air" increased when legislators or witnesses raised their voices. My cameraman would automatically press the button when the decibel level mounted. Participants learned that, too, and often raised their voices when they weren't angry at all.

I realized that if I was to succeed in my assignment, I would have to go beyond the "pseudo-events" of hearings and news conferences and find the kind of concrete depiction of big issues that television demanded. When the *Washington Post* carried a searching series of stories on the scandal of Junior Village, a home where a thousand orphaned and homeless children were warehoused, often neglected, and sometimes abused, I asked for a producer to help survey the institution for a possible television feature. At Junior Village we found misery and children who clung to us, hungry for human contact.

Thanks to the *Washington Post* exposé, Junior Village was eventually closed down. But my producer said the executives in New York didn't see this as the kind of story the "show" wanted. I soon learned that executives in New York, reflecting the attitudes of upper-middle-class suburbanites, which they were, saw welfare abuse, but not welfare, overspending on poverty, but not the poor, as stories for television—unless political controversy was involved.

And so, when a stormy controversy developed about a Head Start project called Child Development Group Mississippi, serving fourteen thousand needy children, I got permission to fly down to Jackson with a camera crew to cover it. Sen. John Stennis and other Mississippi white legislators were denouncing the program as mismanaged and as promoting civil rights. They demanded reduced funding and state control. The parents, whose children received not only teaching, but health care and food, organized in public rallies to defend the autonomy of the CDGM program.

I faced the camera, standing among a couple of dozen children, and started my narration: "These preschool children are, luckily, too young to know about the controversy raging over their heads." Among those I interviewed was Mrs. Sarah Perry, head of the school, who until a year earlier had worked as a maid. My story made the low-rated CBS *Morning News*, at that the only television coverage the controversy got. In the end, the preschool centers were taken over by a board named by Gov. Paul Johnson. Sargent Shriver, married to Eunice Kennedy, sister of the late president, found his home in suburban Maryland picketed by Head Start supporters. He told me that the whole controversy had made him acutely uncomfortable.

As the Johnson administration, under congressional pressure, scaled back antipoverty programs, I sought to portray the impact on the poor. In New York City, poor people picketed the regional headquarters of the OEO. From Harlem I reported the squeeze on a program called HARYOU Act (Harlem Youth Action), which gave young people summer jobs and enlisted them in community action in the hope of turning them from rioters into social activists.

In an interview, Shriver said he was aware of the potentially explosive situation in New York. On camera, he threw up his hands and said, "I wish I had more to give."

In Mingo County, a pocket of white poverty in West Virginia, I reported how the poor were being affected by funding cutbacks. I filmed a community action meeting and reported, on camera, "Among the stolid people of Appalachia, tempers do not flare as they do in urban slums. But these people are worried as they see projects that employ them slow down or stall for lack of money."

At this point the antipoverty appropriation had been hung up in Congress for months. President Johnson staged a White House civil rights conference on June 2, 1966, and dropped in unannounced to say, "We will arouse hopes, as we already have done, and I came here tonight, at the end of a very long day, to tell you we shall not turn back."

But he could not tell them what they wanted to hear—that they would go forward. I had come home to America to witness the amazing phenomenon of the federal government reaching over the heads of states and cities for a concentrated attack on poverty with "maximum feasible participation" of the poor. What I was witnessing, instead, was the gradual demise of that program under the weight of mounting spending for the war.

In the midsixties, Sen. Robert F. Kennedy emerged as the champion of blacks and the poor. His message was that an uncompleted civil rights revolution had gained them the right to sit at a lunch counter, but not the wherewithal to pay for the meal.

I had first met Kennedy in 1954 when he served as assistant counsel to Sen. Joseph McCarthy's investigating subcommittee. I found him then intense, cold, and unfriendly—and "ruthless," the label many pinned on him.

It was a changed man I met ten years later. A year after his brother's assassination, the attorney general came to Berlin to dedicate City Hall square, where the president had delivered his historic *Ich bin ein Berliner* speech, at John F. Kennedyplatz. On a whirlwind day, with three set speeches, Kennedy found time to meet informally with a circle of students at the Free University, winning their hearts with a soft-spoken summons to service in the name of humanity.

After Berlin, off to Warsaw, where Kennedy, speaking about democracy and human rights from atop a car, wowed the Warsovians and made the Communist government edgy. The head of the American government seemed no less edgy about Kennedy's influence among Democrats. President Johnson told him he was out of contention for running mate in the 1964 election. The attorney general resigned, moved to New York, and ran successfully for senator.

By the time I arrived in Washington in 1966, Kennedy had already emerged as an advocate for minorities and the poor—and was thus a part of my beat. In March 1967, as a member of a Senate subcommittee on poverty, he and Chairman Joseph Clark held a series of hearings to dramatize the issue and then flew to Mississippi to look at the face of poverty.

Kennedy's legislative aide Peter Edelman flew down to Jackson to "advance" the subcommittee's trip. There he enlisted the assistance of

Marian Wright, a spirited young civil rights worker, who had testified at the Washington hearing. An associate of the Reverend Martin Luther King, she was the first black woman admitted to the Mississippi bar. Together, she and Peter surveyed poor communities. In the squalor of the Delta a romance was born.

They would marry in July 1968, almost an embodiment of that tragic year. Their wedding in Arlington, Virginia, was the first interracial marriage in that state after the Supreme Court struck down Virginia's antimiscegenation statute. In the preceding months the King aide and the Kennedy aide had both lost their principals to assassins' bullets. The wedding ceremony, under a blazing sun, mingled celebration with mourning. Former Supreme Court justice Arthur Goldberg, for whom Peter had clerked, defined the moment in Dickensian terms: "The best of times, the worst of times... the spring of hope, the winter of despair." And then, to put the blood-soaked American soil behind for a while, the couple took a honeymoon trip around the world on a grant from the Ford Foundation.

But, in the spring of 1967, Senator Kennedy came close to the black people of rural Mississippi for whom it was always the worst of times. I followed him with a cameraman as he entered hovels where roaches scurried across the dirt floor. I saw the senator pick up a little boy and stroke his stomach, distended by malnutrition.

Kennedy went from shack to shack, shaking his head and muttering, "This is unacceptable... simply unacceptable." At one point I thought he was close to tears.

That summer the urban ghettos, including Newark and Harlem, saw new riots. Kennedy's concern for the poor began to take political shape. On NBC's *Meet the Press* he said, "If we can spend twenty-four billion dollars for the freedom of the people of Vietnam, certainly we can spend a small portion of that for the liberty and freedom and future of our own people in the United States."

That sounded like a slap at President Johnson for diverting money from urgent domestic requirements to the prosecution of the war. Speculation started that Kennedy, denied a place on the Johnson ticket, might end up running against him.

The tumultuous year 1968 started with a sense of domestic programs cracking under the strain of the Vietnam War. President Johnson made a secret deal with Rep. Wilbur Mills, chairman of the
tax-writing House Ways and Means Committee, trading support of
the war tax that Johnson wanted for a welfare crackdown that Mills
wanted. Over the New Year's weekend, John Gardner, Secretary of
Health, Education, and Welfare, flew down to the LBJ ranch to
make a last-ditch plea to the president not to sign the welfare bill, or
at least to accompany it with a statement expressing reservations
and promising to revisit the question.

In the end, Johnson said he could not afford to antagonize Mills.
Gardner abruptly left the ranch, not waiting for the signing of the
omnibus Social Security package, and flew back to Washington. All
this I learned the same night, and next morning, January 3, I
reported the clash on the CBS *Morning News* as a sign that the "guns
vs. butter" issue was splitting not only the Democratic Party, but the
Johnson administration.

Mills later told me with some amusement that Johnson had
called him, agitated, at his Arkansas home, swearing he had no idea
how the incident had leaked. Mills said, "I'm not sure I believed him,
but I don't know why he was so upset. It didn't bother me any."

Two weeks later, Gardner, a Republican, resigned from the Johnson cabinet. At a dinner party some time later at the home of Dou-
glass Cater, a Johnson assistant, Doug attacked me before the
assembled guests for having "provoked" Gardner's resignation. When
I repeated that to the soft-voiced, philosophical Gardner, he shook
his head.

"That only shows," he said, "how little they understood about
what was at issue in the cutbacks on social programs."

In signing the welfare restrictions, President Johnson had called
them "severe"—his only concession to Secretary Gardner. The bill
provided for forcing welfare recipients into work or training and
freezing the total number of welfare recipients eligible for federal
assistance. It was a harbinger of a more far-reaching welfare crackdown to come thirty years later in the Clinton administration.

Sen. Robert Kennedy led twenty liberals in a move to repeal the welfare crackdown. On January 30, the day before the formal introduction of the bill, I arranged an on-camera interview with Kennedy in his office. The interview completed, I called the CBS newsdesk. News editor Bill Galbraith told me that the news wires were featuring a statement that Kennedy had made that morning at a press breakfast: "I have told my friends and supporters that I would not oppose President Johnson [for reelection] under any foreseeable circumstances."

Since speculation was rife about Kennedy's intentions in view of his split with Johnson over poverty and the war, this was a pretty big story. Galbraith asked me to have the senator repeat his statement on camera. I told our camera crew to stand by while I went into Kennedy's office to make the request. The senator shook his head and said, "No!"

I said, "Senator, I don't think you understand. I'm only asking you to say on camera what you have said on the record."

"I know," he said with a half smile. "The answer is still no."

On the air that night I reported Kennedy's strange refusal to say on camera what he had already said to the press. I concluded, "Senator Kennedy, it seems, is committed to support President Johnson— but he is not committed in his own voice."

Years later Peter Edelman provided me with the solution to the puzzle. Between the press breakfast and my afternoon interview, word had come of the surprise Tet offensive in Vietnam, threatening America with a disaster. In those few hours, Kennedy had already begun to change his mind about not challenging Johnson. It would take six more weeks, and the emergence of Sen. Eugene McCarthy in the New Hampshire primary as an antiwar candidate, before Kennedy entered the race on March 16. Johnson stunningly withdrew from the race two weeks later.

Early in February, Martin Luther King came to Washington, determined, against the advice of some of his supporters, to unite the civil rights movement with the antiwar movement. On what would be his last visit to Washington, he taught me a lesson about the interaction of television and racial violence.

Having led two thousand antiwar clergymen and laity in a silent dedication at Arlington National Cemetery, having denounced the United States as the world's "greatest purveyor of violence," Dr. King held a news conference to announce a "spring mobilization," a poor people's march on Washington. It would continue indefinitely until the government met the needs of the poor. He said the demonstration would start quietly and then escalate into forms of civil disobedience.

In concert with my network colleagues, I plied Dr. King with questions about whether bridges would be blocked, whether government buildings would be occupied, whether there might be disruptive demonstrations, clashes with the police. We, of course, were looking for that one menacing sound bite that would get the story on the evening news.

The news conference over, I waited for my camera crew to pack up. Dr. King sat alone at the dais, looking morose. I approached him to ask whether he was having a problem. He said, yes, he was, and that I was part of it.

He asked if I was aware that our incessant efforts to elicit violent-sounding statements from Negro spokesmen were having the effect of selecting the most irresponsible "burn, baby, burn" agitators as leaders of the black community. He said it was becoming increasingly difficult for the advocates of nonviolence to make themselves heard.

"And when Negroes are incited to violence," he concluded, "will you think of your responsibility in helping to produce it?"

I listened without comment, recognizing the truth of what he said, and finally I said something like "I guess I see what you mean."

I thought back to my interview with radical-sounding Stokely Carmichael in his storefront office. I thought back to the many congressional hearings on ghettos and poverty I had covered where proposals for a "Marshall Plan for the cities" never made it on the air, but only warnings of "a long, hot summer."

My report on Dr. King's news conference that evening closed with these words: "He still espouses nonviolence, but, seeking to meet the current mood of the Negroes, he appears to be pressing nonviolence to its outer limits."

It was the best I could do in making the exponent of nonviolence seem like a militant. Did I go on seeking menacing sound bites as my passport to the evening news? I'm afraid I did.

That was Dr. King's last visit to Washington. On April 4, Walter Cronkite was originating the evening news from our Washington newsroom. After the "first feed" had ended at 7 P.M., Cronkite remained on hand, as usual, in case a news break required an update of the program for other time zones. As we sat around chatting, word came of the shooting in Memphis, followed quickly by word that Dr. King was dead on arrival at the hospital.

With smooth professionalism Cronkite donned his jacket, combed his hair, and touched up his makeup while an editor rewrote news bulletins and fed them into Cronkite's TelePrompTer. I began gathering reactions. President Johnson canceled his appearance at a fund-raiser and made a statement from the White House, appealing for calm. But rioting and looting erupted in central Washington. I volunteered to go to Fourteenth and U Streets, the center of the rampage, but bureau chief Bill Small said, "You stay here—you're too old for this kind of thing." (I was only fifty-one.)

In Washington, politics transcends mourning. That awful night was not yet over before reporters began assessing the impact on the presidential race. A ranking Democrat said that, with the expected white backlash against ghetto violence, "Kennedy is finished." A politician close to Vice President Humphrey, who had not announced yet, thought his chances were improved.

Johnson, having led the nation in mourning, returned to the Oval Office, where his aide Joseph Califano, as he later told me, reported to him rumors that Negroes were massing to march on Georgetown, home of the upscale Washington establishment.

Johnson rubbed his hands and chortled, "I been waitin' a long time for this day."

A month earlier, the bipartisan commission headed by Gov. Otto Kerner of Illinois, which the president had named to investigate the causes and prevention of riots, had returned with a hard-hitting report warning that America was being divided into two societies. It urged a program of unprecedented dimensions to overcome segregation and discrimination.

The recommendations in the fourteen-hundred-page report look today like a museum piece: federal grants to bring welfare payments up to subsistence levels, federally subsidized insurance for ghetto enterprises, bonuses to integrated schools, and hiring ghetto youngsters as uniformed police aides.

President Johnson considered convoking a joint session of Congress to launch a new and enlarged poverty program. But with "backlash" in the air, he scrapped the idea. Antipoverty director Sargent Shriver, seeing the handwriting on the wall, resigned to become ambassador to France.

The Poor People's March, postponed after the King assassination from April to May, went ahead, mule carts arriving in Washington and camping in the shadow of the Lincoln Memorial. Without the inspiration of its leader, the demonstration turned into an abysmal disaster. Some three thousand blacks, Chicanos, and a few symbolic Native Americans installed themselves in a plywood-and-canvas shantytown called Resurrection City, with the Reverend Jesse Jackson as "mayor." Unseasonably heavy rains turned the community into a sea of mud.

The Reverend Ralph Abernathy, Dr. King's successor, surreptitiously went off every night to the comfort of a hotel. Day after day, I turned up, in boots, with camera crew, trying to chronicle the misery that attracted little interest from television, now fascinated by "white backlash."

The leaders thought up stunts to attract attention. They demonstrated outside government buildings. Jackson led them to the Agriculture Department cafeteria for lunch and refused to pay the bill. "Guerrilla theater," he called it, but there was not much audience.

The assassination of Robert Kennedy took whatever heart was left out of the Poor People's campaign. More than any other white politician he had come to be the voice of the disinherited. Before he could taste the fruit of his California primary victory, he was gunned down in that Los Angeles hotel.

Robert Kennedy had been fatalistic about death ever since the assassination of his brother five years earlier. As his biographer, Evan Thomas, told it, he instructed an aide not to close the blinds in his hotel roon, saying, "Don't close them. If they're going to shoot, they'll shoot." As Attorney General he had been in charge of a task force plotting to eliminate Cuba's Fidel Castro. When President Kennedy was shot by a Castro supporter, Robert had reason to wonder if he had played any part in his brother's death.

On that June 5, I was assigned to stay up all night at the CBS office in what was literally a death watch. Word came about 8 A.M. The CBS *Morning News* was preempted, and with colleagues, I went on the air to report what we knew and to reminisce about Kennedy.

Then I moved to Resurrection City and reported what I was being told by grieving and angry poor blacks—that to take from them both Martin Luther King and Robert Kennedy within a few months meant that this had to be a conspiracy. One of my bosses admonished me for using "irresponsible" language on the air.

Resurrection City now had a new newsworthiness. Conceived by the slain Dr. King, it lay in the shadow of the memorial for the slain Abraham Lincoln, and it would be the last landmark in Washington that the slain Robert Kennedy would pass as his cortege moved over the Memorial Bridge to join his slain brother in the Arlington National Cemetery.

The time had come for the Poor People's campaign to look for a dignified exit. Jesse Jackson negotiated that in secret with Roger Wilkins, head of community relations in the Justice Department. Several hundred poor people, led by Jackson, shuffled up Constitution Avenue, chanting, "I am somebody." Arriving on Capitol Hill, they were met, as planned, by police, who advised on bullhorns that this was an unlicensed demonstration. Quietly, they submitted to arrest by the dozens, our cameras on hand to film them as they went off in paddy wagons—to be released a few blocks away, out of camera range.

Disaster though it was, the march served as a training school for those like Jesse Jackson, who went on to organize antidiscrimination boycotts in Chicago. Marian Wright had been research director, bringing a note of factual reality to this quixotic movement. Having learned that middle-class America didn't care much about poverty, she went on to organize the Children's Defense Fund on the premise that what helps children in general will help poor children disproportionately.

Years later President Ronald Reagan would dismissively say, "We fought a war against poverty and poverty won." I believe that the war on poverty ended not in defeat, but in surrender, a casualty of the Vietnam War and the white backlash.

CHAPTER 12

THE YEAR OF PARENTHOOD AND POLITICS

At 9:12 A.M. on October 6, 1967, at George Washington University Hospital, Li gave birth, by cesarean section, to a boy weighing seven pounds seven and a half ounces, measuring nineteen inches. We had not agreed on a name in advance and eventually chose Jonathan Louis (Louis for the father whom I had barely known).

I remember the circumcision as one of the rare occasions when I experienced another's pain as though it were mine. Li, who had resigned from the OEO to become a full-time mother, sheltered me from most of the trials and chores of parenthood, but I quickly became aware that life at our house on R Street would no longer revolve exclusively around me.

Washington being the kind of town it is, fatherhood at fifty-one was more than a private event. I was called upon to write an essay for radio about the unusual experience. In my essay I noted that this was the third time in three years that I had had occasion to wear a surgical gown, in a baby ward.

The other two times were television-mandated. In Budapest in 1965, I faced a CBS camera in a maternity ward to report on the disastrous drop in the Hungarian birth rate since the 1956 Soviet invasion. Fifty percent more abortions than live births reflected deepening pessimism. In 1966, in Washington, I reported from Columbia Women's Hospital on America's declining birth rate—at 18.5 per thousand, the lowest since 1936.

But in October 1967, it was different when I donned a gown to visit my infant son. Lots of babies were around, but only one interested me.

Washington being the kind of town it is, amid the office congratulations and cigar distribution, I can remember Eric Sevareid, the gloomy dean of CBS, stalking into my office with his own take on fatherhood.

"You understand," he intoned, "that when your son is ten, you will be sixty-one, and when he asks to play baseball, you will probably be too decrepit. I hope that you have considered that."

No, I hadn't, but I stored away Eric's collegial admonition, and on Jonathan's tenth birthday, I took him to the neighborhood softball game. Neither of us enjoyed it very much, and by common consent, we departed to the neighborhood tennis court.

Washington being the kind of town it is, I was able to take Jonathan, as a two-month-old infant, with his mother to Miami Beach on one of my assignments. I was covering the biennial convention of the AFL-CIO. Li had worked for the federation before going into government and had many friends in the labor movement, ready to do the requisite oohs and aahs over our son.

Jonathan spent much time with his mother on the beach (part of the time in a laundry hamper improvised as a shelter from a strong wind) while I listened to a parade of cabinet members, coming to do obeisance to federation president George Meany, sturdy supporter of the Johnson administration. Gaveling down minority opposition to the Vietnam War, Meany rammed through a resolution of all-out support for the administration. At the end, President Johnson himself appeared, basking in a reception about as warm as he could probably get from any assembly in America in this time of polarization over Vietnam.

Years later I explained to a totally unimpressed Jonathan how close he had been to history in the making at the age of two months.

Washington being the kind of town it is, a few days after his birth, a letter addressed to Jonathan arrived from Vice President Humphrey. It welcomed him as "a new citizen of the United States" and endorsed his parents as "wonderful people and very dear friends."

Covering some of the campaign trips of the vice president, whom I had first met in Berlin, had been part of my induction into the American political scene. In October 1966, with President Johnson off on a thirteen-day tour of seven Asian countries, it fell to the vice president to make several swings around the country, drumming up support for Democratic congressional candidates.

I was attracted to his ebullient manner, his unfeigned geniality, and especially his visceral inability to control an errant tongue. It was, indeed, his indiscretions that I found getting on the air on CBS more than the substance of his mainly ad-libbed speeches.

In Salt Lake City, trying to maintain loyalty to a war policy he didn't believe in, Humphrey told a crowd that "the back of aggression has been broken." That was patently untrue. Afterward, seeking to restore his credibility, he told me he didn't mean to suggest that the war was being won, but only that "we are over the hump." When I questioned that, he threw up his hands and said, "What would you do if you were working for Lyndon Johnson?"

In New Orleans, discussing urban riots, the vice president said, "I might start a riot myself if there were rats nibbling on the toes of my children." The implicit criticism of the retrenchments in the war on poverty was clear.

In Kansas City, he held up a newspaper cartoon that showed the president saying to him, "Remember, when I'm away, to feed the dog, put out the lights, and watch Bobby." And he added, to laughter, "I've been doing all three."

In Denver he openly reveled in the freedom he was enjoying with Johnson away. He said, "This is Be-Good-to-Vice-Presidents week. Don't tell President Johnson I'm making this trip."

The vice president's thirty thousand miles of barnstorming for Democratic candidates were unavailing in what turned out to be a Republican year. But the warmhearted, quixotic Humphrey got my private vote. And that was even before he wrote to Jonathan and then called the child's parents to congratulate them.

My relations with President Johnson were something else again. It was disconcerting to find that this avid television watcher seemed to be aware of everything I ever said about him on the air, and ready to take offense.

One evening I did a report on the folksinger Joan Baez, who had come to Washington to agitate for an end to the war. Turned away from Constitution Hall (as Marian Anderson had once been), she sang for a huge crowd at the Washington Monument, which cheered her demand for "peace now." I concluded my filmed report by saying, "And all this in Johnson's Washington."

The next time I met the president in a White House receiving line, he gripped my hand, fixed me with a steely gaze, and said, "Well, Dan, how's it going covering Johnson's Washington?"

One night, after I had been on the air reporting liberals' dismay over cuts in the war on poverty (now retitled the "strategy against poverty"), Johnson awoke me at midnight to say, on the telephone, "Schorr, you are one prize son of a bitch."

The 1966 election also gave me my first taste of pre-candidate politics. Assigned to Detroit on election night, I reported the landslide reelection of George Romney as governor of Michigan. Governors Ronald Reagan of California and Nelson Rockefeller of New York had also won solid victories, so press attention immediately turned to which of them harbored presidential aspirations—which obviously, having just been reelected, they could hardly afford to acknowledge.

Assigned to interview Governor Romney on the morning after the election, I found myself in what seemed an exercise in futility. Would the governor pledge to serve out his term? He had no plans to do otherwise. What did he think about the "Romney for President" bumper stickers that had sprouted overnight? Flattered, but he didn't know where they had come from.

In despair, I finally said that, having lived in Europe a long time, perhaps I had missed something, but I found it difficult to understand the conventional coyness about presidential aspirations.

"Isn't it still the dream of every American boy someday to be president of this great country?" I asked.

"Of course," he responded, "and it is a dream I have shared."

That brief and essentially meaningless exchange won me a fleeting place on the *Evening News* and helped to have Romney soon dubbed an "unannounced candidate." The square-jawed, presidential-looking governor made the mistake, the following summer, of saying the American military in Vietnam had subjected him to "the greatest brainwashing that anybody can get." That effectively ended Romney's presidential bid. The closest he came to the White House was as Nixon's secretary of housing and urban development.

In 1968 I looked forward to a role in covering a tumultuous political year in a country rent by war and racial strife. Li and I returned from a vacation in Switzerland and Israel just in time to hear President Johnson on television on Sunday, March 31, delivering a speech on Vietnam that ended with the stunning postscript that "I shall not seek and will not accept" nomination to another term in office.

Stunning because of the tough-it-out face Johnson had shown to the world. Only a few weeks earlier the president, with the fixation of the Ancient Mariner, had been telling visitors to the White House (including me) that he had polls (pointing to his inner pocket) that showed Americans wanted escalation, not surrender, and that he was trying to restrain the hawks.

The president had said privately, "I'm not going to be the first president to lose a war." But then had come a lot of bad news, not the least of which was the trusted avuncular figure Walter Cronkite, after visiting Vietnam, saying on television, "We are mired in stalemate," concluding that the war was unwinnable.

The war, Johnson's abdication, the assassinations of Martin Luther King and Sen. Robert Kennedy, cast a deep and dark shadow over the political conventions—especially the Democratic conclave in Chicago.

As it happened, I had been outside the United States during every presidential election since 1944 (1948 and 1952 in the Netherlands, 1956 in Moscow, 1960 and 1964 in Germany).

For a television journalist in those days a convention was like the Olympic Games. It was where reputations were made and broken on the strength of how one performed, talking from the anchor booth or roaming the floor with microphone and headphones, stalking interviews to learn the perishable secrets of the closed caucuses. As World War II had conferred fame on Edward R. Murrow, Charles Collingwood, and Eric Sevareid, so the hot lights of the convention hall had nourished Chet Huntley, David Brinkley, and Walter Cronkite.

Compared to those days, when politicians, networks, and journalists all played for high stakes, the conventions of the year 2000 were a dismal bore. With the ticket, the platform, and almost everything else known in advance, the made-for-television meetings in Philadelphia and Los Angeles had little to offer but speeches. I created a small stir at National Public Radio by opting not to attend the conventions in person. I was overcome by nostalgia for 1968.

At the Republican convention in Miami Beach, I chose a fairly "safe" assignment that would not test my inexperience too much. I volunteered to cover the committee drafting the party's platform. The language on Vietnam had become an issue between Nixon and Rockefeller supporters.

"Here in the Voltaire Room of the headquarters Fontainebleau Hotel, behind tight security," I reported live on camera, "the platform writers met until four this morning ducking a head-on collision over Vietnam by an adroit compromise."

I was able to report what the unanimous resolution said—"neither peace at any price nor a camouflaged surrender," and "progressive de-Americanization of the war." What I did not know was how the compromise had been reached. A generation later I still wince about the big story I missed.

A day earlier I had run into Henry Kissinger, Governor Nelson Rockefeller's foreign policy adviser, walking with a man I didn't recognize into a patch of greenery and palmetto trees outside the hotel.

Kissinger introduced him to me with a mumbled name and something about his being a former student of his at Harvard.

We chatted for a few more minutes about what chance Governor Rockefeller might still have of winning the nomination against Nixon. They seemed not inclined to tarry, and we soon parted. Years later I recognized the "former student" as Richard V. Allen, who was Nixon's foreign policy coordinator, later to become President Reagan's national security adviser.

What I had missed, Allen chortled at lunch at the Federal City Club in Washington some years later, was that the walk behind the palmettos was to exchange drafts of a Vietnam plank, on which Nixon and Rockefeller would agree and which would be fed to the platform committee for its unanimous endorsement.

What I had also missed was that this was the start of Kissinger's move from the sinking Rockefeller ship toward Nixon, paving the way for his emergence as President Nixon's national security adviser and later secretary of state.

Allen was immensely amused. "Imagine," he said, "if you had known that Rockefeller's guy was secretly negotiating with Nixon's guy to avoid a floor fight. What would you have done with that?"

Allen was enjoying himself. I lost my appetite.

After a ten-day between-conventions respite with family in Aspen, my favorite vacation place, I headed to Chicago for what promised to be a less serene Democratic conclave. Outside the convention hall and the main convention hotels, young people engaged in passionate protest against the war came up against the clubs of Mayor Richard Daley's police, who conducted what investigative reports would later characterize as a "police riot."

Television made its own contribution to the tension. Wherever sound trucks went at night looking for trouble, trouble would start, as soon as the TV lights were turned on. Finally, CBS News president Richard N. Salant issued orders that if a demonstration started because of the presence of cameras, the crew should immediately douse their lights and leave. Television was not eager to share responsibility for what was happening on the streets of Chicago.

At the Blackstone Hotel, the 110 members of the Platform Committee met, trying to square the circle of a resolution on Vietnam that would be acceptable to the doves led by Sens. Eugene McCarthy and George McGovern and to Vice President Humphrey, who was under the thumb of President Johnson.

That, I thought, was the arena where the main contest of the convention would be fought behind closed doors, and I persuaded my bosses to station a camera outside the room. I felt sure I could get Rep. Hale Boggs, chairman of the Platform Committee, to make a statement as he came out of the tense session—and get liberals in the committee to respond to him.

What was going on, essentially, was that Chairman Boggs, on behalf of the administration, was trying to head off a McCarthy-McGovern resolution that would, in effect, repudiate Johnson by calling for a bombing halt and pressure on the South Vietnamese government to join the North in a coalition government. If the resolution lost in the committee, its proponents said they were prepared to write a minority report and take the battle to the convention floor.

Humphrey, desperately anxious to narrow the gap between him and the liberals, offered what he called a compromise that he claimed had not been cleared with President Johnson. In carefully chosen terms it called for a cessation of bombing. But Chairman Boggs, no doubt at the behest of the White House, sharpened the language, making a bombing halt conditional on the behavior of North Vietnam. With Humphrey's friends running back and forth, seeking the magic words that would satisfy everybody, the process began to look like a proxy negotiation between Humphrey and Johnson.

We awaited the expected breakdown of Platform Committee deliberations and the great battle on the convention floor that would surely follow.

It is hard to remember today how consumed we were by the convention battles—so consumed that we were hardly aware of what was happening in the rest of the world. We paid scant attention when, on August 21, Soviet tanks clanked into Czechoslovakia in a repeat of Hungary in 1956. Their mission was to crush a burgeoning movement for relaxation of totalitarian control. The peaceful revolution was led by dissidents such as Václav Havel, enjoying what they called the "Prague Spring" and inventing slogans like "socialism with a human face."

There was a flurry of interest among the convention reporters when Chairman Boggs, briefed by the White House, told the Platform Committee that President Johnson was taking the invasion seriously, but was not planning to intervene. The Soviets had proclaimed their "Brezhnev doctrine," asserting the right to protect Communist rule in any country of the Warsaw Pact. There was speculation about whether maverick Yugoslavia, or perhaps even Romania, might be next in line for Soviet pressure.

But all of this seemed little more than a distraction to those of us immersed in the titanic struggle that raged inside and outside the convention hall.

On the morning of August 28 I reported that the platform writers were meeting for their fifth day, "their climactic fight over Vietnam policy still before them and deadlines slipping." As I waited outside the committee room for what would happen next, a message was passed to me asking me to see Gordon Manning, the executive in charge of our convention coverage, at CBS News headquarters in the Hilton Hotel.

Manning told me the foreign desk in New York was screaming about its lack of manpower to cover the invasion of Czechoslovakia. NBC, he said, was daily beating CBS, which had only one correspondent in Prague, and he, Peter Kalischer, was ill and asking to be relieved.

"Czechoslovakia is part of your old territory and you know it like the back of your hand," Manning said. "So we would like you to get there as fast as possible."

I remonstrated that I was in the middle of what might be the biggest story of the convention.

"We'll get somebody else to cover it," Manning said.

I said I didn't have my passport in Chicago, that I would need a Czech visa, which would probably be hard to get in these circumstances.

"Stop arguing," Manning said. "Just get going and get to Prague the fastest way you can. Let us know where you want a camera crew to meet you."

I walked out of Manning's office in a daze, thinking about packing, flying back to Washington, telling my wife and infant son that I was off to Eastern Europe again in what might be a hazardous situation.

In the lobby of the Hilton, with all these thoughts racing through my mind, I ran into my friend Art Buchwald, who had just come in from the street, shaken and disheveled. He said, "You should see what's going on out there. The cops are beating up on the kids and anybody else who happens to be around. Schorr, let's go get a cup of coffee. I need something to steady my nerves."

"I'd like to, Art," I replied, "but I can't."

"What do you mean you can't? I'll buy."

"That's a great offer, but I can't."

"What do you mean you can't?"

"I'm in a big rush. I have to go to Czechoslovakia."

Buchwald surveyed me for a moment and said, "Chicken!"

And so, my burgeoning career as a political reporter interrupted, I made my way to Washington, to London, and to Vienna, where I linked up with a camera crew. Visas had been applied for but not issued. Our strategy was to head for the trade fair in Brno, knowing that the government usually waived visa requirements for this event. We spent a day in Brno, filming the fair to maintain our cover.

On film I reported that the Soviets had pulled back the tanks stationed in the immediate vicinity of the fair, where Western exhibitors might see them. We drove on to Prague and checked into the seedy old Alcron Hotel. To my surprise, the reception clerk, whom I remembered from a visit four years earlier, did not ask to see our visas. To my greater surprise I found myself able to broadcast from the studios of Prague Radio for the next two weeks.

Day after day I did radio and television reports on the desperate efforts of the reformist Party chief, Alexander Dubcek, to save what he could of the Prague Spring. He was forced to institute censorship over Czech media and to retreat from modest economic moves toward free enterprise.

Czechoslovakia was under the heel of a force of five hundred thousand, nominally representing the five countries of the Warsaw Pact. I ran into a Polish journalist who had been my translator in Warsaw a decade earlier. "I am ashamed to be here under these circumstances," he said. "Every man in the Polish contingent is ashamed."

A twenty-one-year-old Czechoslovakian airline stewardess told me of how she had experienced the Soviet invasion. She was sleeping at the airport hotel on the night of August 20 when her roommate had burst into the room, shouting, "Wake up. They have occupied us."

"The Germans are here?" she asked.

"No, the Russians."

Then the window was shoved open and there were two Russian soldiers, waving machine pistols. The stewardess, who spoke Russian, asked, "Why have you come here?"

One soldier said, "To save you from imperialism." The other said, "This is our country. We must protect it."

It did not take me long to slip back from my domestic-politics role to East European old hand. I remembered my first visit to Prague in 1955, when a Stalinist regime ruled with a heavy hand and a secret-service car tailgated behind every taxi I took. I was now struck by the relative sense of freedom, even during their second Soviet occupation in twenty years. Back to the days of the founders of Czechoslovakia, Masaryk and Benes, I had always liked the Czechs, the least homogenized of the peoples behind the Iron Curtain, and I sorrowed with them over the suppression of their Prague Spring.

In a taped television address on September 14 that showed signs of cuts and splices in five places, Party chief Dubcek warned his people against quarreling with Soviet troops. But the spunky advocate of "socialism with a human face" asserted, "To those who want to return to the past, we give a stern no. There is no way back for us."

A week later Brezhnev summoned Czechoslovakia's leaders to Moscow. Dubcek was not invited, but insisted on going along. Before his departure I watched him address an adoring crowd in St. Wenceslas Square with a promise not to betray them. I still have one of the buttons distributed at that rally showing the head of a smiling Dubcek in profile.

In Moscow, he was, as expected, fired by the Soviets and exiled to a menial job in the Slovak capital of Bratislava. The Soviets announced a phased pullout of the five hundred thousand Warsaw Pact troops, leaving only a "token" eighty thousand behind. The Party and government structure were shaken up. Controls were reimposed on the press, radio, and television. But, oddly, I was allowed to broadcast from the studio of Prague Radio without censorship.

In a stand-up report in front of the thousand-year-old Hradcany Castle, the seat of government, I said, "Czechoslovakia has entered a strange twilight of lengthening shadows, and no one knows how dark the night will get."

In Chicago, the Democratic convention lurched to its close in a shambles, with bitter acrimony on the floor and police battles with rioters outside. Art Buchwald may have had it right when he suggested that Prague might be a safer place to be.

By the end of September, with Czechoslovakia sullenly quiet, I was ordered to Belgrade, which was going through a war scare. President Tito feared that Yugoslavia, which had stood up against Stalin in 1948, would be the next target of the Brezhnev doctrine, the self-proclaimed right to enforce orthodoxy in the satellites.

I met Marshal Tito at a government reception. He looked stern in his resplendent uniform and wanted it known that, unlike Czechoslovakia, Yugoslavia would resist a Soviet occupation. Yugoslav officers whom I interviewed told how their troops would fall back in the face of a Soviet offensive, but would then fight a guerrilla war— as they had done against the Nazis.

Thousands of reservists were called up and factory militia were armed as though the invasion were imminent, although nothing very bellicose was coming from Moscow. Nor could foreign military observers provide corroboration of Soviet troop concentrations on the Hungarian and Bulgarian borders that Yugoslav officers talked about.

It occurred to me that the fear of invasion, however real, was also serving as a justification to conscript some of the Yugoslav students who had been holding rallies for greater freedom and democracy. And it could be used to pacify some of the strife among Yugoslavia's perennially feuding nationalities.

In any event, concluding that no invasion was imminent, I importuned my bosses, pleading some urgent business, to let me come home from my East Europe-revisited experiences. The business *was* urgent. I made it back to Washington just in time for my son Jonathan's first birthday.

Once again I had to reorient myself from a Europe I knew too well to an America whose political churnings I was still learning. In mid-October, amid feverish rumors of an impending Vietnam bombing halt, I reported that this story was "suddenly displaced" by the news that Mrs. Jacqueline Kennedy was marrying Ari Onassis, a Greek shipping magnate.

"The biggest shock since the assassination," wrote Betty Beale, *Washington Star* society reporter.

I was assigned to travel for three days with Maryland governor Spiro (Ted) Agnew, the Republican vice-presidential candidate, in Kentucky and Texas. If Hubert Humphrey presented the problem of reporting on a candidate I liked, Agnew presented the opposite problem: a politician to whom I took an immediate dislike.

Objectively, there was a lot to dislike. He made nasty references to "fat Japs" and "Polacks." His attacks on opponents had a vicious quality, as he accused Humphrey and his running mate, Sen. Edmund Muskie, of "condoning street riots and draft-card burning." He waved away questions about urban policy by saying, "If you've seen one slum, you've seen them all."

The election was close and hinged on Vietnam, with Vice President Humphrey the prisoner of President Johnson's apparent no-compromise policy. "Apparent" because we would later learn that

Johnson had tried to achieve a cessation of hostilities and an opening of peace negotiations. But the Nixon campaign had induced the South Vietnamese government to refuse negotiations and wait for a better deal from a Nixon administration. At the cost of a longer war, Nixon won the election.

For me and my colleagues there remained the task of chronicling the demise of the Kennedy-Johnson era and seeing how swiftly Nixon would move to demolish the Great Society that Johnson himself had undercut in his pursuit of a mindless war.

Budget Director Charles Zwick advised departments to avoid all postponable decisions that might prejudice the new administration's plans. President Johnson consulted with domestic adviser Joe Califano about how Presidents Truman and Eisenhower had handled the problem of a lame-duck State of the Union message. During the transition, President-elect Nixon had thirty task forces working up his new plans.

As a kind of farewell to my Great Society assignment, I spent several weeks looking at poverty in America. In Big Stone Gap, Virginia, in the center of Appalachia, I reported in depth on one family that, eight years after President Kennedy's promise to remake the region, still lived in a shanty far from the nearest road, subsisting on the earnings of a partially blind barber—and food stamps.

For Thanksgiving I reported on five hundred counties across the country still without food stamps, and the suit of antipoverty lawyers demanding food help from the government.

In Trenton, New Jersey, I prepared a report for *60 Minutes* on a negative-income-tax experiment—aimed at learning whether people whose income was supplemented to a given level would be less inclined to seek work. The counterintuitive answer was surprising, even to me. People who could now afford a telephone, have a bank account, and shop for groceries in quantity felt encouraged to join the mainstream and to look for work.

In his election-night victory statement, Nixon had said, "We want to bridge the gap between the races. We want to bring America together."

"In the ruins of Detroit and Watts and Newark," he said, "lie the ruins of a philosophy of government."

On the CBS year-end television roundtable, moderated by Charles Collingwood, I disputed Dan Rather, who said that the principal failure of federal aid programs was that they had "a dehumanizing quality."

"I would suggest to you," I said, "that the federal government has been the most humanizing governmental factor in American life in the past eight years. Against the apathy of the states and the inability of the cities to cope with their problems, the federal government has gone in with hundreds of programs directed to human beings."

I did not get much support from Roger Mudd, Eric Sevareid, or Mike Wallace. But I knew that, starting January 20, 1969, I would be spending a great deal of time covering the Great Society demolition derby and learning how President Nixon proposed to "bring us together."

L I F E   W I T H   N I X O N
(P R E - W A T E R G A T E)

From the time I went to work for CBS in Washington in 1953, I had found myself, at one time or another, successively in the doghouse with Presidents Eisenhower, Kennedy, and Johnson. The reasons I did not fully understand. Never assigned to the White House, I had little personal contact with the chief executive. And yet, my penchant for probing beneath the surface of things and my visibility on television seemed to generate irritation all the way up to the Oval Office.

As to Nixon, I would eventually perceive that a run-in with this media-hating, paranoid control freak was almost inevitable. But, if there were early auguries when he assumed the presidency in 1969, I missed them.

I had met him as vice president in 1959 on his triumphal tour of Poland after engaging Khrushchev in the famous Moscow "kitchen debate." I was impressed with his restrained conduct during this first high-level American visit to a Communist-bloc country, and I liked his articulate background briefings in a Warsaw palace. In Germany during the 1960 presidential campaign, I heard but did not see the Nixon-Kennedy debates and thought Nixon had come off better in dealing with complicated issues.

During the 1968 campaign I noted, that although pursuing a divisive "Southern strategy" appealing to whites by opposing busing for school desegregation, Nixon also flew to Atlanta after the Martin Luther King assassination to be with the family of the slain civil rights leader. He returned to Atlanta for the funeral and canceled campaign activities for two weeks.

In his victory speech on election night Nixon recalled a poster he had seen held up by a young woman during a stop in a small town in Ohio. It had read "Bring Us Together." The Nixon team encouraged talk of "the new Nixon," more conciliatory than his strident record.

As Nixon took office in January 1969, my private attitude toward him was perhaps best captured in a Herblock cartoon in the *Washington Post*. Herb had habitually depicted him with a sullen five-o'clock shadow. Now he suggested a turn of the page to a new chapter by giving the new president a clean shave.

My inauguration assignment was a stakeout in the Capitol rotunda, helping to fill airtime between the swearing-in ceremony and the parade by interviewing members of Congress about their impressions. These were generally favorable, Democrats and Republicans alike noting his call to "lower our voices," a theme particularly welcome after the spasms of racial conflict, campus violence, and antiwar demonstrations that had grown in numbers and passion with the grim Vietnam casualty tolls.

The public, too, seemed ready for a new start. Along the route of the parade there was only one hostile demonstration. At Pennsylvania Avenue and Twelfth Street, a few blocks from the White House, a few hundred young people threw sticks and stones toward the motorcade. Protestors waved Vietcong flags and shouted, "Ho, Ho, Ho Chi Minh." They found themselves fighting with outraged spectators. Having passed this point, Nixon had the sunroof of his limousine rolled back so that he could stand and wave to the crowd.

In my assignment covering domestic policy, expecting a quick dismantlement of Great Society social, educational, and environmental programs, I was surprised by Nixon's early initiatives. He made a ceremonial visit to the Department of Agriculture and

promised a campaign against hunger in America—a promise honored by extending the food stamp program and convening a White
House conference on nutrition. He established an Environmental
Protection Agency to combat air and water pollution. He proposed a
welfare reform program that would guarantee a minimum income
to the poor and fought for the program until it was shot down by an
alliance of liberals and conservatives in the Senate.

The greatest, perhaps, of his surprises was his declaration of an
anti-inflationary wage-price freeze in August 1971. That was taking
a page from the liberal economists' book. The Democratic Congress
had authorized such a freeze, but Nixon had appeared to spurn it.
Indeed, Secretary of the Treasury John Connally, who had appeared
on the CBS *Face the Nation* program that very Sunday morning, had
responded to my questions by virtually ruling out such action. He
was concealing a decision already made.

That night reporters were summoned to the White House to be
briefed on the controls. Connally acknowledged that he had evaded
my question on television. He grinned and said, "You should know
that a president who made a breakthrough to Communist China is
capable of surprising actions."

By the summer of 1971, however, the bloom was off the Nixon
"bring-us-together" rose. Secretary of Health, Education, and Welfare Robert Finch, a California chum of the president's and his most
moderate cabinet member, had lost a bruising fight to the American
Medical Association in his effort to name Dr. John Knowles, a progressive Boston hospital administrator, as assistant secretary for
health. Finch had also lost his fight to retain vigorous school desegregation guidelines against the resistance of Attorney General John
Mitchell, a godfather of the "Southern strategy." Leon Panetta (later
to be a member of Congress and chief of staff in the Clinton White
House) resigned his position as Assistant Secretary for Civil Rights
under White House pressure, saying, "The Nixon treatment of the
civil rights issue bodes ill for the nation."

Exposed to criticism because of his position, Secretary Finch
had become the target of the militant National Welfare Rights

Organization, which invaded his fourth-floor office, shouting messages of defiance from the window to me and my camera crew on the street. Finch had agreed to meet the protesters in the HEW auditorium, but failed to show up at the appointed time. Instead, he was taken to Walter Reed Army Hospital to be examined for hypertension. I interviewed him when he left the hospital, speaking slowly and softly as though sedated. A few weeks later he was relieved of his HEW post and given a counselor's assignment in the White House, sheltered from the storm outside.

In the face of growing antiwar protests—four students were killed by the National Guard at Kent State University in Ohio—I watched an administration sullenly digging itself in. Education Commissioner James E. Allen openly criticized the incursion into Cambodia in 1970 and was fired. Secretary of the Interior Walter Hickel appealed for more attention to the grievances of American youth and was eased out of his job.

My reporting, which early on had reflected the generally progressive and conciliatory measures of the Nixon administration, came to reflect the increasing belligerence, hostility to social betterment, and retreat from civil rights. But I had no idea that, along with several other television colleagues (the Nixon people seemed to take only television seriously), I was the subject of hostile monitoring in the White House.

In retrospect, I can trace back some of the seeds of the vendetta nurtured in the Nixon White House. The seeds are revealed in the belatedly released Nixon tapes, White House files, and especially the daily news summaries prepared for President Nixon and tailored to his predilections by a team under the supervision of speechwriter Patrick Buchanan.

Disapproving mention was made of my reporting on the administration's retreat on school desegregation, the discharge of Education Commissioner Allen, the vetoed appointment of Dr. John Knowles. I was given bad marks for my reporting on the controversy over national health insurance, and especially my *CBS Reports* documentary "Don't Get Sick in America," which concluded that administration programs were not adequate to meet rising health needs.

The news summary criticized my reporting on the failed Supreme Court nominations of Judges Clement Haynsworth and Harrold Carswell. Especially unpopular was my filmed interview with Sen. Roman Hruska, ranking Republican on the Senate Judiciary Committee. I asked how he responded to criticism of Carswell as being mediocre. Hruska astonished me with his reply: "There are a lot of mediocre judges and people and lawyers. They are entitled to a little representation, aren't they?"

It is evident from the White House files how deep the animus went against certain correspondents. In September 1969, Buchanan perpetrated a practical joke. He fabricated a memo proposing that Nixon arrange meetings with several "susceptible" correspondents. At the top of his list were John Chancellor of NBC and myself. The idea that we might be "susceptible" to Nixon was apparently hilarious.

In the archives one could find memos referring to "Daniel P. Rather" and "Daniel P. Schorr." Nixon lieutenant John Ehrlichman said years later that the *P* was a customary way of referring to unpopular correspondents. It stood for *prick*.

By 1970, signs of palace-guard hostility toward me were breaking through to the surface. HEW secretary Elliot Richardson agreed to debate Sen. Edward M. Kennedy on television about health insurance, then told me the White House had ordered him to cancel because I was to be the moderator. When I disclosed a suppressed report on deficiencies in the food stamp program, Sen. Robert Dole made a speech on the Senate floor accusing me of "false and misleading statements." (Years later he told me he was fulfilling a White House request.)

In March 1971, President Nixon for the first time denounced me in public. I had reported on the *CBS Evening News* that Nixon had decided to proceed with the Safeguard Anti-Missile Defense system despite the advice of his science advisers and his own misgivings. Before a gathering of newspaperwomen he called my report "a lie... totally unsupported by fact." My source, now deceased, had been Dr. Arthur Fletcher, White House science adviser, then about to become director of the National Air and Space Administration.

How did I feel about being a presidential target? In a word, exhilarated. More than half a century old, and with a family, I was still the boy reporter, thrilling to the pursuit of the scoop and the reaction to it. With the great CBS network behind me, I felt that no one could harm me. And what better scoop than one that made the president of the United States mad at you? It never occurred to me that the government would—or could—do anything to harm me.

That changed on August 18, 1971.

The previous evening President Nixon had addressed a dinner of the Knights of Columbus, a Catholic lay organization, in New York, at which he deplored Supreme Court rulings barring government aid to parochial schools. He noted that parochial schools were closing at the rate of one a day, and he promised to help to "stop that trend and turn it around."

The *Evening News* scheduled a filmed excerpt of the speech and asked me to follow it with details of how the administration planned, in the face of Supreme Court restrictions, to come to the aid of the parochial schools. I happened to be having lunch that day with Jack Veneman, undersecretary of health, education, and welfare, a friend of mine. He said he knew of no plan for any significant aid to the parochial schools and doubted there was one. Catholic school lobbyists whom I consulted said they were mystified by the president's speech.

So, after the Nixon speech excerpt, I came on television to say there appeared to be no rescue plan that would get around the Supreme Court's decree. I concluded, "We can only assume that the president's statement was made for political or rhetorical effect."

Next morning a White House press aide called to ask if I could come to the White House immediately to meet with Patrick Buchanan, the author of the Knights of Columbus speech, and education officials prepared to convince me that I was mistaken. Although by now preoccupied with coverage of the wage-price controls, I felt that I could not refuse to go to the White House. There Buchanan and education officials spent an hour outlining to me various initiatives, like paying for schoolbooks for parochial schools.

They amounted to very little. When I repeated them to the chief lobbyist for the Catholic schools, he said, "Were it not for my turned collar, I would say, 'Bullshit.'"

So on August 18 I went on the air again to report on my meeting at the White House. I said that, having consulted the Catholic schools movement, I found no reason to change my mind about political rhetoric.

On that day, I would learn long after the fact, I became the target of a White House covert operation.

On Friday morning, August 20, I arrived at my CBS office to find an FBI agent flashing his badge and saying he was there to interview me. For what reason? He said I was being considered for "a position of confidence and trust" that he assumed I knew about. As he sat across from my desk, notebook ready, my telephone began to ring with calls from relatives, friends, and CBS executives, all saying that they were being asked by the FBI about me. To all of them and to the FBI agent patiently waiting, I said I was aware of no prospective appointment to the Nixon administration and seriously doubted there was one.

The FBI officer said he would report back to headquarters that there had to be some kind of misunderstanding. Only with some difficulty could I persuade my bosses that I was not planning to leave CBS for the Nixon White House, and that the investigation, so suddenly begun and so suddenly halted, was a mystery to me.

It is a mystery no longer. I obtained the FBI's file on the investigation through a Freedom of Information application. Testimony in the Senate Watergate and House impeachment investigation filled in details of a plan to dig up some dirt on me that misfired.

This is what happened:

On August 18, President Nixon, in the Grand Teton National Park on a cross-country trip to California, was advised by Buchanan that the president was getting good coverage on television, except for "one bad shot" by Schorr on CBS on the parochial schools issue. Next morning, Nixon instructed his chief of staff, H. R. Haldeman, to get an FBI report about me. Haldeman's assistant, Lawrence Higby, called FBI director J. Edgar Hoover, saying that the president wanted a "complete background" on me. In FBI parlance, "background" refers to a report on a prospective appointee. Hoover apparently misunderstood what he was being asked for.

His memorandum to field offices said, "The president has requested extremely expedite investigation of Schorr, who being considered for presidential appointment, position not stated." A message to the FBI representative in Bonn, Germany, cited a *Who's Who* biography that listed me as a CBS correspondent in Germany. (By that time, I had been on the air from Washington for five years. Hoover apparently did not watch television much.)

Learning that I was in the United States, the FBI sent telegrams to field offices asking for "identities and locations of all close relatives.... Make certain all periods of adult life are accounted for." A message a day later added, "Investigation this morning indicates Schorr has been transferred back to the United States and is presently residing in Washington, D.C., with his family. He is apparently assigned to the CBS Washington bureau."

Having finally tracked me down, the FBI ran into trouble. Hoover advised Higby, who was now with Nixon and Haldeman in San Clemente, the president's California residence, that neither I nor anyone queried at CBS seemed to know of my pending appointment. In view of these developments, Hoover noted, Higby advised that "the FBI should discontinue its investigation until we hear further from Higby."

By now, documents said, the investigation had been "active" for seven hours, during which twenty-five interviews had been conducted. After a weekend of pondering at San Clemente, Higby called to say the investigation should be terminated, but information already gathered should be sent to his office.

At CBS, we decided not to publicize the bizarre investigation lest involvement in public controversy hamper my reporting. There the matter rested for several weeks. In October, at a dinner party, I met Fred Malek, White House personnel director, who expressed astonishment when I asked if I had been considered for a presidential appointment.

Early in November, *Washington Post* reporter Ken Clawson, who had good FBI contacts (and who would himself soon end up working in the White House communications office), called me to say he had heard of the FBI investigation and was planning a story. I said I could not help him because of the CBS decision not to talk about it. At the FBI, Assistant Director T. E. Bishop was more helpful. According to his internal memo, he told Clawson that the FBI had been "used" by someone in the White House who asked for an investigation "allegedly in connection with possible employment, but actually for the purpose of getting background information on Schorr in an expedite manner."

The FBI still did not perceive the possibility that it had simply misunderstood what the White House wanted. Hoover reported by telephone to Haldeman that Clawson's story was about to break in the *Washington Post*. Haldeman asked Hoover to avoid "any more publicity than necessary" because the press might try "to create a repression-of-newsmen type of thing."

The story appeared on November 11, 1971, on the front page of the *Post*, headlined, "FBI Probes Newsman Critical of President." Nixon, taking charge of the cover-up, called in Charles Colson, the special counsel who had once said that, for Nixon, he would walk over his own grandmother. Together they agreed that press inquiries should be answered with the explanation that, however unlikely it might seem, I was, in fact, briefly under consideration for a position.

Personnel director Fred Malek, who only a month before had guffawed at the idea of my serving in the Nixon administration, was now commissioned to identify a job for which I might, theoretically, have been solicited—adviser to Russell E. Train, chairman of the White House Council on Environmental Quality.

(Since then both Malek and Train have offered me their apologies for the roles they played. In his book, *A Memoir*, published in 2000, Train says, "To put it simply I had been 'had' . . . Good old naïve Train was left feeling like a jerk.")

Attorney General John Mitchell asked Hoover what was going on, and the director advised that the White House had led him to believe that I was being "considered for an important position," with no mention of wanting information "because of some unfavorable articles which he had written about the President."

Presidential Counsel John W. Dean III showed up at the FBI looking for information to bolster the cover story. He asked whether it had ever happened that a job investigation started before the job was offered. W. R. Wannall, head of the FBI's intelligence division, finally divined that "someone at the White House got their signals switched and requested a full field investigation when, in fact, probably all they wanted was background information on Schorr and a check of FBI files similar to that which had previously been requested by Haldeman's office on other news personalities."

(I never learned the names of the other journalists about whom the Nixon White House had queried the FBI.)

Next step in the cover-up was for President Nixon to formulate a new "policy" providing that in the future no one would be investigated for a White House appointment without first being informed and giving express consent. A news conference was called to announce the new "policy" in response to a question, but as luck would have it, no one asked the question. So, Press Secretary Ron Ziegler sought out reporters and told them what the president would have said if he had been asked.

Among those less than satisfied with the White House explanation was "Judge" Sam Ervin, chairman of the Constitutional Rights Subcommittee of the Senate Judiciary Committee. Over strong White House objections, he called a hearing on the subject. I found myself, as though in some theater of the absurd, acting out a scenario I had so often watched, distributing copies of my statement to the committee staff and press, taking my place at a witness table facing up to Senators Ervin and Kennedy. Bernard Shaw, covering the hearing for CBS, asked, jokingly, if I wanted to mark salient portions of my text to be filmed.

I could not rid myself of a sense of through-the-looking-glass as I began to read, "I am Daniel Schorr, resident of Washington, D.C., a correspondent for CBS News for the past nineteen years..."

The White House and the FBI refused to be represented. I recounted how the FBI investigation had changed my life, affecting relations with my neighbors, colleagues, and friends. I told how people hesitated to talk to me on the telephone and how some would ask, "Do you still have your FBI shadow?"

Senator Ervin concluded the hearing by saying that someone in the White House was guilty of "either stupidity or duplicity—these are the only alternatives I see."

In Moscow, where fifteen years earlier I had been in trouble with the KGB, the press was fascinated that I should now have run afoul of the FBI. *Pravda*, the Communist organ, attributed it to American "war psychosis" and surmised that I had been forced "to compromise and restrain [my] criticism of the government."

Equally bizarre was Pat Buchanan, appearing on ABC's *Dick Cavett Show*. Accusing me of "a prime case of bias" against the Nixon administration, Buchanan was trapped by Cavett's question as to why, then, I had been considered for a White House job. He improvised this reply:

"If you've got a guy that's hatcheting you on the air night after night, maybe you say to yourself, 'Why don't we offer the clown a job and give him a big fat paycheck and get him off?' "

It is hard to say whether Buchanan's weird explanation fell under Senator Ervin's rubric of duplicity or stupidity.

All this was before Watergate, although, in retrospect, it was a precursor to Watergate, sharing the pattern of illegality, cover-up, and eventual unraveling that became the hallmarks of the larger White House conspiracy,

On June 4, 1973, a beleaguered Nixon, pondering whether he could afford to release his Oval Office tapes, sat with earphones on his head, reviewing the tapes and making running comments, also recorded, to Chief of Staff Alexander Haig and Press Secretary Ron Ziegler.

He heard himself telling John Dean three months earlier that he had used the FBI "only for national security purposes."

"Yeah," he mused, "the only exception, of course, was that son of a bitch Schorr. But there—actually, it *was* national security." Laughs.

"We didn't say that. Oh, we didn't do anything. We just ran a name check on that son of a bitch."

In the 1974 Articles of Impeachment, the FBI investigation of me would be listed as one instance of abuse of presidential powers (Article II).

If I had known contemporaneously of how the awesome powers of the president were being arrayed against me, I would have been frightened out of my wits. But, instead, I went my merry way, reporting on such matters as hearings on campus unrest in which student leaders said the best way to end violence in universities was to impeach President Nixon.

On August 19, 1971, the day Hoover started his investigation, looking for me first in Bonn, Germany, I was on the air from Washington, reporting that AFL-CIO president George Meany had emerged from a meeting with the administration on wage-price controls, saying that organized labor had no faith in Nixon to manage the economy.

And on September 16, when I reported the Nixon administration was being pilloried by the Senate Agriculture Committee for cutting down on school lunches for the poor, White House counsel John Dean had just completed an "eyes only" list of twenty Nixon "enemies," myself at No. 17, described as "a real media enemy." Dean said these were ready for "go status" under a priority order. The purpose of the list, wrote Dean, was to "use the available Federal machinery to screw our political enemies."

All this, unbeknownst to me and the outer world, was going on before Watergate.

CHAPTER 14

COVERING WATERGATE

Saturday, June 17, 1972, would be a watershed day in my career, but I had no idea of that at the time. That day I returned from St. Louis, where I had covered one of a nationwide series of Democratic platform hearings. This one had been notable for a joint appearance by Sen. Edward M. Kennedy and Rep. Wilbur Mills, chairman of the House Ways and Means Committee, promoting a cradle-to-grave health insurance program.

As I relaxed with family, I listened to my colleague George Herman reporting on the evening news that five men had been arrested in the early hours in a break-in on Democratic headquarters in the Watergate office building. I noted that with passing interest before leaving for New York on Sunday for another platform hearing on Monday. Then I returned to Washington for three days of raucous debate in the 150-member Platform Committee.

By then I had carved out a place in the CBS galaxy of political reporters. Having worked on major documentaries for *CBS Reports* on health insurance, public school financing, neglect of children, and pollution hazards, I would have the role, in this presidential year, of focusing on issues rather than personalities.

This was also a summer when family matters claimed some of my attention. My wife, Li, had left her position in the antipoverty agency in October 1967, shortly before the birth of our son, Jonathan. She had dropped off proposed guidelines for neighborhood health centers literally on the way to the hospital. Since then our daughter, Lisa, had been born. It had been understood, without much discussion, that Li would be the primary caregiver until the children were old enough to permit her to resume her career, while I dealt with the great affairs of state.

Not that I wasn't a presence in our little house on R Street. One evening Jonathan, then aged two, had watched me on television, and when my face had disappeared from the screen, he had clambered behind the TV set, asking, "Where did Daddy go?"

Now Li persuaded me that our house in Georgetown, crammed with toys and in a neighborhood with few children for ours to play with, would no longer suffice. We looked at houses and settled on one on Woodley Road, near the National Cathedral, suburban in atmosphere, yet close to the center of the city. Our block was also something of a journalists' row. Across the street lived James W. "Scotty" Reston, author Elizabeth Drew, NBC's John Chancellor, who would be succeeded in that house by Tom Brokaw, and later, Tim Russert. Farther down Woodley Road, Walter Lippmann had once lived. Around the corner from us was Seymour Hersh; a few blocks away, Judith and Milton Viorst and espionage expert David Wise. One could get penetrating views of the world without traveling far. On our street one knocked at the neighbor's door not to borrow a cup of sugar, but for the latest scuttlebutt.

We planned to move in, after extensive renovation, in the interim between the Democratic convention in July and the Republican conclave in August, both in Miami Beach. On Independence Day I flew to Miami to join the large CBS contingent. The Democrats were plunged into factional fights over the seating of the California delegation. I was being tried out as a podium reporter. From the podium, on the eve of the opening, I reported, "This is the last night for several nights to come that you will see this hall looking so serene." The Democrats fought over delegates, platform, and most everything else as the Humphrey-Muskie opposition to liberal Sen.

George McGovern made futile, last-ditch efforts to block his nomination. His views on welfare might alienate the conservatives. His pro-Palestinian views might alienate Jews. But McGovern had the loyalty of the young party activists who controlled the apparatus.

As the convention made its disorderly way toward the nomination, the last thing in the minds of delegates and press alike was the odd caper at the Watergate in Washington. By now the five burglars, four of them Cuban-Americans, had been arraigned. Their connection with the Nixon campaign committee had begun to emerge. The press in the capital, starting with the *Washington Post*, was having a field day, tracing the secret campaign contributions that had bankrolled the venture.

We journalists in Miami Beach, obsessed with convention maneuvers and (to us) the more crucial question of what new television stars would emerge from these proceedings, were almost oblivious to the bizarre story of the bugging of the Democratic headquarters. White House spokesman Ron Ziegler dismissed the break-in as a "third-rate burglary" by unknown people. More important to us in Miami was that George Meany, president of the AFL-CIO, was refusing for the first time to endorse the Democratic nominee. We saw Democratic doom in his words "I will not endorse, support, or vote for Mr. Nixon; I will not endorse, support, or vote for Senator McGovern."

McGovern's middle-of-the-night acceptance speech found me in the hospital with a bad case of influenza. I returned to Washington to rest and prepare for our move to Woodley Road, which happened on a suffocatingly hot night and, of course, with the air-conditioning not working. Our children had been farmed out to friends for the night.

On August 12 I returned to Miami Beach for the Republican convention—three days as placid as the Democratic convention had been stormy. The GOP platform had been prefabricated by the White House. Where Democrats demanded "new directions," the Republican statement spoke of "exhilarating progress." Where the Democrats demanded "income security" for the poor, the Republicans called for "workfare" for the poor.

It was like looking at two Americas. Analysis showed that 75 percent of Republican delegates were over forty compared to 56 percent of Democrats, and 78 percent of Republicans had incomes over $15,000 a year compared to 63 percent of Democrats. If Republicans seemed richer and older than Democrats, it was because they were.

One could only marvel at the way the White House had orchestrated the convention, planning important events for prime-time television, running "spontaneous" demonstrations for "four more years" as though on a clockwork schedule.

My most exhilarating experience at the convention was obtaining the master scenario, directed behind the scenes by Alvin Cooperman, producer of television's *The Untouchables*. This enabled me to report on CBS what "surprises" were coming, such as President Nixon's appearance at a youth rally or a release of balloons.

I was able to report that John Wayne's aw-shucks ad-lib— "Don't get settled down for a speech because speech-making isn't my business"—was right there in the master script.

My other contribution was to snag Secretary of State William P. Rogers on the podium for a live interview. President Nixon had talked vaguely of some secret plan to end the Vietnam War. National security adviser Henry Kissinger had just returned from Saigon. In our interview Rogers expressed the conviction that a negotiated settlement of the war would come either before or soon after the November election.

The interview upset the Nixon administration. White House spokesman Gerald Warren said, incomprehensibly, that Rogers "was not making any prediction based on any event or any exchange that may or may not have occurred." As it later turned out, Rogers had anticipated the plan to announce shortly before the election that "peace is at hand."

At the close of the convention, Bill Small, my Washington bureau chief, walked with me up the aisle to the exit. He had been assigned to be my producer during the convention and we had quarreled a lot.

"You know," he said, "I think you are one prize son of a bitch. And I wish I had a dozen sons of bitches like you."

That about encapsulated my relations with CBS.

Returning to Washington, I read piled-up newspapers and caught up on Watergate. Bob Woodward and Carl Bernstein said in the *Washington Post* that the operation to bug a telephone and photograph files had been financed by illegal secret contributions to the Nixon campaign, some of them laundered through Mexican banks. Other stories told of the involvement of E. Howard Hunt, a CIA Bay of Pigs veteran, now a White House consultant, and G. Gordon Liddy, an FBI alumnus now on the payroll of the Nixon campaign committee. The "third-rate burglary" was reaching out tendrils close to the Oval Office.

Reporting to the office the next morning, I was called in to see Bill Small. He had become painfully aware that, engrossed in the conventions, we had abdicated to the print press an investigation that had, in two months, developed a substantial potential. Small said that I was to drop all other assignments and to devote myself exclusively to being CBS's "Watergate correspondent," with the hope that we could do some original reporting rather than constantly quoting the *Post* and other papers.

Within a week I was participating in an hour-long Sunday-night "special," reporting from the scene of the crime—the Democratic Party's office:

"At two-thirty Saturday morning, June 17, police found the door here jimmied open. The door has been removed as evidence. . . . The police came through this office with guns drawn. And here they found five men hiding behind a desk. . . . One of them shouted, 'Don't shoot! You've got us.'"

A television investigation, I soon learned, is much different from a newspaper investigation. Woodward and Bernstein could quote "sources." I was constantly being pressed for visuals. For example, I was the first reporter to learn that Liddy and Hunt not only were linked to the burglars, but had themselves been on the scene at the time and had managed to evade arrest. Not earthshaking, but, in terms of the little then known, a story. I proudly briefed Ed Fouhy, Washington producer for the Cronkite show. His initial response was "Fine, but what do we *see?*"

Thus my little scoop became that hated thing in the television trade: a "tell" story—told, like everything Watergate-connected, in front of the crenellated Watergate building. I believe that the constant use of that background by my colleagues and myself, long after anything was happening in that building, was what gave the scandal the name *Watergate.*

When our family drove past the Watergate, our preschool daughter, Lisa, would say, "Daddy, look. Watergatebreakin!" All one word. She thought it was the name of the building.

Democratic chairman Lawrence O'Brien and his counsel, Joseph Califano, anxious to keep the story alive until the election, contrived a way to provide us with visuals. They filed a million-dollar invasion-of-privacy suit against the Nixon campaign committee and got federal court backing to call the principals for pretrial depositions. The lawyers did not expect to learn much from these depositions, but those subpoenaed would have to appear at the office of Williams, Connally and Califano on Seventeenth Street, near the White House.

Notified of dates and times of the depositions, the networks staked out the tiny lobby. Campaign treasurer Maurice Stans came down the elevator, stepped into the blinding lights, and denied doing anything illegal. Former campaign chairman John Mitchell came out, sneering at "Larry O'Brien's press corps." Liddy, we were told, had simply refused to appear. The star would be Howard Hunt, whom none of us in the press corps had ever seen.

Nine A.M., the time set for his deposition, passed, and he did not appear in the lobby. At noon, there was still no sign of him. I went up to the office of Edward Bennett Williams, who said that Hunt had given his deposition. He had arrived early—before the press corps. As to where he was now, Williams said that if we had not seen him leave, he had to be still in the building, probably in the office of another attorney, waiting for us to leave.

In the office of Hundley & Cacheris, deserted during the lunch hour, I encountered a man in a light suit and a panama hat, wearing dark glasses. He scowled.

"Mr. Hunt, I presume," I ventured. "May I introduce myself?"

"You don't have to," he snarled. "We went to the same college."

Confused, I asked, "You went to City College?"

"No. Brown. Aren't you Irving R. Levine?"

"No, he's NBC. I'm Dan Schorr of CBS."

With that he darted into the elevator, I managing to join him before the door closed. We stepped out into the lobby together. I announced that this was Hunt, starting a mad scramble among the unprepared camera crews. He dashed through the streets, followed by me and my camera team, who were doing a great job of filming on the run.

He ran into a Connecticut Avenue office building, where his lawyers' office was located, and into an elevator, failing to notice the "Out of Service" sign. While he frantically pushed buttons, we joined him in the elevator and recorded his tight-lipped "No comment"'s to my questions. Finally, taking pity, I told him the elevator wasn't running, whereupon he started another dash, this time to the nearby Army-Navy Club.

Back at CBS, our film was processed and I received many compliments. I had, at last, come up with a "visual" story. It provided no new information, but the mad dash of a Watergate suspect through the streets of downtown Washington provided a lot of entertainment.

President Nixon, as it happened, held a news conference at the White House that afternoon. He said that "no one in this administration presently employed" was involved in the "very bizarre" Watergate episode. My pursuit of Hunt, whom I described in my report as "one of the most shadowy figures in the Watergate bugging case," got almost as much airtime on the evening news as Nixon.

That's television!

Television can also be timorous in the face of authority—especially authority that can affect its fortunes. In 1971, Daniel Ellsberg offered the Pentagon Papers to CBS and was turned down because CBS lawyers advised that the network might be charged with espionage.

CBS also tended to be nervous when my reporting referred to sealed documents. I learned that Howard Hunt, in his deposition, had refused to tell his whereabouts on the night of the break-in. CBS News president Richard Salant, himself a lawyer, called me to warn that federal Judge Charles R. Richey, who had sealed the document, might demand to know my source and hold me in contempt if I refused to give it.

I said that was a risk one had to take in the news business. Salant said that was the answer he had expected, and he assured me of legal representation if I got into trouble. Judge Richey eventually released the depositions, which contained little beyond Hunt's suspicious refusal to discuss his whereabouts on the night of the break-in.

On September 7, Democratic chairman O'Brien announced, on "unimpeachable" authority, that there had actually been two break-ins, the first in May, and that the main purpose of the June 17 break-in was to replace faulty telephone taps. The "unimpeachable" source soon surfaced—a hitherto unknown participant named Alfred Baldwin III, of New Haven, Connecticut, a former FBI agent.

Baldwin had been hired by the Watergate conspirators to monitor the wiretap from a room in the Howard Johnson Hotel with a line-of-sight view of Democratic headquarters across Virginia Avenue. He had seen the police arriving in front of the building and tried to alert the burglars by walkie-talkie, whose batteries turned out to be dead. During the break-in, Hunt and Liddy were in the nearby Watergate Hotel, escaping to the room in the Howard Johnson when the police showed up.

All this Baldwin and his lawyers had divulged to the Democratic lawyers in the hope of reducing his vulnerability. Baldwin then told the story to the *Los Angeles Times* and later to me in a filmed interview on a deserted beach near his home in New Haven.

Baldwin said he had monitored and summarized two hundred telephone conversations, mostly with clerical and subordinate personnel. (O'Brien did not spend much time in his office.) Some of the conversations were about their sexual exploits. None seemed to justify the risk that the conspirators had taken.

As to how, in retrospect, he viewed his own participation, Baldwin told me, "I was at the bottom of the ladder of a structure that included former FBI and CIA people. And I was working for the former attorney general [John Mitchell], the top law man of the United States. So, I couldn't question the legality of what was going on."

Producer Fouhy and I drove to CBS News headquarters in Manhattan, where the film was processed and put on the air—a revealing glimpse of respect for the law undermined by those entrusted to uphold it.

CBS came nowhere near matching the print press, starting with the *Washington Post*, in unraveling the Watergate scandal, but it may be fair to say we did better than any other broadcast organization. Our work attracted enough interest from Woodward and Bernstein to warrant a luncheon invitation at our favorite Twentieth Street French restaurant. Something worth seeing is reporters trying to smoke each other out about their next stories.

I also became, not by intention, the source of the *Post* team's worst moment. On October 25, the *Post* appeared with its biggest Watergate story to date—reporting that Hugh Sloan Jr., Nixon's campaign treasurer, had given testimony before the grand jury that H. R. Haldeman, Nixon's chief of staff, had been one of those controlling the Watergate "slush fund." This was made up of unreported campaign contributions, a secret fund for secret purposes. It was taken for granted that if the president's chief of staff was involved, Nixon had to know about it.

That morning, I happened to know, Sloan was scheduled to give a deposition at the Arnold & Porter law firm in a suit filed by the public-interest organization Common Cause, to force disclosure of secret Nixon campaign contributions. I staked out the building, only a few blocks from CBS. When Sloan appeared with his lawyer, James Stoner, I asked if he could confirm the *Post* story. Sloan motioned to his lawyer, who flatly denied that his client had given any such testimony.

I reported this on the air shortly after noon. Before doing so, I called my friend Benjamin Bradlee, executive editor of the *Post*. He drew a deep breath and said, "We stand by our story." What happened next at the *Post* is recorded in the Woodward-Bernstein book *All the President's Men*.

Bradlee called in the two and told them that this was his "lowest moment in Watergate." He looked at Sloan and Stoner on CBS, making what seemed to be a flat denial. The editor said, "Those bastards on television.... And there's Dan, dangerous Dan Schorr, whom I've known for thirty years, tucking it to them and ending up tucking it to us."

The denial enabled White House spokesman Ron Ziegler to condemn the *Post* as "irresponsible." Woodward and Bernstein told me they were not resentful of me, but were simply unable to comprehend where they had gone wrong. As it turned out, they were less wrong than premature. Sloan was prepared to finger Haldeman before the grand jury, but had not yet testified.

Robert Redford, who played Woodward in the movie *All the President's Men*, invited me to play myself in this climactic scene, although Sloan and Stoner would be played by actors. I declined. In those days I still worried about journalists crossing the line of reality.

In October, as the election approached, it seemed clear that Watergate, however fascinating to the media, was having little impact around the country. The White House had successfully fended off court proceedings and congressional hearings until after the election. Senator McGovern sank much of his dwindling campaign treasury into buying a half hour of television time to tell voters they were missing the significance of this "executive breach of power." Opinion polls continued to show McGovern far behind Nixon.

CBS continued to be a long step ahead of the other networks in covering the investigation, devoting twice as much airtime as either NBC or ABC. Three weeks before the election, the managers of the evening news, with Walter Cronkite in the forefront, decided to go even further. They wanted to wrap up the Watergate story into a "blockbuster" that would take up half of the half-hour program on two successive nights.

As "chief Watergate correspondent," I was asked to outline how the program should be organized. I wrote a memorandum suggesting four main themes: the "bugging" at Watergate, the "dirty tricks" played on the Democrats, the secret money that financed Watergate, and the "masterminds" behind the conspiracy.

I wrote, "I think we'll end up with the conclusion that the thing lapped very close to the Oval Office, but we do not have evidence that the President gave specific orders or had specific knowledge.... One ugly fact emerges—a kind of shadow government, existing side by side with the constitutional government."

As always, visuals were the hard part. Graphic artists went to work contriving charts and animations. An associate producer and a cameraman were sent to Houston simply to get a shot of an oil company airplane that had flown bags of secret money to Washington.

Friday, October 27, Part I aired, almost fifteen minutes long, Cronkite talking of "charges of a high-level campaign of political sabotage and espionage apparently unparalleled in American history." The print press had said as much, but this was Uncle Walter saying it in America's living rooms. In the CBS newsroom some of us gathered in front of the TV monitor with a tingling sense of seeing the Edward R. Murrow era reborn. The report closed with Cronkite saying, "In our next report—the money behind the Watergate affair."

That report was all ready to run on Monday, but Part II did not run on Monday. In Washington we were told that there were "problems."

We did not know then that on Saturday morning, "Chuck" Colson, after conferring with President Nixon, had called board chairman William S. Paley, dressing him down in coldly biting terms and warning of regulatory and other retaliation to come after the election. Nor did we know that Paley had promised to kill Part II and given orders to Salant to do so. But Salant noted that a second part had been promised on the air, and killing it would invite negative publicity for the network.

What Salant did do was to order Part II shrunk to about half its size. The main elements of the second segment were my analysis of Watergate financing ("a shadowy treasury paying for shadowy operations") and Dan Rather's examination of the president's men. The effect of the excisions was to eliminate much of the supporting material that justified our conclusions.

Associate producer Sanford Socolow sent me by Teletype his edited version of my script and asked me to rerecord it. We had a nasty argument on the telephone about what would go and what would stay. At no point did Socolow tell me why all this was happening. The truncated Part II went on the air Tuesday. Some of us gathered in the newsroom to watch, this time without exhilaration.

We did not know that Colson, still unsatisfied, called CBS president Frank Stanton and told him that after the election the administration would "bring CBS to its knees."

For my sins, I was assigned to Nixon campaign headquarters in the Shoreham Hotel on election night. Watching the boards showing the mounting landslide, I reflected how little Watergate had mattered. Around midnight the reelected president showed up in the Grand Ballroom and responded to a thunderous ovation with a curiously low-key and unsmiling speech.

In his memoirs Nixon wrote, "I am at a loss to explain the melancholy that settled over me on that victorious night." Perhaps he was haunted by portents of trouble deferred.

At first, however, it appeared that the Watergate scandal had successfully been contained and that Nixon might even be home free. On January 10, 1973, ten days before the second inauguration, Howard Hunt, Gordon Liddy, and the five burglars went on trial before federal district court Judge John J. Sirica, known as Maximum John for his tough sentencing proclivities.

As we waited for the judge to enter, I chatted with colleagues, at one point referring to Liddy, who was standing, arms folded, on the other side of the bar.

As he heard his name, Liddy pointed a finger at me and said, "*Mister* Liddy to you, *Mister* Schorr." With memories of his violent reputation, and even though he was safely in the hands of the marshals, I instinctively said, "Yes, Mr. Liddy." I have never claimed to be a hero.

The seven were convicted. Judge Sirica wanted to know who their sponsors were, skeptical of the prosecution's theory that Liddy had misappropriated Nixon campaign funds and gone off, with his cohorts, "on an enterprise of their own." Seymour Hersh reported in the *New York Times* that the defendants had been paid hush money. But none of the Watergate seven nor any Nixon official would come forward to corroborate that.

I told my bureau chief that the defendants had apparently been successfully bought off, there was little likelihood that the higherups would ever be brought to justice, and Watergate was over, for all practical purposes. I went off with my wife for a trip to Europe.

Boy, was I ever wrong!

On March 23, in Austria, I received a message from my office that Watergate was on again, and my presence "would be appreciated."

For one thing, L. Patrick Gray III, acting FBI director, had appeared before the Senate Judiciary Committee for confirmation as J. Edgar Hoover's successor. He had astonished the senators by revealing that the White House had monitored the FBI's Watergate investigation and that he had "probably lied" about the extent of his cooperation with the White House.

For another thing, Judge Sirica announced at the sentencing hearing that James McCord had written him saying that there had been perjury and payoffs to the defendants to protect those higher up.

And for a third thing, the Democratic-controlled Senate voted to set up a special committee to investigate Watergate, headed by the homespun North Carolina former judge Sam Ervin.

So, I returned to Washington, listened to a lot of "clouded crystal ball" cracks, and resumed my assignment.

On April 14, a warm Saturday afternoon, as I lounged with family in our backyard, a call from the office alerted me that John Mitchell had been spotted by a CBS motorcycle courier leaving by limousine from the back door of the White House, apparently headed for National Airport.

Minutes later I was dressed and racing to the airport, there to meet a camera crew. Surmising that Mitchell might be on the next shuttle flight to New York, we piled aboard the plane just as the door was closing and found Mitchell in a window seat, not at all happy about having been found.

Once aloft, I approached Nixon's great friend and former law partner (he had resigned as attorney general to head the Nixon reelection campaign). My cameraman stood behind me. I said I would rather not invade his privacy by sticking a microphone in his face, but asked if he would give us a few minutes on arrival at La Guardia Airport. He nodded assent.

Having deplaned, he faced our camera and denied having approved the break-in plan. He did not deny having been present at some of the discussions of the plan. He also said that the White House had decided to cooperate with the Ervin committee and that he would be a witness.

I was still curious about the reason for the unusual Saturday-afternoon trip to the White House. He said he had not seen the president, but had talked mainly with presidential adviser John Ehrlichman. I asked about rumors that the administration wanted him to be the scapegoat for Watergate in order to protect the president. He replied suggestively, "I certainly would hope not."

(My suspicion proved to be on the mark. In that meeting, Ehrlichman had asked Mitchell to take responsibility for Watergate, and he refused.)

The interview livened up the usually news-hungry Saturday-evening news. It helped to set the stage for what was to follow. Three days later Nixon announced that there had been "major developments" in the Watergate case and asked that none of his assistants, "present or past," be given immunity from prosecution.

This suggested that Nixon was trying to stymie somebody's effort to bargain with the prosecutor for immunity. Two days later it became clear whom Nixon was aiming at. White House counsel

John W. Dean III. He issued a statement saying that anyone who thinks that "I will be the scapegoat in the Watergate case...does not know me."

Stakeout time! My mission was now to find Dean, whom I had never seen. Two days in front of his house in Alexandria were unproductive. (One thing a dozen stakeouts taught me: People who want to duck the press seldom stay home.) On an anonymous tip that Dean had been sighted at the Department of Health, Education, and Welfare—so unlikely that it might be possible—I went down to the building on Independence Avenue that I knew so well and combed the corridors. Eventually, bemused officials introduced me to John J. Dean III, a long-standing employee in the personnel office, no relation. I had some guffaws to face when I returned to the office.

Unable to ferret out Dean, now the pivotal figure in the investigation, I managed at least to learn enough for a "tell" story. Trying to save himself, Dean was bargaining with U.S. Attorney Earl Silbert, offering explosive information. On May 7, I reported that Silbert had rejected the immunity bid. I mentioned that, during the negotiations, Dean's lawyer, Charles Shaffer, had represented him as fearful of going to jail because "his boyish appearance might make him a target for molestation."

In his book *Blind Ambition*, Dean said my report left him "stunned, then angry," but that he suspected that one of his lawyers had put out the story to "force me to go public with my story."

But Dean had another immunity iron in the fire. He reached agreement with Samuel Dash, chief counsel of the Senate Watergate Committee, to tell all he knew in exchange for limited immunity. Prosecutor Silbert went to court trying to block the agreement, but Judge Sirica ruled, somewhat reluctantly, that the executive branch could not limit a congressional investigation.

The Dean immunity deal spurred the television networks into rethinking their original plan to rotate coverage of the Senate hearings to minimize revenue losses. With the president now menaced by Dean, the networks quickly decided that they would all have to cover the hearings, however painful the loss of soap opera revenues.

Audience reaction was interesting. During the first days the CBS switchboard lit up with angry calls from soap opera fans. As days passed, some of the callers seemed to accept the hearings as their new soap opera, commenting on "performance," making suggestions for plot changes, objecting to boring witnesses as though they could be written out of the script.

There could be no better stage set than the musty, high-ceilinged Senate Caucus Room, which harbored memories of investigations past, back to the Teapot Dome scandal. On May 17, the mumbling Senator Ervin rapped his gavel and said the committee would address questions that "strike at the undergirding of our democracy."

For a reporter coveting airtime, the next six weeks were nirvana. Before the opening and after the close of each session and whenever the committee recessed for Senate business, I would step in front of the camera in the anteroom with analysis, background, and anything else that occurred to me. In a confined space I stood shoulder to shoulder with Douglas Kiker of NBC and Sam Donaldson of ABC. At times we were picked up by each other's microphone. (Doug said his producer complained of hearing me better than he could hear him.)

Recesses tended to be sudden and of indeterminate length. At one point I may have set some kind of record by being on the air for an hour and thirty-five minutes, in long colloquies with colleagues back at the studio and in interviews with any senator or staff member who wandered nearby.

When the hearings were in session, we took places at the press table (the same table where I had sat for the Joseph McCarthy hearings two decades earlier). Through earpieces we could get instructions and messages from our control rooms.

John Dean, of course, was the star witness with his recital of having warned Nixon that, with payoffs and perjury, there was "a cancer growing on the presidency." In his third day at the witness table, Dean was wrapping up some odds and ends, identifying documents he had submitted in evidence. Through my earpiece a producer said that this was all dull and that I should think of going out to our camera at some point to explain what these documents were all about.

"The next," Dean droned, "is a copy of a memorandum of August sixteenth, 1971, that was prepared by me for Mr. Haldeman, Mr. Ehrlichman, and others at the White House, which addresses itself to the general problem of dealing with political enemies."

A stirring at the press table...

"The next is a document dated September ninth, 1971. It is from Charles Colson to John Dean, in which Mr. Colson has checked in blue those he would give top priority on the enemies list..."

Over my earpiece a now excited producer told me to find out more about those documents, especially the "top priority" names, and be ready to go on the air as soon as there was a break. Committee staff said copies would be distributed as soon as they could be made (on the slow photocopiers of the time).

Just as the hearing recessed for lunch, copies of the first enemies document were distributed. We three network correspondents rushed out to our cameras, vying to be first, none of us having time to peruse the documents before the red light on the camera went on.

I began sight-reading the document, titled "Dealing with our political enemies," and concluding, "Stated a bit more bluntly—how we can use the Federal machinery to screw our political enemies."

While I was reading this, the second document was handed to me, the "top priority" list with twenty names. On the air, I read down the list, coming to "number fifteen, Stewart Mott...number sixteen, Congressman Ron Dellums..." And then I heard myself reading, "number seventeen, Schorr, Daniel, Columbia Broadcasting System. A real media enemy."

I managed not to gasp, although the impulse was there. I deadpanned my way down the remaining names: Harrison Dogole, "fourth largest private protection agency," Paul Newman, "rad-lib causes," and Mary McGrory, "daily hate-Nixon articles."

I said, "That's it. And now back to you." And then I broke into a big sweat. This was the most electrifying moment in my career.

I feared that, now being a part of my story, I might be disqualified from covering it. That did not happen. But, at my suggestion, somebody else was assigned to package the "enemies" story for the evening news.

Bureau chief Small chided me for using the word *screw* on the air, which had elicited complaints from the Bible Belt. I tried to explain, not very patiently, that I had no way of knowing what word I would be reading next in what was, after all, a White House document.

What interested me was that paranoid word *enemy,* an ominous new concept in American political life where *opponent, adversary,* and *rival* had sufficed before. I do not know what tax audits and possible break-ins would have lain in store for us "enemies" (with other lists they totaled 499 names) had Nixon not soon become preoccupied with his own survival.

The beginning of his end could be marked as Friday, July 13, when White House aide Alexander Butterfield, responding to a direct question in an executive session of the Senate Watergate Committee, disclosed that Nixon had maintained a taping system since February 1971.

Why did he do it? Originally, I believe, to help him write his memoirs and to get a tax break by donating some of the tape to the National Archives. Later, to trap aides into self-incriminating statements. Why did he not destroy the tapes before they were subpoenaed? Because he believed he was protected by unassailable "executive privilege" until the Supreme Court decided, eight to zero, that he was not protected from a criminal investigation.

Impeachment began to loom as a serious possibility after the "Saturday night massacre" of Special Prosecutor Archibald Cox in October 1973. Cox had refused to accede to Nixon's demand that he give up his efforts to subpoena the White House tapes. Nixon ordered him fired and his office sealed by the FBI. Attorney General Elliot Richardson refused to do the firing and resigned. Deputy Attorney General William Ruckelshaus also refused and was fired. Solicitor General Robert Bork agreed to do the firing and became acting attorney general. (In 1982, President Reagan would name Bork to the federal Court of Appeals and, in 1987, nominate him to the Supreme Court. He was refused confirmation by the Senate.)

On March 1, 1974, the grand jury indicted a half dozen Nixon aides, including Ehrlichman, Haldeman, and John Mitchell. I learned that the grand jury, in a straw vote, unanimously favored indicting Nixon, as well. But the new special prosecutor, Leon Jaworski, held that this was not constitutionally possible while Nixon was in office (a matter on which legal experts have disagreed more recently in the Clinton scandal). Unable to indict Nixon, the grand jury named him an unindicted coconspirator.

So intertwined was my life with Nixon's that the day he announced his resignation, August 8, was the day that put me on a collision course with CBS after almost a quarter century of service.

I had previously had painful moments when Paley had our Watergate report truncated and, again, in June 1973, when Paley ordered the abolition of "instant analysis" by CBS correspondents of Nixon appearances. (After Nixon assured a publishers' convention in Florida that "your president is not a crook," I said on the air that "the evidence indicates otherwise.")

On August 8, as Nixon faced three articles of impeachment voted by the House Judiciary Committee (one of which mentioned the FBI investigation of me as an "abuse of power"), the nation wondered whether he would tough it out or resign. Speaker Carl Albert called a meeting with television networks to go over ground rules for broadcasting the impeachment debate.

ABC and NBC were represented by news executives. Arthur Taylor, who had succeeded Frank Stanton as CBS president, came to Washington, saying he wanted to take part himself. None of us Washington correspondents could understand why Taylor wanted to subject himself to an angry debate in which Republican leader John Rhodes accused the networks of wanting to turn the impeachment proceedings into a circus.

As the discussion continued, Speaker Albert received a message and abruptly ended the meeting. Albert said he had been advised that Nixon would announce his resignation that evening, obviating the need to discuss impeachment.

I encountered Taylor when he returned to the office, and we chatted about what lay in store. His principal concern was that, in his resignation speech, Nixon might attack television, especially CBS, as having forced him from office. That, said Taylor, might polarize the nation on the issue of television.

After lunch I met Taylor again, and he said his concern had been dispelled. By what, he did not say. It appeared that Taylor, who had campaigned for Nixon while he was in college, had a contact of his own in the White House who was able to reassure him that Nixon would not attack CBS.

But at what price?

At about six in the evening, bureau chief Sandy Socolow came through the newsroom, telling me to "take it easy tonight—don't be vindictive." When I objected to the reflection on my professionalism, he said I was not being singled out—this word was being given to all the correspondents who would be on the air that night.

Then, a taped Nixon "political obituary" on which I had been working for months with a talented producer, Mark Harrington, updating it every week for the day Nixon would leave office, was unceremoniously scrubbed. It was as though any reminder of the scandal that had driven Nixon from office was not appropriate. Nor were the correspondents, Fred Graham and myself, who had covered Watergate and were identified with Nixon's misdeeds, which CBS seemed not eager to recall that night.

I watched the monitor with a sinking feeling in the pit of my stomach as Eric Sevareid intoned, "On the whole, it seemed to me as effective, as magnanimous, a speech as Nixon has ever made." White House correspondent Dan Rather said, ". . . one of Nixon's, if not his finest hour. . . . He did give this moment a touch of class." "It certainly was a conciliatory speech," commented Walter Cronkite.

Only Roger Mudd, who had been out of touch on Capitol Hill all day, broke the chorus of acclaim, saying that the speech did not deal with the realities of why Nixon was leaving. To which Rather responded that most people did not want "to shoot at lifeboats."

I went home deeply disturbed, trying to sort out what part of my feelings were wounded ego, what part a judgment that CBS had negotiated some deal with the White House out of self-interest. I expressed my dark suspicion in a newspaper interview in Denver and at a bull session with students at Duke University.

Sevareid never spoke to me again. Salant sent word that thereafter I could not speak in public except from a script that had advance management approval. I responded, half-jokingly, that I might open my speeches with the line I had used in Moscow, "This text has been cleared by the censor."

Oddly enough, while CBS and I never really made peace after that, Nixon and I did. When the ex-president went to the hospital with phlebitis in November 1974, my seven-year-old son, Jonathan, perhaps to tease me, asked me to forward a get-well card that he had fashioned. In a handwritten reply of thanks Nixon concluded, "Perhaps you will choose to follow in your father's footsteps, and, if you do, I trust I will live long enough to see you on television."

For the next twenty years I watched Nixon working for his rehabilitation—his "campaign for ex-president," I called it. In 1992, he permitted me to quote from a "private" memorandum he had written criticizing President Bush as insufficiently supportive of Russia's Boris Yeltsin.

In 1993, he had a fax message delivered to me saying my commentary on National Public Radio on his trip to Moscow was the best thing he had heard on the subject.

In 1994, I was invited to a dinner of the Carnegie Endowment for International Peace, where Nixon spoke about Russia. It was the first time I had seen him since his resignation. He responded to a question I asked, and when the evening was over, I could not resist going up to him and asking whether he remembered me.

He put a friendly arm on my shoulder and said, "Of course, Dan Schorr, glad to see you. Damn near hired you once."

And we both laughed, enemies no longer.

CHAPTER 15

SON OF
WATERGATE

Our family vacation fell neatly between Nixon's resignation and his pardon by President Ford. As we drove across Independence Pass, the Continental Divide, we heard on the radio of the sudden Sunday announcement from the White House. Jonathan, then seven, asked, "What's he being pardoned for, Daddy?" I said, "For the bad things he did, and because of this pardon, we may not get to know all the bad things he did."

Returning to Washington, I found that my Watergate assignment was not quite over. President Ford tried to give Nixon back his tapes. The Democratic-controlled Congress blocked that move. Ford tried to ease Nixon's return to private life with $850,000 in "transition" funds. Congress held hearings, cut out such items as a butler and a maid and reduced the budget request by half. President Ford announced a program of limited clemency for draft evaders and deserters. His congressional opponents scornfully commented that this was meant to offset the clemency for Nixon.

How to explain the abruptness of the pardon? Ford had said, in his first presidential press conference on August 28, that a pardon was an option not to be considered before "any legal process has been undertaken." It developed that Special Prosecutor Leon Jaworski had sent the White House a letter making clear that Nixon, unless pardoned, might soon be indicted.

In October 1974, President Ford testified before a House Judiciary subcommittee—the first president ever to appear at a congressional hearing—and acknowledged that the idea of a pardon had been discussed with him before Nixon's resignation.

On August 1, Chief of Staff Alexander Haig had come to him and outlined a series of options. Nixon might tough it out to impeachment and conviction. He could pardon himself and all the Watergate defendants. Haig suggested one other possibility—"a pardon to the president should he resign."

In effect Haig was saying that the only way Nixon would leave quietly was with the assurance that his successor would pardon him. Ford said he had "inquired as to what was the president's pardon power." Haig had produced a legal memorandum saying the president had "authority to grant a pardon even before any criminal activity has been undertaken."

Asked directly by Rep. Elizabeth Holzman of New York whether Ford had, in effect, made a deal exchanging a pardon for a presidency, Ford said angrily, "There was no deal."

Well, not in so many words.

In October, with Watergate and Nixon finally gone, I contemplated my dubious prospects at CBS. I applied to join the *60 Minutes* stable of correspondents and was turned down. I asked to return to a previous assignment as economic correspondent and was turned down. A *CBS Reports* documentary on overuse of prescription drugs, on which I had worked on and off for a year, even though preoccupied with Watergate, was taken away from me and given to Dan Rather. I was told that Rather, having been relieved of his White House assignment, needed to be quickly shown to the public as being engaged in rewarding projects. Rather told me, when he next saw me, that he had been embarrassed by the appropriation of my program, but the decision was not in his hands.

The prospect arose of an autumn romance with the *New York Times*, which had spurned me so long ago.

Aware as I was that my career at CBS was near a standstill because of my flouting its "go-along" rules, I yet remained beguiled by the financial and ego rewards of broadcasting. I might never make it through the glass roof from the journeyman reporter to anchor stardom; I might never crash the "in" group of Rather, Mike Wallace, and Bob Schieffer; I might never be appreciated for myself rather than for "scoops." Yet there remained the satisfaction of getting hard-to-get stories, of having calls returned by important people, of being recognized in restaurants and airports. I had suffered too much childhood insecurity, economic and personal, to be able to walk away from this modicum of fame.

But I needed a patch that I could call my own. And as fate had intervened in 1972 with Watergate, so now, in the fall of 1974, fate made a return visit with what I came to call the Son of Watergate.

In the *New York Times*, investigative reporter Seymour Hersh was making a splash with a series of stories exposing the CIA's campaign a year earlier to bring down the left-leaning President Salvador Allende of Chile. Allende had died during a military coup that installed a military junta led by Gen. Augusto Pinochet. It remained unclear whether Allende's death was a suicide or a murder.

On October 3, CBS bureau chief Sanford Socolow called me in and assigned me to develop what, in effect, would be a television version of Hersh's stories. So, here I was again, playing catch-up with the print press, and in this case, with a neighbor and friend.

First, I needed talking heads. My first stroke of luck was being put in touch with Ray Cline, a CIA alumnus who had recently resigned as State Department chief of intelligence and research in a policy dispute with Secretary Kissinger. On camera, Cline told me that he and most of the State Department had opposed forcible intervention in Chile, but that the oust-Allende policy had been forced down the CIA's throat by President Nixon and Secretary Kissinger, pursuing a policy that "only the two of them seemed to understand."

Elsewhere, I learned that Dr. Kissinger, at a meeting of the secret interagency committee overseeing the operation, had delivered himself of this memorable line: "I don't see why we need to stand by and watch a country go Communist due to the irresponsibility of its own people."

The next morning, Saturday, I was telephoned from the White House with word that, responding to an earlier request, Dr. Kissinger had a few minutes to see me if I came quickly. I wondered whether Kissinger somehow knew of Cline's attack on him, not yet aired.

We met in the cramped, blue-carpeted West Wing office of the national security adviser, which, perhaps because of its proximity to the Oval Office, he seemed to prefer to his palatial State Department suite. He paced back and forth, venting his anger at the leaks that, he said, were subverting national security. He insisted that the United States had used only legal means against Allende. I told him of Cline's attack on him.

"He said that?" asked Kissinger mildly. "That isn't my recollection of his role."

The following Monday, I received a call from Kissinger's executive assistant at the State Department, Lawrence Eagleburger (years later himself secretary of state). In a heavy mock-German accent, Eagleburger said, "Would you like to come to my office? Heinrich has instructed me to show you some interesting captured documents."

In a small conference room in Kissinger's suite, Eagleburger laid out on a table three documents, all stamped "top secret," and said, "I must leave you for a while. You will be on your own."

The documents were interagency memorandums discussing various options for dealing with Allende, from street demonstrations to bribing members of parliament. Each document had a handwritten notation by Cline urging stronger action. "About the morality of bringing down the elected leader of a friendly country," Cline wrote, "in the world of *Realpolitik* sensitivities are not so tender. People are more concerned with who wins power than with morality."

Kissinger, who constantly inveighed against security leaks, clearly had no compunction about using leaks to strike back at his critics. I told the tale—in confidence, I thought—to Seymour Hersh. He embarrassed me severely by writing a story for the *Times* telling how Kissinger had used classified information for his own manipulative ends. No journalist likes to have a confidential source exposed— especially by a friend. It was my belief, apparently mistaken, that friends don't blow each other's confidential sources.

A requested appointment with CIA director Colby came through—with the stipulation that it would be for background only, since the director never speaks on the record. The last time I had visited the spy agency was sixteen years earlier when Director Allen Dulles had invited me to lunch to talk about the Soviet Union.

I drove down the unmarked road in Langley, Virginia, to the blinking red lights at the guard post. My name was checked off on a visitors list. Outside the headquarters building was a statue of Nathan Hale, America's founding spy. In the lobby was an honor roll of the CIA dead, with many lines blank for covert agents anonymous even in death. My camera crew waited there.

An escort officer took me up to Colby's seventh-floor office in an elevator that responded only to the officer's key. The director's office was cream-walled, businesslike, and unostentatious. Colby was different from what I had expected—slighter in build, softer of voice.

He gave me a pat little talk about how covert operations had sprung from the Cold War, had tapered off with détente, but were still needed as a capability. I interrupted to say that I could not see him doing himself any harm by saying these things on camera. He shrugged and said, "Okay."

A moment later we were on our way down the elevator past stunned CIA officers to our camera in the lobby for the first-ever filmed interview with America's spymaster. In the interview Colby talked of how the CIA was absorbing the damage of the revelations about the Chile operation.

"So," I concluded, "you pick up the pieces and go on?"

"It's part of the hazard of the profession," he said in the laconic way of the intelligence professional.

By grace of the director, I was allowed to film my narration in front of the CIA building. I was amused to see a large sign in the lobby, reading, "CBS Filming." It was a signal to cloak-and-dagger people to stay out of camera range.

My two-part report on the clandestine operations world in trouble won general approval at CBS, and I found myself with a new assignment—the intelligence community—just as this hidden world was beginning to come under congressional scrutiny.

My new Son of Watergate assignment was, in a sense, an outgrowth of my old assignment. The agency had been marginally involved in Watergate. The CIA had supplied disguises to Howard Hunt, a CIA alumnus whose burglar team was made up of Bay of Pigs veterans. President Nixon had tried to get the agency to take the rap for Watergate—the June 23, 1972, "smoking-gun" tape. It was so described because it contained the clearest evidence of a cover-up managed by Nixon. On it he discussed with Chief of Staff Haldeman how to get the FBI to call off its investigation by having the CIA take responsibility for the Watergate break-in.

In December, a front-page story by Seymour Hersh in the *Times* told of the CIA having, in violation of its mandate to operate only abroad, conducted surveillance on domestic antiwar protesters and left-wing groups in general. The article said that the intelligence files kept on at least ten thousand American citizens represented one of a number of illegal activities turned up in a post-Watergate internal investigation ordered in 1973 by James R. Schlesinger during his brief tenure as CIA director.

I read the article at breakfast and called Sy to congratulate him. He said he had been working on the story for two years.

There were the usual follow-up events to cover—the complaints by congressional oversight committees of having been kept in the dark about a grossly improper activity, the White House statement that President Ford was calling for a report. My problem was how to "advance" the story. Events came to my assistance.

At 6 A.M. on Christmas Eve the newsdesk awakened me with word that the news wires were reporting the resignation of James J.

Angleton, "legendary" CIA chief of counterintelligence. (Legendary to some; I had never heard of him.) The surveillance operation had come under his jurisdiction.

I found Angleton listed in the telephone directory and sped to his home in suburban North Arlington, Virginia. There I found cameras, one of them ours, already staked out on the lawn, but no one had tried to find out if he was home.

My doorbell ring was answered by a groggy-looking, stoop-shouldered man in his pajamas. His first words were "Well, Mr. Schorr, I certainly didn't expect you to be trampling on the press!" He pointed to a copy of the *Washington Post* on his doorstep on which I was standing.

He allowed me into his home to talk with him, but would not appear on camera, which, he said, would expose him to mortal danger. For the next four hours he rambled on discursively about a world-wide Communist conspiracy. He scoffed at the Soviet-Chinese split as a "charade." He denounced the Nixon-Kissinger efforts at détente with the Kremlin and called Kissinger "objectively a Soviet agent." I wondered not that he was being fired, but that he had lasted so long.

Angleton suggested that his forced resignation was part of a Kissinger-Colby plot to destroy him. This began to sound like a John Le Carré novel, in which the loyal agent is thrown to the wolves by the corrupt spymasters for sinister reasons. I made mental notes on his paranoia for my later story.

Around noon, Angleton, still in pajamas, excused himself to dress, saying he had to go to the office. I felt it fair to warn him, since he feared being photographed, that there were television cameras staked out on his lawn. He shrugged, donned his black coat and fedora, walked out the front door ahead of me, then paused before the cameras as though hypnotized.

Astonished, I picked up our microphone lying on the ground and asked why he had resigned.

"I think the time comes to all men when they no longer serve their countries," he replied.

"Did you jump or were you pushed?"

"I wasn't pushed out the window," he said, as though recalling some episode of defenestration from his twenty-two-year career in the cloak-and-dagger trade.

In the ensuing months I would occasionally hear from Angleton, usually with some incomprehensible reference to some Communist conspiracy. Once we had lunch, under his rules, which required me to arrive at the restaurant before him, choose a rear table where he could have his back to the wall, and leave after him. Most of our conversation was about Communist conspiracies, including a briefing on the Palestinian leader Yasir Arafat as being under KGB control.

By now I knew of his reputation as the destructive force in the CIA whose paranoid fear of moles had virtually paralyzed the recruitment of spies and betrayed some of them to the Soviets.

One night in 1976 he called me at home to complain that I had not been careful enough about shielding him as a source. We never spoke again. When he died, in May 1987, I attended a memorial service in the Congregational church in Arlington. There were hymns, Scripture readings, and a reading from T. S. Eliot by Angleton's good friend Reed Whittemore. But there was no eulogy. No one even spoke his name.

I asked a CIA veteran sitting beside me, "Why no eulogy?"

He looked at me with scorn and said, "It's classified."

The disclosure that the CIA, in its domestic surveillance program code-named Operation Chaos, tapped wires and conducted break-ins caused a public stir that intervention in far-off Chile had not. Over the Christmas holiday in Vail, Colorado, President Ford, it would later emerge, had finally gotten to read the CIA inspector general's report, informally dubbed the Family Jewels.

It detailed a stunning list of 693 items of CIA malfeasance ranging from behavior-altering drug experiments on unsuspecting subjects, one of whom plunged to his death from a hotel window, to assassination plots against leftist third world leaders.

Anxious to keep congressional committees, already gearing up for investigations, from laying bare the worst of these, President Ford, on January 5, 1975, announced the appointment of a "blue-ribbon" commission to inquire into improper domestic operations. The panel was headed by Vice President Nelson Rockefeller and included such stalwarts as Gov. Ronald Reagan of California, retired general Lyman Lemnitzer, and former treasury secretary Douglas Dillon.

A few days later President Ford held a long-scheduled luncheon for *New York Times* publisher Arthur O. Sulzberger and several of his editors. Toward the end the subject of the newly named Rockefeller commission came up. Executive Editor A. M. Rosenthal observed that, dominated by establishment figures, the panel might not have much credibility with critics of the CIA. Ford nodded and explained that he had to be cautious in his choices because, with complete access to files, the commission might learn of matters, under presidents dating back to Truman, far more serious than the domestic surveillance they had been instructed to look into.

The ensuing hush was broken by Rosenthal. "Like what?"

"Like assassinations," the president shot back.

Prompted by an alarmed news secretary Ron Nessen, the president asked that his remark about assassinations be kept off the record.

The *Times* group returned to their bureau for a spirited argument about whether they could pass up a story potentially so explosive. Managing Editor E. C. Daniel called the White House in the hope of getting Nessen to ease the restriction from "off-the-record" to "deep background." Nessen was more adamant than ever that the national interest dictated that the president's unfortunate slip be forgotten. Finally, Sulzberger cut short the debate, saying that, as the publisher, he would decide, and he had decided against the use of the incendiary information.

This left several of the editors feeling quite frustrated, with the inevitable result that word of the episode began to get around, eventually reaching me. Under no off-the-record restriction myself, I enlisted CBS colleagues in figuring out how to pursue the story. Since Ford had used the word *assassinations*, we assumed we were looking for persons who had been murdered—possibly persons who had died under suspicious circumstances. We developed a hypothesis, but no facts.

On February 27, 1975, my long-standing request for another meeting with Director Colby came through. Over coffee we discussed Watergate and Operation Chaos, the domestic surveillance operation.

As casually as I could, I then asked, "Are you people involved in assassinations?"

"Not anymore," Colby said. He explained that all planning for assassinations had been banned since the 1973 inspector general's report on the subject.

I asked, without expecting an answer, who had been the targets before 1973.

"I can't talk about it," Colby replied.

"Hammarskjöld?" I ventured. (The U.N. secretary-general killed in an airplane crash in Africa.)

"Of course not."

"Lumumba?" (The left-wing leader in the Belgian Congo who had been killed in 1961, supposedly by his Katanga rivals.)

"I can't go down a list with you. Sorry."

I returned to my office, my head swimming with names of dead foreign leaders who may have offended the American government. It was frustrating to be this close to one of the major stories of my career and not be able to get my hands on it. After a few days I decided I knew enough to go on the air even without the identity of corpses.

Because of President Ford's imprecision, I didn't realize that he was not referring to actual assassinations, but assassination conspiracies. All I knew was that assassination had been a weapon in the CIA arsenal until banned in a post-Watergate cleanup and that the president feared that investigation might expose the dark secret. I sat down at my typewriter and wrote, "President Ford has reportedly warned associates that if current investigations go too far they could uncover several assassinations of foreign officials involving the CIA . . ."

The two-minute "tell" story ran on the *Evening News* on February 28. While I had been mistaken in suggesting actual murders, my report opened up one of the darkest secrets in the CIA's history.

President Ford moved swiftly to head off a searching congressional investigation by extending the term of the Rockefeller commission and adding the assassination issue to its agenda. The commission hastily scheduled a new series of secret hearings in the vice president's suite in the White House annex. Richard Helms, who had already testified once, was called home again from his ambassador's post in Tehran for two days of questioning by the commission's staff and four hours before the commission on April 28.

I waited with colleagues and staked-out cameras outside the hearing room, the practice being to ask witnesses to make remarks on leaving. As Helms emerged, I extended my hand in greeting, with a jocular "Welcome back!" I was forgetting that I was the proximate reason for his being back.

His face ashen from fatigue and strain, he turned livid.

"You son of a bitch," he raged. "You killer, you cocksucker! Killer Schorr—that's what they ought to call you!"

He then strode before the cameras and gave a toned-down version of his tirade. "I must say, Mr. Schorr, I didn't like what you had to say in some of your broadcasts on this subject. As far as I know, the CIA was never responsible for assassinating any foreign leader."

"Were there discussions of possible assassinations?" I asked.

Helms began losing his temper again. "I don't know when I stopped beating my wife, or you stopped beating your wife. Talk about discussions in government! There are always discussions about practically everything under the sun!"

I pursued Helms down the corridor and explained to him the presidential indiscretion that had led me to report "assassinations." Calmer now, he apologized for his outburst and we shook hands. But because other reporters had been present, the story of his tirade was in the papers the next day.

A week later Henry Kissinger testified to the Rockefeller commission and came out of the hearing room, calling out to the assembled press, "Where's Schorr? I have a new name for him!" Kissinger humor.

The Rockefeller commission issued no report on assassination conspiracies, but instead turned over its findings to the newly created

Senate select committee that was gearing up for a sweeping inquiry into the transgressions of the intelligence agencies over more than two decades. Chairman Frank Church of Idaho came out of Rockefeller's office on May 7, saying, "When Helms says that the CIA never killed any foreign leader, that statement is correct, but not necessarily complete."

With the Senate select committee, a new era began in the monitoring of intelligence agencies long accustomed to reporting to uninquisitive armed services and appropriations committees. A lot of dirty linen had piled up over the years. Assassination conspiracies were perhaps the most explosive subject of all because, as President Ford had suggested, they involved the question of presidential authorization.

In one posthearing briefing, Senator Church said that, in plotting assassinations, the CIA may have been "behaving like a rogue elephant on a rampage." Republican Vice Chairman John Tower disputed the implied effort to exonerate President Kennedy.

Having postponed its broader inquiry for a six-month investigation of assassination conspiracies, the Senate committee released its report at a news conference in November over strenuous objections from President Ford. Near the end of the news conference, I stood up in the aisle to ad-lib for our camera what would be the close of my report on the *Evening News:* "In the end it was as Richard Helms said—the CIA never killed anyone. But it wasn't for want of trying."

The report said that since 1961, the CIA had maintained something euphemistically called an "executive action capability." The agency's science adviser had been consulted on ways to "achieve incapacitation and elimination." In the years from the Eisenhower until the Johnson administrations the agency had been involved in plots, some more advanced than others, to eliminate eight third world leaders:

In 1961, Patrice Lumumba of the Congo (the name I had guessed in talking to Colby). Plans to have him poisoned were well advanced when he was killed by his rivals for power.

In 1961, Dominican dictator Rafael Trujillo. He was killed by insurgents who had received American arms, but it was unclear that these were the guns used.

In 1963, South Vietnamese president Ngo Dinh Diem. He was killed in a CIA-supported military coup, but it was not established that the Kennedy administration had wanted more than his ouster.

In 1970, Gen. René Schneider, chief of staff in Chile. He stood in the way of toppling President Allende. The CIA supported a plan to kidnap him, but there was no evidence that the agency wanted him dead.

In 1973, Allende. The CIA claimed by then it had "separated" itself from the military officers planning to get rid of Allende and install Gen. Augusto Pinochet.

Some thought was also given, at various times, to eliminating President François "Papa Doc" Duvalier of Haiti and President Sukarno of Indonesia. Both of them died in the early seventies, apparently of natural causes. So, at least, the Church committee concluded.

If the CIA was to be believed, it was the gang who couldn't assassinate straight. The best example of that was Fidel Castro, perhaps the most plotted-against—and most unsuccessfully plotted-against—man of the century.

And now it was clear why there had been so much tension about the whole subject of assassination plots—because one could not think of the many attempts to kill Castro without thinking of the Kennedy assassination.

The closed-door "assassination hearings" were held in the most secure room in the Capitol—the windowless penthouse built for the Joint Committee on Atomic Energy. It was a fitting place for digging into a radioactive subject long concealed. The Senate committee learned that, between 1960 and 1965, under the Eisenhower, Kennedy, and Johnson administrations, the CIA had organized eight separate attempts on the life of the Cuban dictator.

Some of them seemed almost childish—an "arranged accident," poisoned cigars, a poisoned drink, an exploding seashell, a diving suit painted inside with lethal germs. Most mind-boggling of all was the

CIA alliance with the Mafia, anxious to regain its grip on Havana gambling.

Johnny Rosselli, of the Florida mob, was enlisted by the CIA. He in turn recruited Chicago gangster Salvatore "Sam" Giancana and Santos Trafficante, the Miami-based Cosa Nostra chief for Cuba. They tried various plans for murdering Castro, including the offer of $150,000 to any Cuban who would kill the Cuban dictator. Nothing worked.

Giancana was subpoenaed to appear before the Church committee. He was killed, gangland style, before he could testify. Rosselli made it to Washington—I actually tracked him down on the telephone in the Watergate Hotel on the day before his scheduled testimony—but he would not talk to me.

The next morning, we staked out various entrances to the Capitol, hoping to catch a glimpse of him. The Capitol police outsmarted us, leading him up back stairways of whose existence I had never known.

Rosselli could escape us, but he couldn't escape the Mafia. At a posthearing briefing, Senator Church told us that the Mafia don, in his "vivid but incomplete testimony," had refused to name his associates in the "get Castro" project. Nevertheless, Rosselli's body was found a few weeks later in an oil drum floating off Miami.

For the senators the most delicate issue of all was how much President Kennedy had been involved in ordering Castro killed. It was why the Democratic chairman, Church, had tried to project the CIA as a "rogue elephant" operating on its own. Former defense secretary Robert McNamara told me he had testified to a contradiction he was unable to resolve—his belief that Kennedy opposed assassinations and that the CIA would not act without authorization.

Sen. Walter Mondale said, "We're not good at assassinations—and thank God!" But the committee gave up trying to establish who was responsible for what President Johnson called "America's Murder, Inc., in the Caribbean."

The investigation triggered by President Ford's indiscretion in January had followed a tortured trail to a hotly disputed Senate report in November, and it would have further consequences.

Studying the report, I noted a curious footnote. It spoke of "the President's friend who was also a close friend of John Rosselli and Sam Giancana," and it said the "friend had close contact with them and with President Kennedy from the end of 1960 until 1962." There seemed to be an awkward effort to withhold the gender, let alone the name, of this "friend" shared by the president and the mobsters.

I sent a memorandum to the Cronkite news producers in New York saying there seemed to be a story hidden there, which I would pursue if so desired. "But, frankly," I said, "I have little zest for what may be a scandal involving our dead President." I received no reply to my memo and concluded that my bosses found the idea as distasteful as I did.

I am amazed today at the restraint I showed then about digging into Kennedy's life. But the seventies were a different time in journalism, when personal scandal was simply not a part of our assignment. I can remember finding Wilbur Mills, chairman of the House Ways and Means Committee, drunk when I showed up at his office for a 9 A.M. interview. It did not occur to me to put that in my story. Soon thereafter he was found, besotted, wading in the Reflecting Pool with an Argentine striptease artist.

In the case of Kennedy, the story I so uncharacteristically passed up was the sensational tale of Judith Campbell Exner, who was the mistress of President Kennedy while also beholden to Sam Giancana, who, in turn, was working with the CIA to eliminate Castro. You think of the opportunities for blackmail! The FBI monitored Mrs. Exner's calls to Kennedy from Giancana's home in Chicago. Eventually J. Edgar Hoover went to the White House to warn the president of the risks he was taking.

President Nixon may have known about the Kennedy-Exner connection from Hoover, who delighted in offering juicy gossip to presidents about their rivals. And that may help to explain what Nixon was referring to in the "smoking gun" tape of June 23, 1972, when he talked of having the CIA take the rap for Watergate, telling Haldeman to remind Richard Helms that "we protected Helms from one helluva lot of things." (Helms was in charge of covert operations during the plots against Castro.)

But the biggest unresolved question to emerge from the Senate investigation was what, if any, connection existed between the CIA plots on the life of Castro and the assassination of President Kennedy by an avowed admirer of Castro. The Warren commission didn't get into the question because the CIA successfully withheld from it any knowledge of the plots against Castro. Gerald Ford, a member of the Warren commission, only learned about the assassination plots on becoming president and finally prying the Family Jewels report out of the CIA.

Oddly enough, it was Congressman Ford who had asked CIA director John McCone, appearing before the Warren commission with his deputy Richard Helms, whether he had "full authority" to disclose relevant CIA information. McCone assured him he had that authority. In 1975, Helms was asked before the Senate Intelligence Committee why he had not mentioned the anti-Castro plots to the Warren commission. He replied, "Because I was not asked."

We are left to puzzle out the connection between the efforts during the Kennedy administration to kill Castro and the assassination of the president. I have spent much time researching this question and have concluded that Lee Harvey Oswald, reading of Castro's public threats of retaliation for the plots against him, made himself Castro's avenger. Follow with me this chain of circumstances:

On September 7, 1963, a CIA "case officer" met in Paris with a Cuban army officer, Maj. Rolando Cubela Secades, who presented himself as a disaffected revolutionary, ready to try to eliminate Castro. They discussed means, including the idea of a poison-tipped ballpoint pen.

That evening Castro showed up unexpectedly at a reception at the Brazilian embassy in Havana and made an off-the-cuff speech accusing Kennedy and the CIA of plotting his destruction. Castro also talked to Associated Press correspondent Daniel Harker, telling him, "Let Kennedy and his brother take care since they, too, can be victims of an attempt which will cause their death."

The CIA apparently saw no reason to connect the two events and to worry about the loyalty of its "agent," code-named AM/LASH.

Conversations went on for several days, and the case officer promised that Cubela's request for a meeting with Attorney General Robert Kennedy would be considered.

Harker's AP dispatch was published in the *New Orleans Times-Picayune* on September 9. Oswald's widow, Marina, has said they received the paper at home and she believes her husband read the story.

After cashing his unemployment check on September 17, Oswald, on September 23, sent his wife and child to Irving, Texas, while he remained in New Orleans, ostensibly to look for work. Instead, in great secrecy, he boarded a bus for Mexico City and went almost immediately to the Cuban consulate.

The FBI learned what happened in the Cuban consulate from American Communist leaders Morris and Jack Childs, paid informants of the Bureau, who met with Castro after the Kennedy assassination. According to Castro, Oswald had talked of intending to assassinate Kennedy and was thrown out by the consul, Eusabio Asque, who believed this to be some kind of provocation.

On June 17, 1964, while the Warren commission was casting about for a possible motive for the assassination, Hoover sent a top-secret letter to commission counsel J. Lee Rankin, reporting what the FBI had learned from its "confidential source" in Havana. Rankin did not share Hoover's letter with the members of the commission. It ended up buried in the commission's files.

In July 1967, long after the publication of the Warren report, with its admission of failure to establish any motive, Castro gave more details in an interview with British journalist Comer Clark. Castro said that Oswald had come to the Cuban consulate twice, each time for about fifteen minutes. On the first visit he had told Consul Asque that he wanted to work for Cuba. He was asked to explain what he had in mind, but he refused. The second time, he said, according to Castro, something like "Someone ought to shoot that President Kennedy," and then, "Maybe I'll try to do it." That was when Oswald was thrown out.

Why didn't Castro alert the U.S. government to a potential assassin? Castro said, "Who would have believed me? People would say that Oswald was just mad, or that I had gone mad.... We would have been blamed for something we had nothing to do with."

So, there you have it: In all probability Oswald, an admirer of Fidel Castro's, read in his hometown newspaper that Fidel was warning of retaliation for plots against him, and the unstable young man took his cue to do the job for Castro.

That was September. On November 22 the CIA officer was having another meeting with AM/LASH (Major Cubela) in Paris and gave him the poison-tip pen to be used on Castro. A chillingly laconic memo in the CIA files records that the CIA officer left the meeting to "discover that President Kennedy had been assassinated," and "because of that, plans with AM/LASH changed."

Major Cubela returned to Havana, where it was announced that he had confessed to plotting with the CIA against Castro, and he was sentenced to prison. The chances are that he had functioned as a double agent, keeping Havana posted so that Castro would have evidence of the plans to assassinate him.

A chilling story and a historic irony—the president who wanted Castro dead and ended up dead himself. And a spy agency too worried about what it may have provoked to level with Congress or the Warren commission until the whole assassination issue broke to the surface more than a decade later.

To the extent that my reporting opened up the issue of assassinations, I feel profound professional satisfaction. About the probability that assassination plots against Castro may have boomeranged and cost the president's life, I feel profound melancholy.

CHAPTER 16

AWASH IN LEAKS

The ship of state, it has been said, is the only kind of ship that leaks mainly from the top. Officials can go berserk over leaks—except the ones that they arrange. Then they are called "deep background." Almost every recent president has, at one time or another, expressed frustration with leaks, which may limit their freedom of action. President Reagan said he was "up to my keister" in leaks. President Clinton said he was "extremely distressed" by leaks of "highly sensitive" information.

President Nixon's extra-official "Plumbers" unit in the White House was so called because its original mission was to plug leaks and hound leakers, such as Daniel Ellsberg, who leaked the Pentagon Papers. "Deep Throat," the Watergate source, or sources, of Woodward and Bernstein, became the personification of the high-level leak.

The leak is probably as old as the secret, but it reached its heyday during Watergate and the ensuing investigations of the CIA, which put a lot of secret information into the hands of loose-lipped members of Congress and staffs.

As leaky a congressional committee as I ever covered was the House Select Committee on Intelligence, rent with internal dissension and struggling to catch up with its Senate counterpart in sensational revelations. Threatened with abolition by the House Rules

Committee in the summer of 1975, the committee, chaired by the free-talking Otis Pike, New York Democrat, turned into a sieve of information about scandals in the intelligence community.

As the committee staff browsed through some two decades of CIA files, stories emerged about the agency's pouring money into an Italian election, getting involved in a civil war in Angola, missing the boat on the Syrian-Egyptian attack on Israel in 1973, and penetrating the White House with personnel "detailed" to the National Security Council. The committee squabbled over documents that the Ford administration tried to withhold on such sensitive matters as the Vietnam War. At one point, the committee threatened to move for contempt citations against Secretary Kissinger and Director Colby. (A compromise was eventually worked out.)

One leak presented me with a mind-boggling challenge. I was told of documents indicating that some CIA officers had worked undercover as journalists by agreement with their employers. Sig Mickelson, retired president of CBS News, identified for me two onetime CBS correspondents—Austin Goodrich in Stockholm and Frank Kearns in Cairo—who, in reality, were intelligence officers. This, said Mickelson, was pursuant to a written agreement between Allen Dulles, an early director of the CIA, and CBS chairman William S. Paley.

With a tenacious but foolhardy dedication to my assignment, I fought successfully to get the story on the *CBS Evening News*, complete with a picture of Paley and his off-camera denial. In the ensuing flap, a former CBS correspondent, Sam Jaffe, said that the CIA had gotten him a job at CBS and that the list of current and former journalist-spies included Walter Cronkite. Cronkite heatedly denied that and demanded that the agency make public the names of spies under journalistic cover—something the CIA refused to do. Before the Pike committee, behind closed doors, Colby testified that at the moment eleven spies were posing as journalists—many fewer than in the 1950s. In succeeding years periodic demands were made on the CIA to stop using journalistic cover, if only because that exposed all correspondents in Communist countries to the suspicion of being spies. At this writing, the CIA has reserved the right to use journalistic cover, but only in rare cases.

One of the more sensational leaks from the Pike committee was the revelation that President Nixon, at the request of the Shah of Iran, had had the CIA instigate an uprising of the Kurdish minority in Iraq. This was meant to put pressure on Iraq's Saddam Hussein, who was in a border dispute with the Shah. When the Shah settled his differences with the Iraqi dictator, the CIA abruptly pulled the plug on the Kurds, withdrawing support for them and leaving them at the mercy of the vengeful Hussein. My report on the Nixon-Kissinger betrayal of these hapless people became the lead story on the CBS Evening News.

At the next open session of the Pike committee, the chairman greeted me on arrival by stating from the dais, in a tone of irony, "Mr. Dan Schorr, who shares membership on this committee from time to time, had a very interesting story on television. . . . It is possible that we have a leak in this committee." The congressmen then discussed whether the leak might have come from the Ford administration to discredit the committee.

Finally Pike said, with mock seriousness, "Mr. Schorr, I don't suppose you want to reveal your source or method at this particular time?"

"No, thank you," I said from the press table.

Whereupon David Treen, a Louisiana Republican, offered a motion that would require me to identify my source in closed session on pain of being cited for contempt of Congress. Chairman Pike announced his opposition, saying, "My guess is that Mr. Schorr is one of those reporters who would rather go to jail than reveal his source." Treen's motion failed in a roll-call vote, and I found myself suddenly perspiring profusely.

Colby, about to be replaced as CIA chief by George Bush, just back from his post as representative to China, gave me a swan-song interview on film. In a period when the agency was being hung out to dry, he had been more candid with Congress than suited President Ford and Secretary Kissinger. In our interview, he deplored the damaging leaks from congressional committees while not blaming the media beneficiaries of those leaks.

"I just don't believe that it's possible for us to conduct secret operations while sharing them with large numbers in Congress," he said. "Congress has to take the position that it represents the American public and isn't just the conduit for every secret."

As the committee worked on its final report, President Ford sent the chairman a secret letter banning the inclusion of information on several covert operations. I was told, of course, of the letter and of some of the operations in question. My favorite was the agency's production of a pornographic film, titled "Happy Days," which purported to show President Sukarno of Indonesia (not named in the report) having sexual relations in his hotel while on a state visit to Moscow. This fell under the rubric of "black propaganda." The reenactment was to be represented as a KGB production, and was thus supposed to alienate Sukarno from his Russian hosts.

In January 1976, the committee finished drafting its report and sent a copy to the CIA, which responded with eighty pages of specific objections and a letter branding the whole report as "biased, pejorative and factually erroneous." In the face of this comment, reinforced with strong words from the White House, a polarized committee approved the report on January 23 by a vote of nine to four. The draft was sent to the Government Printing Office, with plans for public release eight days later.

Six days before the planned release, I obtained a copy of the draft report in typescript, and I showed it on television as I discussed its contents. That act started me down the road to the most tumultuous experience of my career. Colby, on his last day in office, called a news conference to make a bitter protest against "the bursting of the dam protecting many of our secret operations and activities." Sternly he said, "This report should not be issued," implying that some move was afoot to block its release.

By my journalistic lights, this was all academic. Since I had a copy, the report had effectively been issued.

Two days later the House Rules Committee voted to delay release of the report until it received security clearance from President Ford. The recommendation was approved by the House 246 to 184. At an

Israeli reception I asked House Democratic Leader Thomas "Tip" O'Neill how he explained the surprising development.

"This is an election year," he said, "and they're getting a lot of flak about leaks, and they're voting their American Legion posts."

With its printed report locked away in a Capitol vault, the Pike committee held its final meeting on February 13 in an atmosphere of defeat and frustration. Pike could find no upbeat words to say about an eight-month investigation that had ended in defeat. He closed by saying, "Let us adjourn to another room where we can, perhaps, celebrate in a more fitting manner." On the way out I ran into a staff member who wryly remarked, "You've been showing the report on television. Why don't you publish it and take us all out of our misery?"

No previous experience had prepared me for the situation I found myself in. John Crewdson of the *New York Times*, who had given a comprehensive summary of the report in his paper, had been permitted to take notes but not retain a copy. Only I had a copy, and everybody who watched television knew it.

Was it my duty to go along with the House of Representatives, which had been maneuvered into suppressing a report approved by its committee? That would make me the ultimate suppressor of the report. Anyway, I reasoned with myself, almost everything newsworthy in the report had long since leaked, and this was now not much more than a document for historians. And finally, while branches of government may argue with each other about what is secret and what is not, it is not the function of a journalist to keep secrets.

I had in mind the precedent set by the *New York Times*, which had excerpted the Pentagon Papers in news stories, then published an almost complete text through its subsidiary New York Times Books. CBS owned two book publishing firms, and I asked that one of them publish the Pike report as a public service.

I found CBS chillingly unreceptive to the idea. As with the *Times*, lawyers warned of possible legal jeopardy, but unlike the *Times*, CBS heeded the advice of its lawyers. I learned what I should have long since known—that a television network, operating in a regulated environment, concerned about its local affiliates and advertisers, does not display the same First Amendment courage as a major newspaper.

In 1976, the networks were particularly worried about legislation that might favor the growth of cable television at the expense of over-the-air stations. CBS, I began to realize, was not about to risk antagonizing the House of Representatives by appearing to flout its will.

Advising Salant that I would have to find some other way (he later said he didn't remember the call), I appealed to the Reporters' Committee for the Freedom of the Press to help me find a publisher. The trustees put me in touch with a New York lawyer, Peter Tufo, who agreed on the telephone to look for a paperback publisher. A few days later he called to say the book publishers had turned him down, fearful of legal trouble for spilling the nation's secrets. The "good news," however, was that Clay Felker, publisher of *New York* magazine and the *Village Voice*, was willing to undertake publication. (Tufo did not tell me that he was a director of and legal adviser to the Felker publications.)

I agreed to the Felker arrangement, then made two serious tactical errors. First, hoping to provide added protection to the identity of my source, I stipulated that my involvement be kept confidential. That was manifestly impossible since I had shown the report on television and it was widely known that I possessed the only copy "in the free world." Secondly, I told Tufo that, while I desired no payment from Felker, he might discuss with the Reporters' Committee making some contribution for the protection of journalists. In time, the mere mention of money would lead to the charge that I was "selling secrets."

Next morning a messenger was at the door, saying the agreed code words: "I'm from New York to get the package." My wife had thoughtfully taken the document out of the gray CBS interoffice envelope and put it in a more fitting plain brown wrapper. The deed was done. I did not even ask to be advised when and where the report would be published.

I felt that I was nearing the end of some long road in my career, operating in a twilight zone outside my organization to fulfill what I

considered to be my First Amendment obligation. Over that weekend I wrote Salant, saying that, after twenty-three years, I did not
think I had my employer's confidence and would welcome a meeting with him to resolve "what appears to have become 'the Schorr
problem' in CBS." The outcome, I thought, would be either resignation or some miraculous clearing of the air. Salant responded by
inviting me to lunch in New York the following Friday.

But the following Tuesday everything changed. Lawrence
Stern of the *Washington Post* called to say that the *Village Voice*
was out with a twenty-four-page supplement. The headline covering the whole front page read, "The Report on the CIA That President Ford Doesn't Want You to Read." Stern asked me to confirm
what he already knew from a friend on the Reporters' Committee—that I had supplied the document. Totally unprepared, I
stammered an appeal for fraternal understanding of my wish to
protect my source. Stern made clear that I was not a colleague,
but a story.

Copies of the *Voice* arrived from New York. I brought one to
bureau chief Socolow's office. He pointed to the subheadline reading, "The Pike Papers: An Introduction by Aaron Latham," and said,
"Are you thinking what I'm thinking?"

I could figure out what he was thinking. Latham worked for the
Felker publications. He was also a friend (later, husband) of CBS
correspondent Lesley Stahl. Many evenings he would be in our
newsroom, waiting for Lesley to finish work. In the center of the
newsroom stood a photocopier that had been used to make extra
copies of the Pike report for CBS executives.

I responded with an elaborate shrug.

Realizing that I could no longer conceal my involvement, I
called my lawyer friend Joe Califano for advice. He counseled level-
ing with CBS, but doing so through the intermediary of a CBS
lawyer so that we could assert lawyer-client privilege in the event of
legal proceedings. I immediately called CBS's Washington counsel,
Joseph DeFranco, and asked to see him the next day—urgently.
Meanwhile, I asked Socolow to dismiss from his mind any theory he

had formed about the origin of the report, saying that he would soon know more.

I realized that my ill-advised effort to conceal myself as the source was diverting attention from the report and what it revealed about the CIA. The story had become that there was a conspiracy to thwart Congress's efforts to keep its secrets. Seizing the opportunity, the White House announced that President Ford was offering Speaker Albert the services of the FBI in tracking down the leak. Secretary Kissinger told a news conference, with one of his magnificent displays of outrage, that "we are facing a new version of McCarthyism," a connection that I could not divine.

Next day, Friday, February 13, my lunch with Salant in New York having been postponed, I drafted a public statement acknowledging my role in transmitting the report as "an inescapable decision of journalistic conscience." Salant called to say I would have full support against any effort to compel me to reveal my source, and later on we would discuss my problems with CBS. "If any," he added reassuringly.

I was now painfully aware of the blunder I had committed— that by turning an act of disclosure into a covert operation I had jeopardized the principle I was defending. Trying to publish a proscribed document without organizational support is not easy. But that was no excuse.

My other great mistake I discovered when I opened the pages of the *New York Times* on Sunday. Staring me in the face was an editorial captioned, "Selling Secrets." It spoke of "cash sale...commercial traffic...the attempt to launder the transaction by devoting the proceeds to high constitutional purposes." In dismay I wrote a letter to the editor, published the following Sunday, saying, "Is it not downright hypocritical for a paper that has so successfully profited from secrets (the Pentagon papers) to apply a term like 'laundering' to one who avoids a profit and diverts it to a cause he believes in?"

The *Times* editorial page tends to be a pacesetter for others. In quick succession came the *Chicago Tribune* with "peddling...to the highest bidder," the *Buffalo Evening News* with "inexcusable merchandising," and climactically, the *Peoria Journal-Star* with "Was Daniel Schorr an accomplice to a crime?"

Here, suddenly, I found myself on the wrong side of the barricade from my journalistic world. For the first time I could understand what countless targets of the press have meant when they said we had it wrong. And, worst of all, my isolation from the media world served to encourage plans in Congress to punish me.

Rep. Samuel Stratton, a conservative Democrat from upstate New York, announced plans to have me summoned to the well of the House of Representatives and peremptorily cited for contempt of Congress. He thought better of that idea after concluding that a "virtual trial" on the floor of the House would afford me too much of a forum. Instead he proposed an investigation, looking toward "some kind of punitive action," to be conducted by the Committee on Standards and Official Conduct—the ethics committee, which, in the ten years of its existence, had never investigated anything. After a short debate, the Stratton resolution was adopted by a lopsided 269 to 115.

My wife was testifying at the time before a House subcommittee on children's health. During her testimony the buzzer sounded three times, signaling a quorum call on the floor. A short time later as the members filed back into the hearing room, Rep. James Scheuer, at whose home Li and I had originally met, told my wife, "They just voted to investigate Dan."

Troubles did not come singly. The Justice Department told the press it would "determine if there is any reason to investigate a possible violation of law." President Ford's counsel, Philip Buchen, mentioned the possibility of violation of a statute prohibiting "unauthorized disclosure of signal intelligence."

President Ford scheduled a press conference, and Socolow, fearing that the president might attack me personally, urged me not to attend. I insisted on going, although promising not to ask any questions. The president denounced the leaking of the Pike report and promised tighter measures to safeguard "critical intelligence secrets."

I was still assigned to the "intelligence beat," but it was becoming increasingly difficult to work. On February 18 I had a brief chat with CIA director George Bush when he arrived in the Capitol for a closed-door briefing for the Senate Committee on Foreign Relations. An Associated Press photographer took a picture of us that dominated the front page of the *Washington Evening Star.* The caption, referring to my run-in with Richard Helms, spoke of "another confrontation" with a CIA chief. Bush made a friendly call to my home, expressing astonishment at the caption and apologizing if his thoughtful expression as he considered my question was interpreted by someone as anger.

That evening, as it happened, the Bushes and the Schorrs were dinner guests at the Netherlands embassy. The ambassador greeted us nervously, relieved to learn that we were on good terms and that he need fear no "incident."

I continued working, as best I could, despite the tension surrounding me. But the next day, Socolow interrupted me in the midst of assembling a story for the *Evening News* to say that, on instruction from New York, I was immediately to stop working on the intelligence beat.

I learned the reason for the abrupt order two weeks later from the trade journal *Broadcasting.* The executive committee of the CBS radio affiliates had voted unanimously to demand that I be taken off the air and that my dismissal be considered. The television affiliates came through with a similar message. CBS stations joined in attacking me on the air. WBT-TV in Charlotte, North Carolina, said, "We don't think newsmen should be able to break the rules with a claim of individual conscience." WSAU in Wausau, Wisconsin, said, "It could well have harmed the national interest, and Schorr's action should not go unanswered." John M. Rivers, president of WCSC in Charleston, South Carolina, was candid enough to say on air that congressional anger at the networks might cause Congress to make concessions to cable television.

Within two hours of the House vote to launch an investigation, Socolow advised that Salant wanted to see me in New York the next morning for unspecified reasons, and he would accompany me. Meanwhile, my telephone was ringing with incessant requests for comment on the House action. To one and all I responded much as some of my interview subjects had—with an assertion of confidence in our constitutional system and expectation that I would be vindicated.

Some calls were anonymous, some abusive, even threatening. The CBS switchboard in New York relayed word of a call threatening to "waste that traitor." My wife and I returned from dinner at the home of friends to be met by a distraught babysitter, saying she had been frightened by a stranger at the door who asked my whereabouts and refused to leave his name. The police promised to patrol around our house during the night, and they advised me to get an unlisted telephone number.

Much of the night my wife and I were awake, listening for prowlers, deciding not to have our children walk home from school for a while. In the morning I called Socolow and said that, without wishing to seem alarmist, I didn't feel like starting my car and could he pick me up on his way to the airport.

At CBS News headquarters on West Fifty-seventh Street, Salant waited with three other news executives. Without indicating the purpose of the meeting, they put me through an interrogation on the whole course of events surrounding the publication of the Pike report. At one point Salant asked whether I viewed the Pike report as personal property. Sleepless though I was, I had the wit to reply that, since government documents carry no copyright, it was, as far as I could see, public property.

After two hours of questioning, Salant said, "If you will step outside, we will consider our decision." Then, changing his mind, he said, "No, I don't want you wandering the halls. You stay here, we will step out."

Decision? Decision about what?

I had not long to wait. Five minutes later the four filed back into the office and gravely took their seats, looking for all the world like a jury in a capital case. From twenty years of associating with him, I knew that Salant's clearing his throat and looking down at his desk while speaking meant that he had something unpleasant to say. He offered me the choice of resigning with a payout of my contract, which had three more years to run, or remaining on the payroll without "any further duties at CBS News."

Dazed with fatigue, I tried to absorb that, without benefit of counsel, I had been tried and found guilty of some unstated charge. I pleaded that public dismissal at this juncture would surely prejudice my position in the forthcoming congressional investigation. Salant replied that he was sorry, but that was the way it had to be.

I declined to say anything more without consulting my lawyer. Salant said that I would have until the next day, Saturday, to make my decision. Only a week before Salant had said that our problems, "if any," could wait for the conclusion of the congressional inquiry. Now I had been fired in a weird star-chamber proceeding that clearly reflected fear of Congress and the CBS affiliates.

I flew back to Washington to tell the news to my family. Eight-year-old Jonathan asked whether this meant that he would no longer be going to the studio with me on Sundays for the sandwiches that followed the program *Face the Nation*.

While I was in New York, Li had prevailed on the telephone company to do a rush job of giving us an unlisted number, and the house was strangely quiet. Our friends, Judith and Milton Viorst, unable to reach us by phone, brought over a bottle of wine. They said they didn't want us to feel shunned by friends, as had happened during the McCarthy days. Richard Dudman of the *St. Louis Post-Dispatch* brought a note of personal support and word that his paper was going to denounce the campaign of vilification against me. Such gestures in a time of trouble are not forgotten.

There was also Joe Califano, a friend in need as well as an attorney in need. Attorney for the *Washington Post* and a leading First Amendment lawyer, he undertook to represent me whether or not he was reimbursed by CBS. On Saturday morning we met at his office and agreed that our first need was to prevent a public firing that would whet the congressional appetite for my scalp. Telephone discussions between Califano and Salant stretched through the day and into the evening while we fended off calls from reporters inquiring about my fate. (Today it seems almost inconceivable that in 1976 I was a running front-page story.)

Finally, Salant agreed to announce that I was being relieved of reportorial duties in order to deal with the House investigation, with the secret understanding that I would resign when the inquiry was concluded. On Monday, Joe and I flew to New York to work out the details. Salant presented a statement for my signature that committed me to resign when CBS, "in our sole discretion," decided that there was no further risk of governmental proceedings. Joe and I looked with astonishment at this undated resignation that would put both sides in the position of covering up the true state of affairs. Salant and the other executives would not be moved. Apparently they needed to satisfy Paley that I was, at long last, being terminated. (In a subsequent interview, Paley told me that he had tried to fire me for twelve years, ever since I had embarrassed him with Senator Goldwater in San Francisco, but that Salant had kept resisting him.)

I called my business agent, Richard Leibner, who came to CBS and spent two hours negotiating the financial details of my termination. Sensing that to CBS my resignation mattered more than money, Richard did a brilliant job of getting on paper not only the payout of the three years of my contract, but also fifty-two weeks of severance pay and the status of retiree for pension and health benefits.

On the way back to Washington, Califano, undergoing baptism in the font of show business, said that what CBS had done was utter madness—giving away hundreds of thousands of dollars for nothing more than the assurance of dismissal, which always lay in its power.

But, meanwhile, CBS and I were joined in an uncomfortable agreement to dissemble in public about the true situation. As I walked into my office in Washington, the news wires were already running bulletins (bulletins, imagine!) saying that I had been "suspended," which was the way they read "relieved of duties." I contributed to the duplicity with a statement that I could not work as a reporter "while personally engaged in a controversy over a reporter's rights."

At lunch the next day, Califano shook his head and asked, "How are they going to explain all this when it comes out that they really fired you in February?"

But, with suspension, the tide of opinion began to shift toward the beleaguered reporter. In the *New York Times*, Tom Wicker, under the caption "Defending Schorr," said that CBS had succumbed to a Ford administration campaign. A CBS survey of its mail showed that letters, which had been running eight to one against me, were now seven to four in my favor. In my own "mailroom," our dining room table, we watched the pro messages climb past the anti heap, which included lots of "Benedict Arnold" and "Communist traitor" appellations.

As the House ethics committee, with a $150,000 appropriation, began hiring retired FBI agents as investigators, editorial opinion shifted markedly. The *New York Times*, which I blamed for helping to provoke the administration attack on me, now ran an editorial captioned, "Overkill on the Hill." Mary McGrory wrote of the House on "a lunatic course."

Califano told me to count my blessings and keep a low profile. I told him I was already committed to speak at a lunch of the Washington (formerly Women's) Press Club. In my speech, reviewed in advance by Joe and with two of his associates in the front row to remind me, I appealed to the assembled journalists:

> I do not ask you to approve of how I went about doing what I tried to do. My own agonized critique indicates some possible improvement in my tactics. But what the government can do to one journalist, it can do to all journalists. When you hear the whip crack, send not to know for whom this backlash cracks. It cracks for you.

Among the questions from the floor, one that I remember was from a woman wanting to know if it was true that I had given the Pike report to the *Village Voice* because my daughter worked there. I replied that, while Lisa was precocious, she was only five. There was laughter, and it struck me that I hadn't heard laughter in a long time.

It struck me that being a cause célèbre was not like being a celebrity. People would not simply tell me that they recognized me from the tube, but some would stop me in the street to say "Hang in there" or simply "Thanks!" Much in demand as a lecturer, I traveled around the country, constantly amazed to find reporters and cameras waiting for me at airports. The questions followed a uniform pattern as though they had all read the same clipping file:

"Why did you sell the Pike report?"

"Wasn't it arrogant to defy Congress and your own employer?"

"What do you say to those who say you are arrogant and abrasive?"

Having worked for freedom of the press, I now began to long for freedom *from* the press. But not from ordinary people. In 1976 I made seventy-three speeches across the country, trying to explain that the nation suffers more from excessive secrecy than from excessive disclosure. I tried to explain why I had to do what I did, however badly I did it. My fondest memory was speaking at the University of Arkansas commencement in a light rain and seeing the gowned graduates in the steeply banked Razorback Stadium give me a standing ovation.

CBS executives, apparently discomforted by my sudden popularity, began spreading word that I wasn't such a hero, that I had tried to implicate Lesley Stahl and Aaron Latham in the transmission of the Pike report. The CBS people knew better, of course, from my first debriefing by Joe DeFranco, in which I took full responsibility. It seemed as though CBS was, retrospectively, trying to come up with a justification for having fired me. The Lesley Stahl matter had not been mentioned in the discussions surrounding my termination. The facade of comity between CBS and myself was beginning to crumble.

Despite my ambiguous position, I decided to attend the black-tie dinner of the Association of Radio and Television Correspondents. The dinner, in reality, is a showcase for network executives to meet their correspondents' important governmental contacts. I had, long before, invited the former CIA director Bill Colby to be my guest. When I called to let him off the hook and avoid embarrassment, he said he looked forward to attending the dinner with me.

As we walked together through the predinner reception, mouths dropped and heads spun. Congressman Pike came up to us to say, "I cannot believe what I'm seeing." Colby replied casually that we were two professionals on the shelf who had shared interesting experiences. After dinner I took Colby to the hotel suite where CBS was having its after-dinner party. Chatting with CBS executives, he seemed fully aware of the sensation he was creating and fully aware that he was making CBS look silly for having suspended me.

The next afternoon, Nina Totenberg, a reporter for National Public Radio, who had been present at the dinner and the CBS party, called to ask my comment on what she had heard from somebody at CBS—that the network had "bought out" my contract and that I would not return when Congress was finished investigating.

I declined comment. She said she was sure enough of her source to broadcast the story that evening. Califano had heard that CBS was now split between "pro-Schorr" and "anti-Schorr" factions, and it appeared that the anti-Schorrs had decided to torpedo our delicate "suspension" arrangement by leaking it.

(Since then Nina and I have become NPR colleagues. She has never offered to identify her source, nor, to satisfy my curiosity about the leak, have I asked her.)

A few minutes after Nina's call that problem was erased from my mind when a physician called from New York to say that my long-ailing mother, eighty-five years old, had died in the hospital after a heart attack. My wife and children were off skiing in Aspen; my brother and sister-in-law were also traveling. As I worked on the phone trying to fetch my scattered family and arrange for a funeral in New York, I was constantly interrupted by calls on the other line inquiring about Nina's story, which was now being quoted by the news services.

Later that night Califano arrived unexpectedly at my home, asking if he could help. I blessed him for his thoughtfulness. He said, "You handle your mother's funeral. I'll take care of yours." And for the next two hours, I talked to relatives and rabbis while Joe talked to reporters.

My mother, widowed when I was six and my brother an infant, had struggled against poverty to raise her sons, finding comfort in my brother's success as a social worker and mine as a journalist. After a series of disorienting heart attacks she had not understood the drama enveloping her firstborn. In her dementia, the last time I visited her nursing home, she told me that I was the editor of the *New York Times*, and persisted when I shook my head. Perhaps just as well. Our early life of privation had left her permanently anxious about her sons' job security.

During "sitting shivah," the week of mourning, I canceled public appearances. At Tulane University, I had been scheduled to debate Bill Colby. He defended me better than I could have defended myself, telling the New Orleans audience, "Schorr carried out his obligation to the First Amendment and to himself as a newsman, and he should not be punished for publication of the Pike report."

The first public event that I attended after the mourning period was the annual white-tie Gridiron Club dinner, to which I was invited because there would be a reference to me in the satiric show. Clark Mollenhof, veteran reporter for the *Des Moines Register and Tribune*, sang a parody: "I want a leak just like the leak they gave to dear old Dan." Secretary Kissinger sought me out to say, "I think you got a bum rap. The blame should fall on whoever leaked the report, not the journalist who received it."

With Kissinger's permission, Califano passed that remark on to the press. A furious Bill Small called Joe to ask why he was cooperating in an attack on CBS. My bosses were clearly feeling uncomfortable now that my ratings had improved. Les Brown wrote in the *New York Times* about the division in CBS over the idea of reinstating me in view of "the drift of public opinion on Mr. Schorr."

In mid-May I asked Califano to propose to CBS that we end the pretense of suspension by an immediate resignation. Bill Small, apparently now reflecting the view of the "pro-Schorr" faction, said he was willing to tear up our February agreement—but without my resigning. The tide had, indeed, turned. With lecture invitations multiplying and various awards being conferred, Joe joked that, if CBS wanted me back at work, I might not have time.

There comes a point in growing fame where one breaks out of the world of news into the world of entertainment. Johnny Carson delivered gags about me on NBC. An NBC prop that now hangs on the wall of my study says, "Schorr Made Congress Read Its Own Report." In a Norman Lear situation comedy, a fictional CBS reporter said his network was shorthanded since my departure. Columnist Art Buchwald made a joke about something as inconceivable as "the night Daniel Schorr replaces Walter Cronkite as anchorman." Perhaps the ultimate was finding my name as the definition for *TV reporter* in the *New York Times* Sunday crossword puzzle.

Meanwhile the ethics committee plodded on with its investigation, interviewing members and staff of the defunct Pike committee. Reporters—including me—were invited to discuss with the committee how the press does its work. None of us would appear voluntarily. The committee held a few public hearings, but postponed a decision on whether to subpoena journalists.

In July, I left with my family for five weeks in Aspen—a benefit of being suspended with pay. Watching the Democratic convention in New York, I heard Cronkite report that "my colleague Dan Schorr received one Oregon vote for the vice-presidential nomination." In my annual lecture for the Aspen Institute, I tried to head off a subpoena, saying, "If subpoenaed I shall not give testimony about the source of the House intelligence report.... I hope there will be no confrontation with Congress over sources."

Califano relayed word of what was happening in the ethics committee hearings. The chief investigator, David Powers, testified that 420 interviews had revealed chaotic security procedures in the final hectic days of drafting the Pike report. Powers said he had established that Crewdson of the *Times* had only made notes on the report, so the only missing copy was the one in my possession.

On July 29, the last hearing day before adjournment for the Republican convention, Rep. James V. Stanton of Ohio, a member of the Pike committee, created a stir by testifying that I had remarked to him about having received the report from the CIA. Califano's associate John Kuhns called to say a subpoena for me now seemed inevitable. But Chairman John J. Flynt Jr., of Georgia, adjourned the hearings for the summer without announcing his plans.

In Los Angeles, where we were visiting my parents-in-law, I met the Democratic presidential nominee, Jimmy Carter. He said, pleasantly, that I was missed in this campaign. I replied that my future seemed to depend on his Georgia compatriot, Congressman Flynt. Carter replied, "I have never been able to figure out what Jack Flynt has in mind." Three days later I was called to the telephone during lunch with my civil libertarian friend Stanley Sheinbaum to be told by my wife that the ethics committee had just voted, eight to four, to subpoena me and personnel of the *Village Voice* to testify in public session on September 15.

The word *jail* suddenly took shape from a mist of abstraction. I returned to the home of my parents-in-law to find them disturbed. They were refugees from Nazi Germany, and my father-in-law had spent some time in the Dachau concentration camp.

I agreed to be interviewed by anchorperson Connie Chung at KNXT-TV, the CBS-owned station in Los Angeles. She asked, "Are you prepared to go to jail?" I replied, "I hope it won't come to that. But I cannot betray a source." My family watched at home, and my wife later told me that six-year-old Lisa had asked, "Do they really want to put Daddy in jail?"

When we returned to Washington at the end of August, the ethics committee was asking the House for an additional $100,000 and Chairman Flynt was telling reporters he thought he knew who had leaked the Pike report. After Labor Day, Califano and I started a week of intensive prepping for my hearing. He and his assistants pored over research papers. I was given the office of a junior associate, Charles Robb (later, senator from Virginia), in which to study the hearing transcript and to draft my opening statement.

On September 13, two days before the hearing, we assembled in Califano's conference room. He, pencil in hand, slowly read my draft statement to his associates, making verbal changes along the way.

Then I was asked to read the statement, pretending that I was before the committee. Next day they all tested me on questions that the congressmen might ask. An important caution was about the "Stanton booby trap." If I specifically denied talking to Congressman Stanton about my source, it might be claimed that I thereby opened myself to questions about whom I had talked to. The correct reply was that I had discussed it with nobody, and not to respond to questions about any specific person.

A pile of telephone messages awaited us as we came out of the conference room. Public television said it planned to carry the hearing live nationwide, even though limited by the committee to a single camera. The Newspaper Guild of America had started a petition campaign on my behalf and had collected fifty-five hundred signatures. Four reporters of the *Fresno Bee*, themselves in jail for protecting a news source, signed the petition in their cell. Rep. H. John Heinz III of Pennsylvania provided a room in the Rayburn House office building, not far from the ethics committee, where journalistic stars such as Dan Rather, Carl Bernstein, Seymour Hersh, Mary McGrory, and I. F. Stone spoke out in my support at a news conference.

Chairman Flynt, receiving all the petitions and telegrams, telephoned Califano to complain about pressure on the committee. Califano replied that it wasn't his pressure. To my amazement, what seemed to be happening was a belated backlash against the secrecy backlash, a surge of sentiment for an unfettered press. No longer, it seemed, was I an isolated target for the national-security buffs.

Next day, September 15, my wife and I met Califano and his associates at Joe's office and proceeded to Capitol Hill in two taxis. Outside the Rayburn building, in a drizzle, was a long line of spectators that had started, we were told, at 6:30 A.M. As we mounted the marble steps, Califano suddenly stopped and said, "Hey, isn't there something wrong with this picture?" As my heart started beating more rapidly, Joe continued, "Isn't it always the *Italian* gangster and the *Jewish* lawyer?" Very funny.

In the crowded hearing room I heard committee counsel John Marshall say, "Mr. Daniel Schorr to the witness stand." And there I was, Califano beside me, facing up past the covey of photographers sitting on the floor to the congressmen ranged along the raised dais. I did not feel anxiety so much as nervous tension of the sort that comes with an important live broadcast in prime time.

I read my oft-rehearsed statement smoothly, explaining why protection of sources is vital to a free press, concluding, "If you will allow one last personal word: To betray a source would be, for me, to betray myself, my career, and my life. To say that I refuse to do it isn't saying it quite right. I cannot do it."

Marshall plunged ahead with his prepared scenario. First, the demand that I produce the Pike report and, when I refused, the warning read by Chairman Flynt that "willful refusal" would subject me to "prosecution and punishment by a fine or imprisonment, or both."

Next, the expected "Stanton booby trap." I denied that I had discussed the source with anyone, but refused to make that denial specific. Once again the warning of possible prosecution.

Finally, the demand that I say where I got the report. And, for a third time, Chairman Flynt read to me the warning of a citation for contempt of Congress and the punishment that might follow.

During the lunch recess Congressman Flynt considerately made available to us an office in which we could talk and relax. I was relieved to be told by Califano that I had "done fine." Counsel Marshall looked in on us to praise our "professionalism." After lunch there were a few more questions from Marshall that I refused to answer.

As the members started their questioning, the atmosphere in the hearing room began to change. On live television my nemeses acted almost apologetic about their seven-month pursuit. South Carolina Republican Floyd D. Spence asked my understanding for Congress's problem trying to keep its secrets. To his question whether I would disclose a source if a life depended on it, I replied, as coached, that I was not an absolutist and would be given pause if I thought a life depended on it. "That's the answer I wanted," said Spence with satisfaction.

Hostility evaporated and the hearing turned into a sort of seminar on the role of the press and the constraints on the press, and I found that I was beginning to enjoy myself. As the end of the hearing neared, I was amazed to hear Thad Cochran, Mississippi Republican, say, "I support you a hundred percent...in your refusal to name your source." James Quillen, Tennessee Republican, said, "I understand your sincerity, Mr. Schorr, and I respect it."

I felt a weight being lifted from my shoulders. I had turned from recalcitrant witness into teacher of free-press values. In closed session the committee voted, six to five, not to recommend a contempt citation. Four members, led by Chairman Flynt, added a statement reprimanding me and saying, "We have created a most unlikely hero."

"Unlikely hero" was right. What saved me, I think, was the public television decision to carry the hearing live. There is something about the picture of a covey of politicians staring down on a lonely person defending a principle that elicits sympathy.

Now many of those who had excoriated me joined in praising me. Richard Salant, who a month earlier had insisted on my resignation, now telegraphed a message of "gratitude for a superb appearance." In Williamsburg, Virginia, CBS president Arthur Taylor likened me to the Virginia patriots who had "run risks for freedom."

At home, I heard Jonathan explain to his younger sister, "Daddy had a secret and gave it to a newspaper. And Congress got mad and wanted to put him in jail. But the consumers of America wouldn't let Congress send him to jail."

It had cost the taxpayers $450,000 to generate the Pike report on abuses on the CIA and another $250,000 to try to learn how the report had reached the public. It had cost CBS $150,000 for Joe Califano to represent me. And years later, when Hillary Paley, planning to marry Joe, took him home to meet her father, his first words were, "Mr. Califano, you charged me too much for representing Dan Schorr."

It was time for my deferred resignation, but my employers had other plans. Salant asked me to come to New York the following Monday to discuss reinstatement. Meanwhile, Mike Wallace asked me to tape an interview about my First Amendment triumph for *60 Minutes*. It turned out to be a hatchet job of accusations, undoubtedly reflecting the anti-Schorr faction in CBS. He repeated Salant's line about the Pike's report being CBS property. Califano strongly urged me not to return to CBS, saying I would be giving up a financially advantageous termination agreement for an uncertain position that could be ended at any time.

So great was my emotional investment in CBS that I agonized about my decision. But, Califano argued persuasively that I had no future there, and Wallace's antagonistic interview with me seemed to confirm that.

I called Salant at home and told him, "Dick, I've known you too long to leave you in the dark until tomorrow. It is my intention to go through with the resignation." I heard a gasp of consternation. He said it had never been his intention to close the door on my return and that he should not have let the corporate lawyers write the termination agreement.

At one point we both lapsed into silence, broken when Salant groaned, "Oh, Christ! See you tomorrow."

In Salant's office in New York the next day, Califano presented my one-sentence letter saying I was resigning "in accordance with the letter of agreement of February 23." Salant said he wouldn't accept it—that automatic resignation had never been his intention.

"But you fired me in February," I said.

"Then I'm rehiring you now," he replied.

It was like saying that he wanted me out when my ratings were low and wanted me back now that my ratings were high. I shook my head. It was simply not to be. I agreed to a new and friendlier exchange of letters, in which I said, "I leave CBS News with sadness, but without rancor," and he said, "I share your sadness. Your years of reporting for CBS News have been unusually distinguished."

In his memoir, Salant described me thus: "... a very special reporter, super-aggressive and determined. He fought with everything he had to get a story and to get to the bottom of it, and then to get it on the air. He used his shoulders to shove not only competing news organizations' reporters aside, but even his colleagues at CBS News. He was not universally loved. But he was very good."

Salant was still unable to acknowledge that he had fired me and then tried to undo the dismissal. He wrote, "I will have to leave to others more objective and less defensive than I to decide whether Dan voluntarily resigned or whether I fired him—or whether it was a little of both."

So, twenty-three years after Murrow had asked me to join the "Tiffany network" and fifteen years after his departure, my love-hate affair with CBS News was over. Washed away by one controversial leak too many? Undone by a reporting style that proved indigestible to a network worried about affiliates and regulation? Unable to adapt myself to corporate tugs on the reins? Unwilling to exempt my own network from my investigative reporting?

All of that, I guess. Finally, I had an answer to Scotty Reston's 1953 question, "Had enough?"

CHAPTER 17

LIFE WITH TED

At the age of sixty, with no thought of retirement, I pondered my next career. For a while I coasted on the momentum of fame. I accepted a short-term Regents professorship in journalism at the University of California, Berkeley, conducting a graduate seminar, "The Impact of Television on Society." At my first meeting with the two dozen students who had signed up for the seminar, the first questions were not about my lofty subject, but how I would grade, how much reading I would require, and whether I would demand a term paper. These were not the Berkeley change-the-world radicals of the sixties, but the pragmatists of the seventies, seeking the maximum graduation credits for the minimum investment of time.

I learned, too, that my students were less interested in academic pursuits than celebrity pursuit. They were less focused on the trouble with television than the trouble I had been through and how close I had come to going to jail for daring to tangle with the CIA. One student brought her mother to my weekly conference hour for no other reason than she wanted to be able to say she had met me.

My family stayed in Washington, the children being in school, and I lived in the Faculty Club, deserted at night. To occupy my evenings, Dean Ed Bayley farmed me out for lectures in other

Berkeley faculties and to other campuses all over California. To all I carried my now well-rehearsed message about the importance of defending the freedom of the press.

I wound up my four-month academic stint on June 19, 1977, with a commencement speech in the journalism school. Dean Bayley took pleasure in introducing me with a reference to how hard he had worked me and how the school had gotten more than its money's worth.

Without time for lengthy farewells, I was off to Chicago, met by a helicopter, and whisked to Columbia College for one more commencement speech and an honorary degree for "standing up to power with rare courage and integrity."

But man does not live by kudos alone. And Berkeley had taught me I was not marked out to be a teacher, as I lacked the requisite patience and passion for guiding young minds. I was perhaps too great an egoist to find vicarious satisfaction in the advancement of unenthusiastic students.

So, after a quarter of a century with a steady paycheck, I was a freelance again, lecturing and writing for op-ed pages and magazines. The *Des Moines Register and Tribune*, seeking to trade on my name recognition, offered to syndicate a weekly column. One of the first clients, the conservative *Arizona Republican*, explained in an editorial titled "Why Daniel Schorr?" that people needed to know what the outrageous left wing was saying. The *Seattle Post-Intelligencer* carried my picture at the top of the front page with the headline "TV's Daniel Schorr Returns to Newspapers."

Not for long, alas. To newspapers looking forward to verbal bomb-throwing, my column, "Daniel Schorr at Large," was a great disappointment. My first column, on February 8, 1978, criticized President Carter for not keeping his promise to name judges solely on the basis of merit. Other columns analyzed the conflict over national health insurance, discussed the Korea influence-peddling scandal in the House of Representatives, and outlined the CIA's dilemma in dealing with the Soviet defectors who might be double agents. I wrote from places where I had other reasons to go—from the oil fields of Prudhoe Bay, Alaska, from

NATO maneuvers in Germany, and from the scene of a neo-Nazi march in Skokie, Illinois.

In short, I wrote not as a rabble-rouser but as a journalist, and for many newspapers, that did not match their perception of the troublemaker who had defied constituted authority. After two years, with my subscribers' list never exceeding a hundred, the Des Moines syndicate declined to renew my contract.

During that time I also made a peripheral return to television. I narrated some public television specials and appeared on panel programs. A service for nonnetwork commercial stations, the Independent Television News Association, arranged for me to tape commentaries twice weekly. This ITNA connection opened the way to my next career.

The head of ITNA, Reese Schonfeld, called me from New York in May 1979 to say he had an interesting proposal for me. He was in negotiation with an Atlanta media entrepreneur, Ted Turner, about creating a round-the-clock news service for the fast-multiplying cable-television stations hungry for programming.

I knew little about Ted Turner and less about cable television. Turner, I learned, had inherited a billboard advertising company from his father, an alcoholic and a suicide. Ted had sold that company and acquired marginal television stations in Charlotte, North Carolina, and Atlanta. From the Atlanta station he had created something called a superstation—distributing its programming by satellite to the cable systems. Station WTBS (for Turner Broadcasting System) had no news programs, but did lampoon news figures such as Walter Cronkite. Turner also had interests in yachting, baseball, drinking, and women. At first blush, not where a traditional newsman would want to spend his waning years, nor, indeed, was I the kind of person who would appeal to a flamboyant media entrepreneur.

But I did need a job. For several days I temporized by putting questions to Schonfeld for relay to Turner about what would be required of me, how much freedom I would have, whether I would be drawn into lobbying and promotional activities. Finally, Schonfeld said that Turner was leaving for Las Vegas for the annual convention of the National Cable Television Association and suggested that I go there for a brief meeting and Turner would try to resolve all my doubts.

The reason for the time pressure became clear. Turner had scheduled a press conference for 4:30 P.M. next day in Las Vegas at which he would announce his plan to create a news network in a year. My presence at the news conference, I gathered, was intended to lend journalistic legitimacy to his announcement.

I was leaving for a lecture in Los Angeles that evening and agreed to stop off in Las Vegas next morning on the way home. Schonfeld, as though fearful of losing me, accompanied me to Los Angeles and, early next morning, to Las Vegas.

In a penthouse suite in the Las Vegas Hilton I was greeted by this human tornado, Ted Turner, who interspersed our "negotiation" with bites of breakfast, telephone calls, and a brief "Good morning" to a woman friend who appeared from elsewhere in the suite. In rapid-fire fashion, he outlined his media philosophy: Over-the-air networks would decline as audiences turned to videos and other outlets for entertainment on demand. The network future belonged to whoever would deliver what was happening now—live news and live sports. That was why he wanted to be the first to deliver all news, all sports, all the time.

Yes, he had not taken news seriously in the past, but he was taking it seriously now. He was offering me a chance to get in on the ground floor as the very first employee of the venture he would call Cable News Network. He offered me a vice presidency, stock options, management of the Washington bureau. He shrugged when I said I wanted only a journalistic position—senior news analyst.

My last question was how I could be sure that I would not be obliged to violate my professional standards. He said, "Look, you write an agreement that says you won't have to do anything you don't want to, and I'll sign it."

I went down to the lobby to call my business agent and lawyer. With their help I hand-drafted an agreement that said, "No demand will be made upon him that would compromise his professional ethics and responsibilities." Turner, hardly glancing at it, scrawled his signature and we were off, Turner racing through the corridors, I puffing along behind to a conference room crowded with cable operators and media reporters aware that Turner was launching some new enterprise.

That was May 21, 1979.

Could a grizzled veteran of newspapers, radio, and television in his midsixties find happiness with a fast-talking Southern buccaneer in an untried new universe of communications? At any rate, once again I had the security of a steady salary—for however long it might last.

How fragile was that security came home to me in August, when I arrived in Denver to address a dinner of cable television people and was greeted with a news agency dispatch reporting that Turner was missing in a storm during a yachting race off Ireland. Fortunately for both of us, he made it safely to port.

In that promotional start-up year, Turner and I made a strange couple. He bought a Jewish country club in Atlanta for his CNN headquarters and, as he showed me around, joked that I should feel at home there. We appeared together on a late-night NBC talk program, and Tom Snyder asked me how I would characterize my new boss. I said he was a modern version of Bill Paley, with the same combination of business acumen, programming awareness, and grasp of possibilities opened by technological change. I noted Turner's eyes widening in appreciation.

Once, we met at Washington National Airport to fly together to Atlanta, and I was embarrassed to find that he had a coach ticket while I was traveling first-class. He agreed to get upgraded, grumbling about the waste of money. On board he showed me pictures of his plantation near Charleston, South Carolina, and his children. I told about my family, and Turner asked how my wife and children would see me at work since cable had not yet come to Washington.

"I know," he said, "I'll give you a dish." And four days later a crew showed up at my home to install a satellite receiver. Later he joked, "Did they fix it so it can only bring in CNN?"

Sometimes our conversation became quite personal. He told me he had grown up hating newspapers because his alcoholic father would come home with newspapers carrying editorials that condemned roadside billboards—his father's failing business. Perhaps because of his antinewspaper animus, Turner developed a theory that the printed press was doomed in an era of oil scarcity because it was an "energy inefficient" way of delivering information, using fossil fuels at every stage, from making wood pulp to carting away yesterday's papers.

Deeper than his hatred of newspapers was his hatred of the television networks, which he called "purveyors of murders, rapes, and disasters." He said that when he had first set foot in his Atlanta station, "I didn't know a transmitter from a camera," but he thought it had served him that he came to television with a "totally new approach."

Schonfeld, the president of CNN, was on hand in April 1980 when we moved into the space rented for our Washington bureau on Wisconsin Avenue north of Georgetown. Partitions were not up yet, and telephone lines were strung haphazardly—and hazardously—along the floor. In mid-May we started dry runs, switching back and forth to the anchor desk in that former Jewish country club in Atlanta. My first report speculated on the possibility that should the Democratic convention deadlock between President Carter and Sen. Edward M. Kennedy, Secretary of State Edmund Muskie might emerge as a dark-horse compromise. Seen by few, happily.

On June 1, CNN opened for business with an interview with President Carter that we had taped the preceding day. It celebrated, among other things, the first Southern-based national television network, and from Carter's state, at that.

It was an auspicious day not only for CNN, but for my twelve-year-old son, Jonathan, who joined me at the White House to meet his first president. The "news" in that interview was that the president said he would make every effort to forestall a convention fight with Senator Kennedy, which would only harm Carter's chances of beating Ronald Reagan.

Two days later Schonfeld had me come down to Atlanta to anchor, heedless of hazard, coverage of the California, Ohio, and New Jersey primaries. With untried facilities and untrained reporters we put on a show more daring than effective. I was consoled by the knowledge that there could not have been more than a few thousand viewers, curious enough about the new kid on the block to tune in.

From our hastily improvised coverage in Atlanta of the primaries, I flew to Newark to join Senator Kennedy on his campaign plane. On the way to Cleveland I taped an interview in which Kennedy challenged Carter to a debate—a challenge that the president ignored.

Next, in these heady days, to Venice for the G-7 summit of the seven industrialized nations. President Carter strove to hold together European allies nervous about the American confrontation with the Soviet Union over the war in Afghanistan. European leaders were more nervous still about the prospect of a more hawkish Reagan as the next president. As Carter emerged from the meeting, I asked if he thought that his stock might be going up in Europe because of Reagan jitters. He nodded and said, "I hope not just in Europe."

I stood before our camera to record an ad-lib commentary and ended by saying, "This is Daniel Schorr, CBS News, Venice." Then I broke out laughing. Four years away from CBS had not overcome the habit of a quarter century.

From Venice I went to Belgrade, as Carter made up for having missed the funeral of President Tito. A few hours in Madrid for reasons still unknown to me (although I enjoyed a guided tour of the fabulous Prado art museum). And home to plunge into the political campaign.

Covering the Republican convention in Detroit and the nomination of Ronald Reagan was an adventure in bricks without straw. Other networks had planned their coverage for months, nay, years. While they were ensconced in glass-enclosed "skybooths," CNN had to make do with an open position in the spectators' gallery. Bernard Shaw and I would be interviewing a Republican official or exchanging thoughts when the band would start playing and leave us looking helplessly into our live cameras.

We got through the Republican convention in Detroit and the Democratic convention in New York. And then I found myself traveling to observe the candidates of both parties. I flew to Shreveport to interview Reagan, marveling at his smoothness. Asked his reaction to being endorsed by the Ku Klux Klan, he said, in even tones, that he had not sought the endorsement and that he rejected it.

My most memorable moment of the 1980 political season was the presidential debate on October 26—for most of the country a two-man debate, but a three-man debate for the fledgling CNN.

President Carter had refused to include in the debate the independent candidate, Rep. John Anderson, a moderate Republican from Illinois. Maverick Ted Turner, seeing no reason to exclude a fellow maverick, gave orders that we find a way of including him in the debate. This was a considerable challenge requiring a considerable technical feat. We would carry the Carter-Reagan debate from Cleveland. We would interject responses from Anderson, seated with me on the stage of Constitution Hall in Washington, which had been rented for the occasion.

Imagine, if you can, how this was supposed to work. We would carry the two principals responding to the first question in Cleveland. Then, we would switch to Constitution Hall, where I would put a similar question to Anderson, and he would respond. Then we would cut back to Cleveland, now on tape, having fallen behind. Our technicians eventually lost track of what they were doing, and the result was a technical disaster.

With all the zaniness of the venture, CNN was hailed in the press for valor and independence. On the wall of my study I still have the five-foot-high poster inviting people to come to Constitution Hall to see "John Anderson debating the issues with Ronald Reagan and President Carter."

As the election approached, I hoped that my life at CNN would settle into some kind of routine. But that was not to be. A week before the election Schonfeld called me from Atlanta to say he had heard rumors that the fifty-two hostages imprisoned in the embassy in Tehran were about to be released. He had heard that Dan Rather of CBS was on his way to Frankfurt, Germany, where the hostages would be brought. My boss said that I should leave on the first flight for Frankfurt because "CNN will not be beaten on this story."

I made some calls and ascertained, first of all, that Rather was in New York and not going anywhere. Further, my best sources in the State Department and the White House assured me that there was no sign of any imminent break in the negotiations with Iran that Undersecretary of State Warren Christopher was conducting through Algeria. Further, it was most unlikely that the Iranians, after Carter's futile rescue effort, would help his election chances with an "October surprise."

All this I communicated to Schonfeld, who responded only, "I want you on the next plane to Frankfurt. A camera crew will meet you there."

Two hours later I was headed to Dulles International Airport and an overnight flight to Frankfurt. From nearby Rhine-Main U.S. Air Force Base, we set up a "live shot" showing where the hostages would presumably arrive and how they would then be transported to the air force hospital in Wiesbaden. Having done my absurd duty, I then settled down in an airport hotel, whittling away some of the time with colleagues from my old days in Germany, and waiting for permission to come home.

On election day I was permitted to return, arriving in the afternoon. The exit polls were already projecting a clear Reagan victory. I did not spare Schonfeld in expressing my frustration about the useless trip to Frankfurt. He replied meekly, "You have to try."

Two weeks later I broadcast the American intelligence assessment that Iran was stalling the negotiations in Algiers to insure that the hostages were not freed on Carter's watch. That turned out to be accurate. Four days before the Reagan inaugural I flew again to Frankfurt, this time with plenty of company. On January 20, inauguration day, Iranian television showed the Algerian planes in Tehran, ready to take off, with the liberated Americans. In a live report from

Frankfurt, I spoke of a "sense of rage beyond suspense that Americans, from the president on down, can be kept on tenterhooks and manipulated up to the last moment of this grisly episode." A little subjective, but no one minded.

Moments after President Reagan was sworn in, the planes were in the air. President Reagan, as a gesture to the outgoing administration, asked ex-president Carter and ex-secretary Muskie to fly to Frankfurt to receive the "returnees" officially. They were brought to Wiesbaden, to a hospital festooned with yellow ribbons hung from the trees and bushes. No contact with the news media was allowed. I spent much of the night outside the hospital in subfreezing cold, trying to describe on live television in America a scene that I could not see because CNN had neglected to provide me with a TV monitor. Other than the hostages being whisked from buses into the hospital, there was not much of a scene anyway, except for military police making sure that no one approached the building.

Families of the returnees had been advised that, after 444 days of captivity, it was better to delay reunions until after a few days of decompression. A day later ex-president Carter visited them in the hospital and came out visibly shaken by what he called "mistreatment much worse than I could imagine."

After six days of medical attention and debriefing, the fifty-two were taken to West Point, New York, for further decompression before being exposed to the press. I returned to Washington with Carter and Muskie, and, with the help of a plane charter, I got to West Point in time. I then followed the released hostages to Washington for President Reagan's exuberant welcome home on the White House lawn. He promised the returnees "swift and effective retribution" for any future attack on an American diplomat—a promise that he was unable to keep.

From the White House lawn, I closed my live report about the returnees: "They have floated this week on a sea of yellow ribbons and an ocean of love that stretched across three continents. Tomorrow is the first day of the rest of their lives as they try to put behind them an experience they can never forget."

Despite the frigid night outside the hospital in Wiesbaden, I counted it as one of my greatest experiences in journalism to be so close to a story of such human endurance. Occasionally I still run into Bruce Langen and others of the former prisoners, and after two decades, I still feel a special warmth about them.

The cornucopia of airtime that a twenty-four-hour news service provided took some getting used to after a quarter century of scarcity at CBS. I settled down into a routine of a daily news analysis, titled "From the Desk of Daniel Schorr," plus a weekly, and eventually daily, live program called *Ask CNN*, responding to questions phoned in by the audience. Plus an "insert" into whatever program was on the air whenever required by a development or the simple need to fill time.

An event such as the shooting of President Reagan on March 30, 1981, mobilized CNN's slender resources for saturation coverage. With Bernard Shaw at the anchor desk, I spoke from George Washington University Hospital, interviewing press spokesman Lyn Nofziger or anyone with a snippet of information about what was happening in the operating room.

When not in the hospital, I was back at the office researching tangential stories. There was the question of who controlled the nuclear trigger when the president was incapacitated. Not the vice president, I learned. In a secret arrangement, a line of authority ran through the secretary of defense and the Joint Chiefs of Staff.

I spent much time researching the profile and background of the would-be assassin, John Hinckley Jr., learning of his obsession with violent movies. He would hole up in a hotel room with junk food, his eyes glued to the television screen. I learned that he had several times seen the violent film *Taxi Driver* and had developed a fixation on Jody Foster, the female lead. Paul Schrader, who had written the screenplay, told me on the telephone that the moment he had heard of the attack on the president, he had said, "There goes another taxi driver!" I received compliments for a piece of original reporting.

Media violence was an interest I shared with Ted Turner. He would send me notes praising my reports on the air. When I wrote a lengthy article on media violence for the magazine *Washingtonian*, he sent me a handwritten note, saying, "The best single article on the subject I have ever read. Congratulations. I'm proud to be associated with you. Keep on truckin'."

At Ted's urging, I testified before a House committee on "the symbiotic relationship between television and violent behavior," and he quoted from my statement when he appeared before another congressional committee.

But then a disagreement arose between us. Turner felt strongly enough about media violence to make it the subject of his first personal editorial on his network. It concluded by saying that violent movies had to be "stopped." He added, "If you are as concerned as I am, you should write your congressman and your senator and tell him you want something done about these destructive motion pictures."

To criticize violent films was one thing; asking Congress to ban them raised First Amendment questions. His editorial ran eleven times over the Memorial Day weekend. I sent word that, lest I appeared to be associated with a call for censorship, I felt it necessary to reply to him on the air. Word came from Turner's office that he didn't know what I was talking about, but go ahead. My reply ran just once—at a late hour.

Word of the intramural dispute got into the newspapers. Turner sent me a clipping with a note indicating that he was still mystified about why I felt it necessary to reply to him. "I know that you are strong on violence in television and the movies," he said. "So, what do *you* think should be done?"

But then he dismissed the matter and concluded that he should do no more editorials. There seemed to be no hard feelings. When he came to Washington to speak at a lunch or a dinner, he still invited me to be present. Sometimes he pointed to me as "that liberal who works for me."

Once Turner came to Washington for a meeting with Senator Goldwater, chairman of the Senate communications committee, seeking help on a piece of legislation dealing with the cable industry. He later told me that Goldwater asked him, "Why don't you get rid of that son of a bitch Schorr?" Turner said he replied, "Senator, I need your help, but nobody tells me who I hire and who I fire."

Against the loyal, independent Turner one had to balance the casually bigoted Turner. Once he had lunch with the Reverend Jesse Jackson, who was urging him to hire more Afro-Americans. Flippantly, Turner said he was a minority, too, having to contend with three big networks, that he was also one of the poor, having lost $15 million the previous year. And, Turner added as Jackson shook his head unbelievingly, one answer to minority unemployment might be to have blacks carry missiles from silo to silo, "the way Egyptians used to carry stone blocks during the building of the pyramids."

Turning to Jane Fonda, his second wife, the civil rights leader said, "Your husband is a rich racist brat."

"He treats everybody that way," she replied.

Characteristically, several months later Turner became a life member of the National Association for the Advancement of Colored People, saying, "I think everybody, black or white, rich or poor, Jewish, Italian, truly should be equal."

And, in truth, Turner's bigotry seemed mainly for shock effect. CNN's chief executive officer, Reese Schonfeld, was Jewish, as was Turner's senior news analyst, and Bernard Shaw, black, was his favorite anchorman.

By 1982 I found myself quite at home with a twenty-four-hour news service and its unpredictable demands. The death of Soviet premier Leonid Brezhnev would summon me at 5 A.M. for the ten-minute drive from Woodley Road to Wisconsin Avenue and a long on-camera ad-lib from memory about Brezhnev's position and his friendship with President Nixon. The attempt on the life of Pope John Paul II in Rome had me on the newsroom set, chatting about his Polish resistance background and speculating with colleagues about who (perhaps the KGB) had been behind the assassination attempt. The bomb attack on the American marines in Beirut called for a lengthy explanation of the tangled Middle Eastern situation and America's role in Lebanon.

I became, in the most literal sense of the word, a generalist, enabled by a long career to say something about almost anything.

I also became something of a Reagan watcher, intrigued especially by his unheeding carelessness with facts. He told and retold as factual a story about a heroic tail-gunner who insisted on going with his pilot long after Reagan must have known he was remembering a scene in a motion picture. He went on telling a story about a Chicago "welfare queen" driving a Cadillac to pick up her check long after he must have known it was an invention. I assumed the task of covering his news conferences, then going out on the White House lawn, clipboard in hand, to list for the CNN audience some of the errors he had made.

For example, on May 13, 1982, I ticked off the following errors in a single exchange on the subject of arms control:

- Reagan said that a Democratic-controlled Senate had refused to ratify SALT (the Strategic Arms Limitation Treaty). Not so. President Carter withdrew the treaty after the Soviet invasion of Afghanistan.
- Reagan said the treaty would have "allowed the Soviet Union just about to double their present nuclear capability." Not so. It would have meant a modest increase, at most.
- Reagan said his administration was concentrating on submarine-launched missiles because "these instruments can be intercepted—they can be recalled." Not so. There is no way a submarine-launched missile can be recalled. He was apparently thinking of "fail-safe" arrangements for recalling bombers headed toward their targets.

This kind of spot analysis did not make me popular around the White House. I began finding it difficult to get seated at a news conference, let alone be recognized for a question. Press Secretary Larry Speakes would positively glare at me when he saw me, which was often, because my "senior" position required me to go on Reagan's major trips, such as summit sessions of the G-7 industrial powers in Versailles and Ottawa.

A keenly nostalgic moment in June 1982 was Reagan's visit to the Berlin Wall, whose beginnings I had witnessed twenty-one years earlier. "That ugly gray gash," the president called it. Like President Kennedy with his *Ich bin ein Berliner*, Reagan had learned a few words of German for the occasion, a sentimental phrase, *Berlin bleibt Berlin* (Berlin is still Berlin). I was saddened to see that, in those two decades, West Berlin had become a seedy city rather than a heroic city, isolated as it was behind the Iron Curtain. Reagan would challenge Gorbachev to "tear down this Wall!" and would live to see it come down in 1989.

A round-the-clock network with a little budget relies heavily on talking heads—our own and the many invited guests. In my five years with CNN I must have interviewed, or participated in interviewing, many dozens. Once CNN put out a piece of publicity bragging of all the "hard-to-get interviews" I had done, ranging from foreign figures such as West German chancellor Helmut Kohl to American figures such as H. R. Haldeman, President Nixon's former chief of staff.

Looking back, I remember a few odd moments in these interviews. There was Henry Kissinger, recovering from open-heart surgery, breaking the news that "the doctors found I have a heart." There was the Lebanese ambassador, looking around uncomfortably and finally saying, "There must be some misunderstanding. I was told I would be interviewed by Dinah Shore." There was FBI director William Webster in January 1985, puncturing a scare about a Libyan "hit squad" reportedly on its way to assassinate President Reagan. Webster said it was a hoax, "probably planted" by double agents.

The one interview I remember best was an unprecedented hour-long conversation with Supreme Court justice Harry A. Blackmun. We had met in the summer of 1982 in a "Justice and Society" seminar in Aspen and had become friends. During one of our walks he talked of the "remoteness" of the court from the people. I seized the opportunity to suggest that he could help to make the court more accessible by explaining it in a taped interview for television.

After several more meetings, he finally agreed. He chose Thanksgiving Day for the taping "because the Chief [Warren Burger] will be out of town and won't be able to stop me." On the appointed day we arrived in three CNN trucks. Blackmun was waiting in the underground garage to show us where to park.

The justice was more open about the workings of the court than I would have expected. He spoke of the justices acting like "prima donnas," sometimes playing "hardball" as they argued their positions. He talked of tension in the weekly secret conference. Once Justice Sandra Day O'Connor, hearing a beep, asked if the room was bugged. Blackmun had to tell her that the beep came from his hearing aid.

His emphasis was on the high tribunal as the last, best defender of the individual rights of Americans. I finally summoned up the courage to ask about what must have been his most trying experience—the 1973 *Roe v. Wade* decision legalizing abortion. That decision, he said, brought in the greatest volume of mail of anything in the court's history—75 percent of it negative.

"Well, of course it hurt at first," he said. "It doesn't hurt so much anymore. . . . Of course, a lot of it was abusive. You can think of any name to call someone, and I have been called it. Butcher of Dachau, murderer, Pontius Pilate, King Herod. You name it, it's all in there."

Each year on January 22, the anniversary of *Roe v. Wade*, he would make a point of walking back from lunch to see the annual antiabortion demonstration. He said he had never been recognized by the protesters.

I was on hand at the White House in April 1994 when President Clinton announced Justice Blackmun's retirement. I asked, "How are you going to get along without your daily fix of hate mail?" Blackmun turned and said something to the president, who then said, "He offered to take some of mine."

Covering the political conventions of 1984, CNN had come a long way since the hasty improvisations of 1980. When the Democrats gathered in San Francisco, we were ensconced in sky-booths with office space and all the paraphernalia of a media-age event, which this indeed was. I counted a total of 14,500 newspeople, outnumbering delegates and alternates by three to one. The limousines rolling to the VIP entrance disgorged more anchormen than statesmen—and to greater recognition and acclaim.

At the Democratic convention I found myself involved in what I first thought to be a minor tiff with CNN management. Burt Reinhardt, who had succeeded Reese Schonfeld as president of the company, sent word to me that Ted Turner wanted me to share my place on the set with John Connally, who was being retained as "guest commentator." I demurred. Connally, former governor of Texas, former secretary of the treasury under Nixon, onetime candidate for president, had been tried and acquitted on a bribery charge. That aside, I said that mixing a journalist and politician was mixing apples and oranges. I would be glad to interview him across a table, but not to share the same side of the table as a partner.

Reinhardt did not press the matter. Back in Washington between conventions, he brought it up again and said that, at the Republican convention in Dallas, he would insist on my appearing with Connally as "co-commentators." I flatly refused, said that under these conditions I would not go to Dallas, and for the first time, invoked my 1979 agreement with Turner that permitted me to veto an assignment.

What I had learned in the interim fortified me in my decision. Turner was playing up to Connally, hoping to induce the Texas wheeler-dealer to help raise money for an attempt to take over CBS. The trade press had reported Turner's discussions with various ultra-conservatives, including the evangelist Jerry Falwell, Sen. Jesse Helms of North Carolina, and Reagan communications director Pat Buchanan, to arrange a leveraged buyout of CBS with the use of junk bonds.

In Dallas, Connally was given a "guest commentator" role, but not with me. Ironically, he figured in one story I aired from Dallas. Former president Gerald Ford, a convention speaker, told me in an interview that in October 1973, when Vice President Spiro T. Agnew was forced to resign in disgrace, Nixon's first impulse was to name Connally as vice president.

With Nixon himself in trouble over Watergate, raising the possibility that the country could be left without either a president or vice president, Nixon decided on Gerald Ford, House Republican leader, who would presumably be speedily confirmed.

But, Ford said, Nixon had told him bluntly that in 1976 he planned to designate Connally, not Ford, as his successor. All this Ford detailed in a taped interview. Connally confirmed the accuracy of the story to me, but declined to give me an on-camera interview. I took pleasure in making the point to my bosses that Connally was a news subject, not a news partner.

After Dallas my relations with CNN management were strained, but as we pitched in to cover the Reagan-Mondale campaign, I assumed that the episode would be forgotten. It wasn't.

In February 1985, my agent, Richard Leibner, advised that he had been in touch with Burt Reinhardt about my annual contract renewal, and Reinhardt had said he wanted to drop the contract clause permitting me to reject assignments. I responded that this clause was part of my basic understanding with Turner and that I saw no reason to give it up.

I awaited further discussion, but it never came. In March, Leibner called to say that Reinhardt wanted me to take terminal leave until my contract expired in May, meaning that my employment was over.

This was totally unexpected. Maybe it shouldn't have been. CNN, now five years old and well established, no longer needed me for validation. And, unwilling to serve Turner's imperial ambitions, I had lost utility for him.

Word got around quickly. On that Friday evening, newspapers called for comment. I told reporters that the issue was CNN's effort to limit my editorial freedom. Newspapers quoted me as saying, "Turner is not sensitive to the necessity to insulate news coverage from his business interests. Turner comes from a new tradition of media tycoon."

A few days later the trade magazine *On Cable* appeared with me on the cover, voted by readers the "outstanding news personality" of the year. I went to the dinner in New York to receive the honor.

So here I was, nearing seventy and once more out of work. Bill Headline, CNN Washington bureau chief, called to say, with some obvious embarrassment, that "they" wanted me to return the satellite receiver that Turner had given me six years earlier.

The ten-foot-diameter dish, anchored in my front yard and a conversation piece for passersby, no longer served any purpose since cable had meanwhile come to Washington. After consulting a lawyer friend, I advised Headline I would be glad to return the dish, but since it had been a personal gift from Turner, I would like a letter from him requesting it. Also I would expect CNN to pay for relandscaping after it was dug up. Also, since the dish had attracted local newspaper attention when it was first installed, the removal would probably also be noted by the media.

Headline said he would relay all this to "them." A few days later he called with the message "They say to keep the f— dish." It still stands there, a memento.

Five years later, at a reception at the State Department, Ted Turner made his way across the crowded room, threw his arms around me, and said, "Real glad to see you, Dan. Remind me—are you mad at me or am I supposed to be mad at you?"

CHAPTER 18

DIDN'T YOU
USED TO BE...?

Some thirty years with CBS and CNN, and now I was off television. One evening, as I arrived at a Connecticut Avenue restaurant with my family, a man stopped me and asked, "Hey, didn't you used to be Daniel Schorr?"

Nearing seventy, I faced the question of whether there could be life after television. For the first time in a long time I felt the twinge of financial insecurity that dated back to my youth. Jonathan and Lisa were in the expensive Sidwell Friends School. My wife was starting work on a book. My longtime broker assured me that between Social Security and investment income we could live comfortably if I never worked again. My anxiety was irrational, but who ever said anxiety had to be rational?

That summer Li and I obtained scholar-in-residence grants for a month at the Rockefeller Foundation's magnificent study center in Bellagio, overlooking Lake Como. Li, taming a balky computer, was starting work on her book *Within Our Reach: Breaking the Cycle of Disadvantage*, a study of poverty programs that work and how to identify their attributes.

We learned for ourselves what other wife-husband collaborators had told us about the tensions that can develop. I was constantly wanting to smooth out Li's language; she was constantly accusing me of not understanding her. Apart from that, we had a wonderful time, making friends among the other scholars and artists from several countries. We counted it a blessing when we received the Bellagio fellowship again ten years later. This time I was working on my own book while Li worked on her second book—all by herself.

By the time we returned to Washington, my next career was beckoning. In signing up with Ted Turner in 1979, I had insisted on including in my contract permission to continue doing occasional commentaries for National Public Radio. Now Robert Siegel, the news director, offered to expand our relationship with additional weekday commentaries and with contributions to the new weekend programs that NPR was preparing to launch.

I met at lunch the prospective host of *Weekend Edition Saturday*, Scott Simon. We agreed that my principal contribution would be a nine-minute colloquy on Saturday mornings reviewing the week's news. Jay Kernis, the producer, asked whether I would be willing to do it live when necessary. I replied that I assumed that it would always be live, to avoid being outdated and because I have always felt that the tension of being live makes for a more interesting discussion.

I soon became much impressed with Simon, gentle in manner, smooth in delivery, talented in writing. He also displayed that rare gift that Ed Murrow had of deferring to a guest in a way that made him feel knowledgeable and important. A dry run of our colloquy went well, and it has gone well since. We have the ability to conclude just as the countdown clock reaches zero. Sometimes Scott uses the last fifteen seconds to tease me. For example, knowing of my ignorance of sports, he once asked, the day before the Super Bowl, who I thought would win.

"Gee, Scott," I said. "Who's playing?"

NPR is an organization of young people, many of them a third my age. I am accorded some of the respect of an elder statesman, consulted on almost everything from Russia under Stalin to America under Roosevelt. Occasionally, someone will put his head in my door with a question like "You didn't cover the Spanish-American War, did you? No, I guess that was before your time."

To capitalize on my age and long experience, I developed the practice of putting current events into historical context whenever possible. For example, when we ad-libbed our way through pauses in the Iran-contra hearings, it fell to me to make comparisons with Watergate and famous hearings back to the Teapot Dome scandal. When we covered Clinton impeachment hearings in the House and the trial in the Senate, one of my duties was to review the Nixon impeachment proceedings, aborted by his resignation. When the nation was consumed with the struggle over the custody of the six-year-old Cuban boy Elian Gonzalez, I tracked the history of the impassioned Miami Cubans back to the debacle of the Bay of Pigs invasion in 1961. During the stormy election controversy of 2,000, I was the expert on close elections, such as Kennedy-Nixon in 1960, if not Tilden-Hayes in 1876.

Age, I found, conferred other benefits. A New York advertising firm called to offer a seven-figure multiyear contract to do commercials for Avis car rentals. When I asked how I had been chosen, the executive said a poll of typical car renters had shown that they tended to trust older people with reputations for integrity more than their contemporaries. For a moment I was intrigued by the idea of competing on television with the O. J. Simpson commercials for Hertz. But then I said that selling myself that way would destroy the reputation for integrity that was my principal asset. The ad man said he was not surprised by my response—just asking.

When, years later, David Brinkley resigned from ABC and was soon thereafter seen in commercials for Archer Daniels Midland, "supermarket to the world," I was glad I had avoided that ethical problem.

Age had also led me into an unlikely friendship with the world of rock music. One day in 1986 I got a telephone call from someone whose name was unfamiliar to me. As he spelled it, I repeated, "Z-A-P..." I saw my daughter, Lisa, look up with wide eyes. She whispered,

"Daddy, is it Frank Zappa?" Holding the phone to my chest, I asked, "Who's Frank Zappa?"

Unfazed by my ignorance, the famous musician, whose compositions stretched the boundaries of rock and classical music, said he wanted to come to Washington to discuss my collaboration in a late-night television show that he was planning. A few days later we had lunch and then repaired to my office at NPR, where seeing me with Frank Zappa set mouths dropping and heads swiveling.

He outlined his idea for a program that would feature him and his band in Los Angeles. There would be one segment called "Night School." Intended for rock fans who were generally turned off by the news, it would have me in Washington responding to questions from his band about what was *really* going on in Washington.

Why me—a senior citizen totally alien to the rock culture? Because, said Zappa, the "kids" don't trust their contemporaries and see in me a straight-talking maverick like Zappa. The show never got off the ground; Fox Broadcasting figured—accurately—that it might be "controversial."

But Zappa and I became friends. I came to see, behind the dirty words and rage against corrupt government, a musician of true talent who cared about young people and wanted to lead them to active citizenship.

When he came to Washington on an East Coast concert tour, he invited me to come onstage during a break and appeal to the "kids" to register and vote to take government back to the people. When I completed my little homily, Frank asked whether, while I was there, I wanted to sing something. The audience erupted in cheers. Ham that I am, I sang "It Ain't Necessarily So," from Gershwin's *Porgy and Bess*, with an improvised accompaniment from the band.

After a year at NPR I began to wonder whether I would ever again be involved in covering a great scandal in government, like Watergate and the CIA misdeeds. I did not have long to wait.

On election night, November 4, 1986, as I scanned the news wires waiting for results, I noted an item from Beirut, quoting the weekly magazine *Al-Shiraa*, reporting that the United States had been supplying arms to Iran and that Robert McFarlane, President Reagan's former national security adviser, had visited Tehran in May. Considering that the Reagan administration was supposedly backing Iraq in its war with Iran, the report was mystifying. Furthermore, one of the fifteen hostages held by Iranian-backed terrorists in Lebanon had been released the day before, and President Reagan had spoken of "sensitive channels" that had helped to secure his release.

Pointing to the news ticker, I ventured to a colleague that something might be going on that could well overshadow the off-year election. Next day I said on NPR that there were reports of some deal with Iran involving military hardware and a McFarlane mission to Tehran. The leak to an obscure Lebanese magazine, I said, had apparently come from Iranians opposed to the deal.

Another piece of the puzzle fell into place when a plane loaded with supplies for the Nicaraguan rebels called *contras* was shot down over southern Nicaragua. Three crew members were killed, and a fourth, Eugene Hasenfuss, captured by government forces, said he was working for the CIA.

"A whiff of Watergate," I broadcast. The outlines of a complicated conspiracy began to take shape. TOW antitank missiles and other military hardware had been sold to Iran in the hope of winning the release of American hostages in Lebanon. Only two of the fifteen were released. McFarlane, accompanied by a National Security Council staffer, Oliver North, had flown to Tehran with a planeload of missiles, plus a Bible and a kosher chocolate cake picked up in Israel on the way as goodwill tokens. McFarlane hoped to make contact with Iranian "moderates" sympathetic to the West.

The "moderates" were a delusion. The Iranians unloaded the missiles and kept the White House delegates cooling their heels until they left in frustration. On the way home North told McFarlane (both retired marine lieutenant colonels) that not all the news was bad. North had overcharged the Iranians for the missiles, and the excess profit would be used to purchase arms for the Nicaraguan contras that Congress had refused to authorize.

McFarlane was shocked. Then, in February 1987, he tried to commit suicide by an overdose of sleeping pills. As he recovered, ex-president Nixon was one of the first to visit him in the hospital. I was the first journalist to interview him after he came home. I did not ask about the suicide attempt, but we talked about disillusionment with government service. Henry Kissinger, whom he had once served as an assistant, used to tease him about marines not being very intelligent. As national security adviser himself, McFarlane had nurtured the idea of a marine engineering a strategic breakthrough to Iran as Kissinger had done with China.

"Bud" McFarlane was a conscientious public servant who had become mixed up with a cynical, conniving crowd. And it hurt. He wrote a book about public service that did not sell well. He went out to marine installations, hawking the book from the back of his van.

"Hell hath no fury like a Congress scorned," I said in a commentary as a joint Senate-House committee geared up for hearings on "Iran-contra." What I had done for CBS in the Watergate hearings I now did for NPR—sitting through thirteen weeks of testimony, often repetitious, often irrelevant, ready at the drop of a gavel to join my colleagues in dispensing analysis.

I remember some of the one-liners better than the tortured arguments. Oliver North's secretary, Fawn Hall, on why she shredded documents: "Sometimes you have to go above the written law, I believe." Secretary of State George Shultz: "When you get down into the dirt of the operational details, it always comes out 'arms for hostages.'" House committee chairman Lee H. Hamilton: "You locked the president out of the process." And the star of the hearings, Oliver North: "I came here to tell you the truth—the good, the bad, and the ugly."

Thirsting for his presence in the televised hearings, Congress had granted North immunity from prosecution for his testimony. Until then he had been seen on television only as a furtive figure, ducking into cars, flashing a defiant thumbs-up sign.

But as he took the stand on July 7, flanked by his aggressive lawyer, Brendan Sullivan, who asserted himself by announcing that he was "not a potted plant," North performed the miracle of resurrection by television. Whispering into a microphone at the press table, I noted North's self-confident, often impassioned utterances. I also observed how he would slide away from probing questions, falling back into his assertion of patriotic motives, obedience to authority, and reverence for the commander in chief. He talked also of the pressures on him and the threat of assassination.

I noted also that North never seemed to be at a loss on how to respond to a question, even if he didn't know the answer. A senator asked him to translate the code name *Joshua* in a document. He said it stood for an Israeli official. But the key to the code showed that *Joshua* was President Reagan.

Most of us at the press table thought North was a fraud. We were too close to see what the nation saw—a handsome marine with a distinguished war record who stated his convictions in soaring eloquence, standing up with pride and dignity against a cabal of persecutors and pettifogging politicians. As telegrams of approval and support piled up, I ad-libbed, "As they taught us in school, magnetic North should not be confused with true North." Today, Oliver North is a radio talk-show host, onetime candidate for the U.S. Senate, and it is hardly remembered that he was convicted of perjury, the verdict overturned on appeal on technical grounds.

Looking back, I see North and Iran-contra embodying the Cold War "Reagan doctrine," which justified support—even illegal support—of anticommunist "freedom fighters." Iran-contra shared with Watergate a willful president establishing an extra-legal government inside the government to accomplish his ends. Nixon said an act is not illegal when the president does it. Reagan said that he acted like Lincoln, who did what he deemed necessary, such as freeing the slaves and blockading Southern ports, without constitutional authority.

I enjoyed participating in the coverage of these grand inquests that left the humdrum affairs of the world suspended while we watched powerful forces contending for mastery. My record of hearings that started with the McCarthy Red-hunting committee in 1955 and ran through Watergate and Iran-contra can be said to have reached a climax with the eighteen-week effort to drive President Clinton from power.

There is something quite awesome about the idea of unseating a president. There is no doubt that President Nixon would have been impeached by the House and convicted by the Senate in 1974 had he not chosen to resign. But Clinton, softer in manner, had a tougher core than Nixon. He would accept rebuke or reprimand, but would not willingly leave, regardless of the humiliation to which he would be subjected.

I knew Bill Clinton very little, but what I knew was appealing. When he started his weekly radio talks on a Saturday in 1993 at 9:07 A.M., I wrote to him pointing out that this was the precise moment when I was reviewing the week with Scott Simon and that I could not possibly compete with him. A few weeks later the time was changed to 10:07 A.M., and George Stephanopoulos called to tell me that, at a staff meeting, the president announced the new time, saying, "We just can't do that to Dan Schorr."

At a White House dinner, my wife was seated next to the president and I across the table. She later told me they had a lively discussion of her book, which he had obviously read. When I saw Clinton several weeks later, I remarked that my wife had been quite taken by her discussion with him at the dinner table. He put his hand on my shoulder and said, "Dan, marrying Li was the smartest thing you ever did." I cannot imagine how he knew and remembered the first name my wife usually uses only with friends.

As the impeachment process wore on, first in the House Judiciary Committee, then in the full House, and finally in the trial before the Senate, one could only marvel at how this gifted man had contrived his own destruction—or something close to it. The events are still too fresh in our minds to require much review here. But let me quote what I broadcast on February 21, 1999, after it was over:

> For five weeks and a day, including three Saturdays, I sat with
> my colleagues Neil Conan and Nina Totenberg crammed into a
> narrow space in the Senate Office Building, reporting on the

impeachment trial and yearning for the day when it would be over. And when that time came, we stood up, shook hands, reporters, assistants, and technicians.

As I headed towards the door, a feeling overcame me that took me back to 1945, when I was discharged from the army. I had hated every moment of living under military discipline, but it had spared me having to make decisions. So it will be with life after impeachment, but not without some looking back.

I remember the many times I heard senators vow they would consult conscience and Constitution and not be influenced by constituent views. But then there was Robert Byrd, who wrote a speech supporting conviction, then changed his mind. He still believed President Clinton was guilty, but, he said, "Senators carry the proxies of the people. Senators must listen to what Americans are saying."

It was, in the end, the people who saved Clinton from the passions that ran so strong in the Congress. And the next opinion survey gave Clinton a 68 percent job-approval rating.

I said, "Most Americans have long since made up their minds what happened—a president having a rather adolescent affair with a consenting intern which he then tried, rather clumsily, to hush up."

To illustrate my work as analyst, let me quote from others of my NPR commentaries over these fifteen years. First, November 9, 1988, after the election of George Bush:

The election seems to have left America more exhausted than exhilarated. Democracy has again worked, but not very happily. The president-elect seems fully aware that he must put together what a nasty campaign has rent asunder.

February 12, 1990:

Along with Gandhi, Zakharov, and Martin Luther King, Nelson Mandela ranks as one of the century's celebrated prisoners of conscience. Growing in stature in confinement, he emerged to find himself a figure of almost mythic proportions. . . . Mandela seems conscious of how much power he holds in his hands. He appealed to the crowd in Cape Town to "disperse with discipline" lest others say that "we can't control our own people."

December 23, 1991:

The Gorbachev era in Russia comes to an end with a singular inelegance, looking less like a succession than an eviction. President Yeltsin takes obvious pleasure in humiliating the man who kicked him out of the hierarchy four years ago, saying he was finished. And Gorbachev, filling his last Kremlin days with brooding, seems too full of bitterness to reflect on the meaning of this moment in Russian history.

July 3, 1992:

Between the last Monday in June and the first Monday in October we are left to reflect on a Supreme Court as full of surprises as a box of Cracker Jack. Its members often defy the expectations of everybody, including the presidents who appoint them. . . . President Eisenhower appointed Earl Warren and William Brennan, who led a liberal revolution, and Mr. Eisenhower lived to call these the two biggest mistakes of his presidency.

November 3, 1992:

President Bush called it "the most unpleasant year of my life." He is not alone. For millions of Americans the campaign for president, once an exhilarating festival of renewal, has turned into a tawdry spectacle of media saturation, full of sound and fury, clarifying little. Voters seem to be voting their resentments rather than their hopes.

January 21, 1993:

President Clinton has been conducting a national revival meeting that has accumulated for him a vast, but perishable reser-
voir of goodwill. He has brought the country to Washington
and Washington to the country, with an adroit mingling of Jefferson solemnity and Clinton folksiness.... Soon he will feel
the weight of all the hopes and expectations he has partly generated, partly come to personify.

April 21, 1993:

A tragedy almost beyond comprehension like the destruction of
the Branch Davidian compound at Waco requires culprits.
Attorney General Reno was all over television Monday shoul-
dering responsibility, President Clinton belatedly joining in
Tuesday. But that won't do. That's formality. America wants
real culprits. Surely the history of religious fanatics from
Masada to Jonestown teaches the potential for self-destruction
among zealots under pressure.

June 22, 1993:

"I think we're coming toward agreement" on gays in the military, says President Clinton.... However tantalizingly close
agreement may seem, several devils remain in the details. It is
one thing to repeat the Don't Ask, Don't Tell mantra. It is
another to make it work in practice.

April 7, 1994:

Richard Nixon would surely have wanted a state funeral like
those of Eisenhower and others back to Lincoln, could he have
foreseen the wave of sympathy and respect that welled up from
a fickle public after his death. But Nixon, who never left his

public ceremonies to chance, would not have risked the pain of another rejection had he talked to President Clinton about a state funeral and been rebuffed. The focus today is on burying the thirty-seventh President. What kind of president will be sorted out by history. But one is left wondering how a man so creative could be so self-destructive.

May 29, 1995:

Bosnia is developing into the defining crisis of the post-Cold War era, testing whether the international community has the power to control barbarism at all.... The melancholy fact is that the Bosnian Serbs have seized enough artillery to be able to shell Sarajevo with redoubled intensity. A definition of futility is having only bad options and worse options.

October 7, 1995:

The trial and acquittal of O. J. Simpson exposed and may have exacerbated racial tensions. All through the trial two-thirds of whites were convinced of his guilt, two-thirds of blacks didn't believe it. So, when you saw reactions to the verdict—black jubilation, white dismay—you could see how far along we are on the road to two societies, about which the Kerner commission warned us a couple decades ago.

June 17, 1996:

Let's hear it for Russia's infant democracy. The election wasn't canceled by a power-hungry president, as some had predicted. There was no widespread vote-rigging, as many had predicted. And not even the televised Russia-Germany championship soccer game prevented a voter turnout of 70 percent, which a mature democracy like ours could well envy.... What Russian voters seem to want is stability and a better life. And most of

them seem willing, for lack of anyone better, to stick with
Yeltsin.

November 6, 1996:

Senator Dole was gracious in defeat and President Clinton was
humble in victory. And the pageantry of democratic continuity
and renewal was splendid. But behind the hoopla lurked some
ominous signs of deepening alienation of Americans from their
government. It could be read in the 49 percent turnout—lowest since the lackluster Coolidge year of 1924.

September 4, 1997:

Saint of the gutter and saint of the media. The death of Mother
Teresa casts a strange light on the Princess Diana frenzy sweeping
Britain and much of the world. Mother Teresa was celebrated,
but not a celebrity. Mother Teresa left the world owning only
two pairs of sandals, two pairs of eyeglasses, a wooden wash-
bucket, a well-thumbed Bible. Princess Diana left an estate estimated at $65 million. This is only to say that there is a difference
between a life well lived and a media image well cultivated.

October 11, 1998:

The Serbs are making trouble in the Balkans. Iraq is pursuing
Saddam Hussein's dream of weapons to cow the world. Russia
and a large part of the world are in the grip of an economic crisis. The post-Cold War era—let's face it—has been a big bust
so far.

April 11, 1999:

About the two heavily armed young men who shot up
Columbine High School and then themselves, we still know

painfully little. Identifying young people at risk of becoming violent remains a most inexact science. What is predictable is that a schoolyard killing spree will almost always involve guns. As Attorney General Janet Reno says, "We've got to get guns out of the hands of young people."

April 14, 1999:

If you want to know why ground forces for Kosovo are such a sensitive issue, it is because Americans have a thing about not wanting their people in service to die. . . . In announcing the start of the air war on March 24, President Clinton clearly believed it necessary to assure Americans, in the most emphatic terms, that there would be no ground forces. That was a gratuitous gift to President Milosevic that undoubtedly helped him to design his order of battle.

April 17, 2000:

To understand the passions of the Miami Cubans over the boy named Elian, you have to go back to April 17, 1961, and the CIA's misconceived, misdirected landing of Cuban exiles without air cover to overthrow Fidel Castro. President Kennedy later said, "How could I have been so stupid to let them go ahead?" But from the Bay of Pigs there developed a dysfunctional relationship between embittered exiles and government leaders, under constant pressure to compensate for betrayal by supporting the cold war against Castro.

In my years with NPR the worst tribulation was the libel suit I got us into. On a Saturday morning in April 1992, I was on the air with Scott, discussing the journalistic ethics of "outing" homosexuals and AIDS victims. I made reference to a disabled marine veteran who, in 1975, at a rally for President Ford in San Francisco, had seen a woman aim a gun at the president. He had knocked the gun from

her hands. Newspapers identified him as homosexual, precipitating a
family crisis.

Based on incomplete research into the seventeen-year-old incident, I named the man as Larry Buendorf. Unfortunately, I forgot
that there had been a second attempt on Ford's life in Sacramento,
and it was *there* that Larry Buendorf, special agent in charge of the
Secret Service detail, had grabbed a gun from Lynette "Squeaky"
Fromme and arrested her. The hero of the San Francisco incident
was Oliver "Billy" Sipple.

Had the error been brought to my attention, I would have gone
on the air immediately with an abject apology. Buendorf did not
call. Instead, five months later he sued me, Scott, and NPR for libel.
NPR retained Floyd Abrams, noted First Amendment lawyer, to
defend us. Six months later the federal district court threw out the
case on a motion for summary judgment. Judge June L. Green ruled
that while we could have been "more diligent" in our research, the
error did not rise to the level of "reckless disregard for the truth."

Stupidity is not necessarily malice.

Somewhat to my surprise I found that in my commentator's
niche at NPR I was attracting some attention. Lecture dates
increased, and even Hollywood made modest advances to me. I
played a news anchorman in three films—*The Net, The Game,* and
Siege. When the *Boston Globe* asked why I was violating my expressed
principle of separating fact from fiction, I said, "I have no defense. I
did it because it amused me." I also narrated several television documentaries, one for public television about the politics of the Cuban
community in Miami. I did a five-hour series on Watergate for the
cable Discovery Channel. I worked with the highly professional PBS
Frontline unit on a documentary titled "Smoke in the Eye." This was
an investigation of how—and why—the CBS program *60 Minutes*
had for weeks sat on an interview with a tobacco-company whistle-
blower, Jeffrey Wigand, who had arraigned cigarette manufacturers
for lying about the addictive quality of their product.

It fell to me to interview Mike Wallace, who had done the
Wigand interview. Although Wallace had done a hatchet job on me

in his interview in 1976, I made it clear that I would treat him civilly and professionally. I let him explain that he had never felt so much heat on any story before. He stated that CBS was facing a lawsuit with billions at stake—maybe double or triple the worth of the CBS corporation. He said that he did not resign in protest because he wanted to continue the fight inside the company.

Walter Cronkite told me, in an interview in his CBS office, that *60 Minutes*, in buckling under, had violated "a journalistic imperative" and "dealt a blow to all investigative journalism."

The story of the titanic battle inside CBS was told as fiction in the motion picture *The Insider.* In the film, producer Lowell Bergman, who had arranged the interview with Wigand, upbraids Mike Wallace for not resigning over the issue. Wallace says, "I don't plan to spend the end of my days wandering in the wilderness of National Public Radio."

That seemed to refer to me, the only former CBS correspondent now with NPR. Wallace telephoned to tell me he had never used those words. Bergman said that some liberties had been taken in the fictional screenplay, but that the quotation generally reflected Wallace's attitude, scornful of those who made an issue of principle.

In a commentary for NPR's *Weekend Edition Sunday* in November 1999, I concluded, "It may be Mike Wallace who is wandering in an affluent wilderness. I have found the promised land."

CHAPTER 19

STAYING TUNED

In May 1999, Kevin Klose, president of National Public Radio, invited me to a meeting of the NPR board and surprised me with a bronze plaque, emblazoned, "Lifetime Achievement Award." I, ever the copyreader, responded that I wished to amend the wording to "Lifetime Achievement So Far..."

I was only half joking. I wanted it known that, octogenarian that I was, and "Keeper of the Past," I had some commentaries left in me and could not imagine life without world-watching. Sedentary generalist more than jetting journalist, I no longer feel a need to compete for attention or airtime, no need to prove myself.

Talking to visiting students, I could make mouths drop simply by reciting familiar items that I lacked at their age: no ballpoint pens or nylon hose or plastic wrap or frozen food or computers (*software* was not even in the dictionary) or jet planes or nuclear bombs.

And no television!

In 1939 I saw experimental television demonstrated by RCA at the New York World's Fair. My girlfriend stood before a camera holding a microphone. On a monitor fifty feet away I could hear her and see her grainy image. I commented, with something less than prescience, that television seemed to be an amusing toy, but without much practical application. A more perceptive E. B. White wrote in

Harper's magazine that television would have a profound effect, "a new and unbearable disturbance of the modern peace or a saving radiance in the sky."

More "disturbance" than "saving radiance," I have tentatively concluded after my multimedia six decades. Live television forces our political leaders to react before they have had time to think. Scenes of suffering Kurds in Iraq relentlessly pursued by Saddam Hussein's forces obliged President Bush in 1991 to halt the withdrawal of American forces. On television, the body of an American airman being dragged through the streets of Mogadishu forced the withdrawal of American forces from Somalia. One shudders to think of what the 1962 Cuban missile crisis would have been like if President Kennedy and Nikita Khrushchev had had to play out their tense confrontation breathlessly before live cameras.

All those years I worked in television I deplored the medium's affinity for violence, an affinity that grew as the ratings race became more fierce. The motto in local television newsrooms was "If it bleeds, it leads." The level of video violence was a constant source of conflict with the public health community. A surgeon general's report in 1972, one of many, found a "causal relationship between viewing of violence and aggression," especially among the young. In 1993, Pope John Paul II got thunderous applause during a speech in Denver when he said, "The media must accept some of the responsibility for the epidemic of killings sweeping the country." That got little play on national television.

In 1969, the National Commission on Violence found that some violent people are influenced by exposure to television. My report on that for the *CBS Evening News* was cut to eliminate that embarrassing conclusion.

In 1958, almost twenty years after E. B. White pondered about television as "radiance" or "disturbance," Ed Murrow rendered his scorching verdict in a speech to the Radio and Television News Directors' Association in Chicago.

"I would like to see [television] reflect occasionally the hard, unyielding realities of the world in which we live," he said. "The instrument can teach, it can illuminate; yes, and it can even inspire. But it can do so only to the extent that humans are determined to use it to those ends. Otherwise, it is merely wires and lights in a box."

In 1993, speaking to the same association in Miami, CBS anchor Dan Rather gave an updated version of Murrow's speech, saying that "we all should be ashamed of what we have done and not done, measured against what we could do."

He said, "They've got us putting more fuzz and wuzz on the air, cop-shop stuff, so as to compete not with other news programs, but with entertainment programs, including those posing as news programs, for dead bodies, mayhem, and lurid tales."

Those were some hefty stones Dan was throwing in that luxurious glass house he inhabits.

Television has done things to us. It has created a new breed of politician, regular of features, smooth of voice, quick of sound bite, handcrafted for a medium that screens out the verbose and the reflective. Has it occurred to you that no politician today stammers, as Winston Churchill did? And no candidate says, "I have no comment on that," as more self-confident politicians such as Roosevelt, Truman, and Eisenhower often did? Television won't allow that.

Television has also produced a new breed of citizen, ready and able to respond to its demands for man-in-the-street comment or eyewitness description of disasters. In the early days of television I had trouble getting spontaneous interviews. The average layman, confronted with a camera, would stutter and break into a cold sweat. How far the medium has come in training people to its needs struck me after the school shootings in 1999, when I marveled at the articulateness, even eloquence, of teachers, students, and parents who could have been expected to be in shock.

Television has also created a new breed of journalist, more knowledgeable of the medium than of the world. This journalist may be more adept at the ad-lib than searching analysis, more expert in camera angles than English grammar. The "press" has become part of the "news media," and finally, simply "the media." As journalism was shunted to the corner of a vast entertainment stage, it tended to attract people who were, at least in part, entertainers.

The typical television journalist today may be an "anchor," reading off a TelePrompTer a script written by someone else, able to exchange banter with the weather reporter and the sports reporter. Or a talk show "host," able to prod guests into saying provocative things, or assembling "journalists" who will scream at each other. A journalist today can come from anywhere—from the revolving door of the White House, from a failed campaign or office. A journalist today can even be a movie actor, such as the star of *Titanic*, Leonardo DiCaprio, recruited by ABC to interview President Clinton about the environment.

It is a long way from the *The Front Page* and "Hello, sweetheart— give me rewrite." It is a long way from impecunious reporters with press cards in their greasy hatbands to the era of multimillionaire television-news stars, more celebrated than most of the figures they celebrate.

I never aspired to be an anchor—probably a good thing—but I did aspire to be a featured commentator like Eric Sevareid and David Brinkley. In 1953, when I joined CBS, I asked a young producer what a newspaper reporter needed to know to succeed in television.

"Sincerity," he said. "If you can fake that, you've got it made."

I became reasonably proficient in the right style of clothing, the right amount of Max Factor makeup. I learned how to interview while walking, how to film "reaction shots" after the interview, how to use the TelePrompTer (looking down at the desk occasionally to make it seem more natural). But, time and again, a director had to tell me to comb my hair or button my collar. And, I guess I never succeeded in faking sincerity very well.

Some of the great moments for TV journalists were more theater than journalism. In 1964, John Chancellor, removed by the police from the floor of the Republican convention from which reporters had been barred, closed, off camera, saying, "This is John Chancellor, NBC News, somewhere in custody." Similarly, in 1968, Walter Cronkite, from his anchor booth overlooking the Democratic convention, thundered at police who had rudely handled Dan Rather, "Those thugs!" Or CNN's Bernard Shaw, standing nervously at a hotel window during the Allied bombing of Baghdad in 1990. Or, for that matter, myself coming to my name on the Nixon enemies list while on the air.

But moments of unpremeditated drama are not sufficient to satisfy the medium's demand for something more exciting than actuality. From that demand has sprung the semifictional form called docudrama, and the "reality-based" syndicated shows such as *America's Most Wanted* and *Hard Copy*. Over the years many viewers have become increasingly confused about what is reality.

The assault on reality reached some sort of milestone in 1998 when fiction invaded the three network news programs, the last bastion of nonfiction in television. The *ABC Evening News* showed what purported to be surveillance film of an American diplomat in Vienna, Felix Bloch, handing a briefcase, presumable full of secrets, to a Soviet agent on a Vienna street corner. Peter Jennings neglected to say that the scene was a reenactment using ABC personnel.

NBC's *Dateline* program staged an explosion and a fire in a collision between a car and a General Motors truck. It was simulating a problem with the gas tank of the truck, but neglected to say so.

And CBS, employing what must have been the first-ever news department "casting director," used an actor to depict the ordeal of Terry Anderson, the Associated Press reporter who had been taken hostage in Lebanon. There were apologies all around, but the pressure for "action" is inexorable.

I had long been aware of how people could lose their grip on reality. In July 1969, CBS sent me to the Netherlands, one of several correspondents deployed to various parts of the world to provide quick reaction to the moon landing. We set up our camera in a quaint café in Amsterdam, telling a group of patrons that we would show them watching the landing and would then report their reactions to the historic event for America.

The Apollo spaceship touched down, and live by satellite, I turned to one of the burghers and asked what he thought.

"To be frank," he said, "I liked it better the first time. The picture was clearer."

It took a moment for me to grasp that he was referring to a simulation of the landing projected from Houston earlier. I gave a hasty return cue to Walter Cronkite. My mission had been less successful than Apollo's, but I had learned something—that many people are no longer sure of what is real and what is pretend. And many don't think much about the distinction.

For many, television has become the arbiter of reality, a way of validating their existence. To be recognized by television some will wave their hands, some will call a news conference ("pseudo-events," historian Daniel Boorstin calls them), some will stage demonstrations, and some will kill. Sometimes prison rioters will list as their primary demand that they be allowed to air their grievances on television.

Television has become a target for terrorists. The young militants who occupied the American embassy in Tehran in 1979 got their kicks from seeing the dozens of TV cameras outside the gates. The hijackers who took a TWA plane to Lebanon made a deal with ABC for an interview with the pilot in the cockpit with a gun to his head. In another hijacking episode, a passenger was shot and thrown onto the tarmac to keep the attention of television.

Anthony Quainton, former head of the State Department's Office for Combating Terrorism, associated an increase in casualties during hijackings and hostage takings during the 1980s with a desire to force media attention. Obviously, television must report hostage takings, but sometimes it is done with such excess as to suggest that television itself has been taken hostage.

It is no accident that, in episodes of civil strife—in Prague, Bucharest, Moscow—a decisive part of the battle became the struggle for control of the television station.

Television is not an ideal medium for information. It appeals more to the senses than to the intellect. Our notion of the world tends to be dominated by what the camera can show. Israel's harsh reaction to Palestinian rioting in the West Bank stirred a vigorous reaction in the United States. In the 1980s, Syria perpetrated a massacre in the rebellious town of Hama in which thirty to forty thousand people were killed. It was a front-page story in the *New York Times*, but had little impact in America because Western television was not allowed to witness the brutality.

If the American civil rights movement of the 1960s succeeded in penetrating the mind and conscience of America, it was because the racists in Mississippi and Alabama were ill-advised enough to let their clubs, fire hoses, and attack dogs be seen by the news cameras.

Television has some peculiar effects. Anyone who has been much on the tube can tell you of being regarded as something other than a human being. During the Watergate period of the 1970s, when I was getting a great deal of exposure, parents would point me out to their children at airports and other public places as though I were on display. In one airport lounge, a businessman pulled me out of a chair, saying jovially, "Come on over here. I want to show you to my partner. He doesn't believe it's you." He would not have treated an ordinary person that way. But I was not a person; I was a personality.

As an alumnus, I observe with fascination the way technology continues to expand its power to provide vivid pictures. Investigative reporting can now be done with the help of a tiny camera concealed in the reporter's hair. Not only videotape but live pictures can be manipulated to create something that can truly be called "virtual reality."

In January 1994, ABC's Cokie Roberts was seen in a coat, reporting from the steps of the Capitol. She was actually in the ABC studio, but a magical device called the Chiron had made it possible to transport her to the Hill. On New Year's Eve, ushering in the year 2000, Dan Rather broadcast from Times Square. If you were in Times Square, you would have seen that behind him was a Budweiser billboard and an NBC sign. On television, his backdrop was a CBS logo.

This is not just a matter of doctoring a picture, such as the darkened image of O. J. Simpson on the cover of *Time* magazine. It is the digital era in which a Woody Allen or a Forrest Gump can be seen talking to President Kennedy. But that is just entertainment. When newspeople can make images on the tube be whatever they want them to be, it is downright scary.

Indeed, on the Internet, a journalist doesn't have to be human at all. I have seen Ananova, the attractive computer-generated virtual newscaster, who blinks her saucer eyes as she delivers the news on the Web.

As media companies gobble up other companies, becoming ever more remote from the people they profess to serve, I am depressed at the way journalism has fallen in the esteem of the American public. What was once regarded as a monitor of the establishment is now regarded as an establishment itself. A 1997 Roper poll reported fewer than 20 percent of respondents considered journalistic ethics as high, 82 percent believed reporters are insensitive to people's pain, 63 percent believed the news too sensationalized.

Even as I look back on six decades dominated by the rise of television, another communications revolution is upon us—the age of the Internet. It offers the public unprecedented access and control in what they want to see, hear, and read from their computers. Before long, I am told it will be possible to stop the action on a live telecast, search the Internet for related information or query the TV's software about some ambiguity or unclarity, then pick up where you left off.

Like television, the Web is creating new kinds of journalists. Anyone with a Web site can be a publisher. *Slate* and *Salon* have reporters and editors, but such is the multiplier effect of the Internet that any individual can be a "journalist" to millions, free to spread gossip and rumor.

Into the annals of Web journalism must go the date January 17, 1998—the first time a piece of gossip on the Web affected the course of history. Matt Drudge, a self-styled gossip-monger, told the millions standing around the Net's figurative water-cooler that *Newsweek* magazine was sitting on a bomb about to explode in the White House. It was the first public mention of the former White

House intern Monica Lewinsky, involved in an affair with President Clinton. Sunday morning Drudge was quoted on ABC by Bill Kristol, and soon the story was everywhere.

Newsweek was, indeed, sitting on the story for further checking. Matt Drudge, whose *Drudge Report* obeyed no institutional ethic, went on hearsay. The awesome multiplier effect of the Web created a new kind of journalism, as television had in a different way.

In the Internet age, people can select the information they want. But how will they know what they don't know—and maybe should know? And learning swiftly in real time what is going on, will they know why it happened and what it means? You will see that I am sneaking in a plug for the old-style interpretive journalist who helps people make sense of complex events.

In my days as an investigative reporter, my motto was "Find out what they're hiding and tell those who need to know." In my more sedentary days, the motto has changed to "The people know a lot. Tell them what to make of it."

In the old days people would recognize me and say, "I've seen you on television." In recent years it is more likely to be someone who swivels around in a restaurant and says, "I would know that voice anywhere," and then something like "Thank you for explaining things." I find that most satisfying.

From the day I reported that suicide outside my window in the Bronx, journalism has been a profession that I have loved, not always wisely, but well. In the twilight of a life and a career, I find new enjoyments in the way my wife, my son, my daughter, have distinguished themselves by serving the public weal.

Sometimes I shake my head about journalism that comes closer and closer to entertainment. But, as best I can, I am staying tuned.

14 28 DATE DUE DAYS

OCT 2 0 2001			
NOV 0 3 2001			
MAY 0 3 2002			
JUN 2 1 2002			
AUG 2 7 2002			
NOV 2 9 2002			
JAN 1 7 2003			
MAR 2 4 2003			
APR 1 9 2003			
GAYLORD			PRINTED IN U.S.A.